DATE DUE

Nov. 30, 2010	
JAN 1 1 2010	

DEMCO, INC. 38-2931

TAKE THIS JOB
AND SHIP IT

TAKE THIS JOB
AND SHIP IT

HOW CORPORATE GREED
AND BRAIN-DEAD POLITICS
ARE SELLING OUT AMERICA

SENATOR BYRON L. DORGAN

THOMAS DUNNE BOOKS / ST. MARTIN'S PRESS
NEW YORK

THOMAS DUNNE BOOKS.
An imprint of St. Martin's Press.

www.thomasdunnebooks.com
www.stmartins.com

Library of Congress Cataloging-in-Publication Data
Dorgan, Byron L.
    Take this job and ship it : how corporate greed and brain-dead politics are selling out
America / Byron Dorgan.—1st ed.
        p.   cm.
    Includes index.
    ISBN-13: 978-0-312-35522-7
    ISBN-10: 0-312-35522-X
    1. Labor supply—United States.   2. Contracting out—United States.   3. United
States—Commercial policy.   I. Title.
    HD5724.D595 2006
    382'.30973—dc22   2006040295

First Edition: August 2006

10   9   8   7   6   5   4   3   2   1

CONTENTS

ACKNOWLEDGMENTS

I WAS INSPIRED TO WRITE THIS BOOK BECAUSE I'M WOR-ried about the future of our country. I hope this book will help sound the alarm.

It took me nearly a year to write this book, and along the way I had some very special help and encouragement. First, it was the patience of my family: my wife, Kim, and children, Brendon and Haley. And of my son Scott and his family: Denise, Madison, and Mason; and my brother, Darrell. I thank all of them for their encouragement and their love and patience.

A special thanks to two wonderful agents, Wayne Kabak and Mel Berger, at the William Morris Agency, who felt that this was a book and a point of view that needed to be written.

And thanks to Thomas Dunne at Thomas Dunne Books/St. Martin's Press for believing in the power of this message and for helping me navigate the interesting world of publishing. And to Sean Desmond at Thomas Dunne Books, who helped with every phase of the manuscript.

———

Finally, thanks to Tony Bender, my friend, collaborator, editor, critic, and a wonderful wordsmith. When I decided to write this book I was determined to write it myself. But I knew I needed an editor to work with and to help me do research, editing, rewrites, and collaboration on the direction of the book. I chose Tony Bender, from North Dakota, who has a populist spirit and a keen intellect. He is a friend from a small town with a very big talent.

I believe it was Hemingway who said something like "Genius is in the seventh draft." Well, I didn't reach seven drafts, but it was close. I hope you enjoy the book.

Byron L. Dorgan
U.S. Senator
March 2006

TAKE THIS JOB
AND SHIP IT

ONE

A STAR-SPANGLED RUT

A POIGNANT STORY IS TOLD ABOUT THE SORROWFUL days following President Roosevelt's death in 1945.

In a long line of mourners waiting to pay their respects to the dead president lying in state at the U.S. Capitol was a fellow who had waited for hours.

A reporter, who was writing a story about the outpouring of love for FDR, saw this workingman standing quietly, holding his hat in his hands, with tears in his eyes.

The reporter, notebook in hand, asked, "Did you know President Roosevelt?"

"No," the man said through his tears. "But he knew me."

What a simple yet profound way of expressing that this was a president who truly cared about ordinary folks, about the working people of America.

So, who knows America's workers today?

Who is looking out for them now?

When their jobs are shipped overseas, who stands up for the American worker?

Who takes notice for example when the nine hundred Ohio workers lost their jobs because Huffy Bicycle Company decided to move those jobs to China, where they could pay Chinese workers thirty-three cents an hour to make bicycles?

Did anybody know that on the last day of work, as they drove out of the plant parking lot, in a quiet but powerful message, each of the Huffy employees left a pair of shoes in their empty parking space. It was their way of telling the company, *"You can move our jobs to China, but you're not going to be able to fill our shoes."*

So who knows those workers and millions like them? Our president? The Congress? Corporate executives? I don't think so.

If this is a nation experiencing a crisis of confidence—and I believe it is—it is because these days many American workers feel ignored, abandoned, and vulnerable.

They feel so very alone because they know they are governed by the callously indifferent who not only don't "know them," but who really don't think workers matter much.

These days we are told to suck it up and stop complaining. Things are going fine here in the United States. The president says so. So do a lot of economists, columnists, and business leaders. The world is flat, we're told. It's a good thing. Who could argue otherwise?

"We're number one!" . . .

"Our biggest export is wastepaper!"

That's right. America's largest export (by volume) is now "wastepaper" mostly headed for China. And another big export of ours is good American jobs, also headed mostly to Asia.

If you're thinking that sending wastepaper and American jobs—millions of them—overseas isn't exactly a sign of robust economic health, you're right!

Moreover, we are ringing up a trade deficit of over $700 billion a year (highest in history). That means every single day we buy about $2 billion of foreign products more than we are able to sell to other countries. To pay for that, each day we sell some of our country to foreigners. It is a strategy I call "The Selling of America."

And in this new global economy, no one is more profoundly affected than American workers.

In 1970, the largest U.S. corporation was General Motors. Most people who went to work there stayed for all their working lives. They collectively bargained, were paid well, and received good retirement and health-care benefits.

Today, the largest U.S. corporation is Wal-Mart. According to published reports, the average salary is $18,000 a year. First-year employee turnover is reportedly near 70 percent. And a large number of their employees have neither health-care nor retirement benefits. Some progress!

Add to all of that, in the past five years we've lost over 3 million U.S. jobs that have been outsourced to other countries and millions more are poised to leave. The bulk of these are jobs producing goods abroad under conditions that would never be allowed in this country. These products are then shipped to be sold in the United States from countries that still have not opened their markets to us.

So the plain truth is, things aren't really going so well. More people are seeing their jobs sent overseas. We are sapping our manufacturing strength. Many of our corporations are stripping their workers' pensions and reducing salaries. Workers and families are losing confidence in the future—a future we are financing by selling part of our country every day.

Despite those who tell us everything is just great, many of us can sense we're headed in the wrong direction. And we need to take action before our economy implodes.

That's the purpose of this book. I want to both sound the alarm and offer some hope. We've faced big challenges in the past and overcome them once we understood them. And we will again!

It's not going to be easy. Those who have spent billions to pave the road that allows them to produce in low-wage countries and sell in our established markets without all the restrictions they face in our country will attack views like mine as uninformed. They love this nonsense about "the world is flat." Well, the world isn't flat. Not when our trade agreements aren't fair. We are up to our neck in debt. And we are on a course that is unsustainable. The question isn't whether it changes, but rather, when.

Some say that global trade is now an unstoppable force of nature, and those of us who rant about the unfairness and the mountain of trade debt are Luddites. But that ignores the reality of our current trade mess. I do support trade, and plenty of it, provided it is fair, free, and mutually beneficial to us and our trade partners. However, that's not the case today. And we do desperately need change.

Change doesn't mean closing our borders and retreating from the global economy. But it does mean standing up for our country's interests and establishing a set of rules for trade in the global economy that reflect our country's interests. It means establishing a trade strategy that is designed to lift others up without pushing American workers down. We can do that. But we need to start now.

And oh yes, one more thing. As I write this, Wham-o has just announced that it has been bought by the Chinese. You remember Wham-o. It gave us Hula Hoops, Frisbees, Silly String, Slip 'N Slide. I understand the Chinese wanting our textile jobs, technology jobs, and manufacturing jobs. But our Frisbees and Hula Hoops? We put Hula Hoops in the Smithsonian Institution, for God's sake. Is nothing sacred? Okay, I'll stop. Trade is truly a serious issue and deserves our serious attention.

So, this book is about what's wrong and how to fix it. It is about summoning that can-do American spirit to force change and reform and grow our economy in the right way.

FDR—OFFERING HOPE TO A NATION

During the Great Depression and the beginning of World War II, FDR's infectious confidence taught an entire country how to believe again, to endure, and to triumph.

He gave Americans a sense of self-worth and a sense of purpose.

He made us believe in ourselves and in our country, to realize our American Dream.

It was rooted in family, faith, and a good job. It was about the confidence in the future to build schools, roads, communities, and churches. This was a country at work, a country of builders.

Our history is both an anchor and a teacher. The place where I grew up still reminds me of the commonsense lessons I learned there. About work and about community. My hometown in southwestern North Dakota is a small farming community—only about three hundred people—but like most small towns, what it lacks in population it makes up for in heart.

I learned a lot in Regent—as much from the hardworking farmers who congregated there as I did in school. I tell people I graduated in the top ten of my senior high school class. There were nine of us. You see, in a small town you're never very far from the top or the bottom.

In my hometown, pride was not the sin of vanity but rather was born of the satisfaction that comes with a job well done. It was a community that rose from the prairies and was still barely two generations old when I was a kid. From crude shacks and some sod houses in those early years there evolved a thriving, bustling Main Street—hard work and values had built something special.

On the Saturday nights of my youth, I remember a small-town Main Street that was full of cars and trucks when farmers came to town at the end of a long week. The barber cut hair until midnight on Saturday nights. The two bars and the single café were epicenters of conversation and news as friends gathered in town after a hard week's work to talk about the weather, the crops, and the kids.

In those days, no politician would have presumed to lecture about values to the folks in my hometown. They *lived* their values every day. They honored family, faith, and hard work. When there was a job to do, they did it. When the town needed volunteers, they pitched in. They looked out for one another.

These are the lessons of my past. And the lessons from my small hometown, repeated all across America in the twentieth century, were the building blocks that created the greatest nation on earth. These lessons of greatness were gained through struggle.

During the post–Second World War period, we saw an America propelled ahead by the GI Bill, by a growing manufacturing industry that produced good jobs that were protected by the strength of unions organizing for good pay, benefits, and worker protections. All of this produced strong families and built the world's economic superpower.

Work was valued.

There was no social program as important as a good job that paid well.

All of this paved the way for the development of a broad middle class. Wage earners became the consumers and supported a strong, vibrant manufacturing sector that, in turn, produced good jobs with good benefits.

In short, the economy worked.

It became the major difference between our country and so many others.

I watched as many of the soldiers returned to our small town after the Second World War, got married, got a job, built a home, and raised a family. Even in that small town we were part of the great American experiment, engaged in a democratic debate about how to improve life in our country.

They, and others, decided that workers have rights: the right to labor in a safe workplace, the right to organize and bargain collectively, the right to a minimum wage, the right not to have to compete with child labor working in the mines or the factories. All of these rights were the result of great struggles over the past century. And they have roots in America's hometowns.

TIMES HAVE CHANGED

Fast-forward to 2006 and try to explain to the folks in Regent how those things have changed. The good jobs American families relied on are evaporating. The giant corporations have discovered more than a billion people around the rest of the world they can employ for pennies an hour, and if these poorly paid foreign workers dare try to organize a labor union, they can be fired or even jailed. In some cases these companies can hire children and work them twelve hours a day, seven days a week in unsafe, often harrowing conditions. Bad for the children, but great for the bottom line, and that's all that matters, isn't it?

The practical folks in my hometown would say, "Are you nuts? We Americans are being asked to compete against Chinese or Indonesian workers who make thirty cents an hour? We can't compete with that, and we shouldn't have to!" Yet that is exactly what is happening in this country, and few people seem interested in sounding the alarm. American families are taking it on the chin while the big corporate interests are raking in the big profits.

In my small town, dignity and respect were earned by one's labors. Farmers, mechanics, and businessmen stood as relative equals, but a man without a job never stood as tall.

As a young boy, I used to watch our local blacksmith, Adam Krebs. He would heat iron in the forge, then pound the metal into the shape he wanted. I learned that the way you bend metal is to heat it, then pound it. American politics is a bit like that, and that is the purpose of this book. I want to apply some heat to our present trade policy. I want to pound it, bend it, shape it, and fix it. With a trade deficit of over $700 billion a year, millions of lost jobs, and millions of families who have seen their American dreams shattered, it's long past the time to question those who claim everything will work out just fine. In fact, it's time to wake up and take action.

DANGEROUS TIMES

There is little evidence that this president or this Congress understands the grave danger to our economy. This awakening must begin with the American people—with you.

These are dangerous times. We have built the strongest economy in the world. We have one of the highest standards of living, and yet both our fiscal policy and our trade policy have almost overnight made us the world's biggest debtor nation, and that threatens America's future.

Budget deficits in the 400-to-500-billion-dollar-a-year range, coupled with trade deficits over $700 billion a year, are rapidly sapping America's strength. The budget deficit is financed entirely by borrowing, and the trade deficit is financed by foreign capital purchases of our bonds, stocks, real estate, and other assets. The combined $1.2 trillion deficit in one year is a sign of real trouble. Even in a country as rich as ours, that's one hell of a lot of money, and things aren't getting better.

We hear platitudes and wishful theories, including a new mantra from some conservative circles that deficits don't matter. Nonsense. Any working person with a checkbook can tell you that deficits matter. And if they won't, their banker will! Yet, in both Washington, D.C., and on Wall Street these days, up is down, black is white, greed is good, and deficits don't matter.

Somehow they think we can remain great as a nation of consumers, not as producers.

Folks in my hometown know better.

Wealth is measured by what you produce, not what you consume. America is a nation of builders, a nation of innovators, inventors, and creators, and driving that great engine of commerce is the American worker. Take those things from us, and you strip the country of its greatness. Whose self-destructive idea is this, anyway?

Well, for the past thirty years, America's largest corporations—along with the think tanks and the politicians who parrot their views—have shaped American trade policy for their own interests. They tell us that we now live in a global economy and our goal is to push for "free trade" policies. But as the globalization has galloped forward, and new trade agreements are negotiated, our trade deficit grows larger and larger, and more and more American firms move U.S. jobs overseas in search of lower wages and lower costs. The danger this poses to the American economy should be self-evident. But blithely they carry on, oblivious to the obvious.

Corporations are too busy counting their profits, politicians are too busy collecting their campaign contributions from those same corporations, and consumers are too distracted rushing to Wal-Mart and Target to buy their imported products. We American consumers watch our Japanese television set, wearing our Chinese T-shirts, Taiwanese trousers, Mexican shorts, and Italian shoes. We drive a Korean car to the store to pick up our Mexican vegetables, Australian beef, and a six-pack of Heineken.

And then we wonder what happened to all of the good jobs here at home.

THE INSANITY OF SELF-EXTINCTION

One man who is greatly concerned by this downward spiral is Warren Buffett, one of America's most successful businessmen and investors. When I visited with him recently, he told me that he believes our fiscal and trade policies, left unchecked, pose a real danger for our economy. He has made the same emphatic points in his letter to the Berkshire Hathaway shareholders. Looking at Warren's success over the past thirty years, we might want to start paying some attention. Warren is our country's second-richest man. But he lives simply in Omaha, Nebraska, and over the past three decades he has, by all accounts, been uniquely successful in predicting future economic trends in America. And today, as he looks forward, he sees trouble with these trade and fiscal policies.

Yet there seems to be little sense of urgency in most of Corporate America and none in the White House or Congress. Part of it might be that there is no politician, lobbyist, or journalist who is losing his or her job to outsourcing. It's the other folks who pay the price.

Self-extinction never makes sense, yet in today's economy, the role of the corporation (one of the dominant forces in our lives) has changed. Corporations today, larger and stronger as a result of mergers, have more economic muscle. And many think of themselves as international citizens, no longer uniquely interested in the impact their decisions have on the American economy. And none are raising their heads long enough during the hunt for profits to see the big picture.

The big picture is this: Slowly but surely, in the race for short-term profits, America's manufacturing base is being dismantled. Manufacturing is the backbone of a great nation. It's the manufacturing base that allowed America to retool swiftly and defeat Germany and Japan in the Second World War. Shipyards and foundries helped defeat fascism. They employed Americans who bettered their lives and created an economic juggernaut. Today, that economic strength is facing destruction in the name of globalism and in the search for high profits under the mantra of "free trade."

I admit "free trade" has a marvelous sound to it. It sounds distinctly "American." Give us a wide-open marketplace, and with American ingenuity and hard work, we'll triumph. That's the mantra. In fact, trade, as I will describe in greater detail later, can indeed provide great benefits to all of us. It can spur competition and innovation and provide new products for the marketplace. All of that is true.

The thing is, though, free trade must be fair trade, and these days it is *not*, and we in the United States are paying a huge price.

Our own negotiators have agreed to trade pacts that are decimating the bedrock of America—the middle-class workers whose sweat and brawn and toil built this country. The steelworker in Pittsburgh, the coal miner in West Virginia, the craftsman in Minnesota, the textile worker in Georgia, the metal fabricator in Ohio, and yes, the American farmer. Those good jobs are leaving America at a dizzying pace. And yes, some of them are being replaced—though with jobs that pay less and require less skill.

If you think that the worry about exporting American jobs is sheer nonsense, consider the recent article in *Foreign Affairs* by Princeton economist Alan Blinder, a former vice chairman of the Federal Reserve Board who is considered a mainstream economist.

Blinder says that in the new global economy it is not just manufacturing jobs that are at risk. His calculations are that "the total number of current U.S. service-sector jobs that will be susceptible to offshoring in the electronic future is two to three times the total number of current manufacturing jobs (which is about 14 million)." In short, Blinder calculates that between 42 and 56 million jobs could be sent abroad. And even if the jobs remain here, those who perform them will be competing with those in foreign lands doing the same work for far less money. That means a future with downward pressure on wages for those Americans whose jobs aren't sent offshore.

That's a sober warning from a highly reputable economist. And that is why we must begin to take this seriously.

THE BRUTAL LESSONS OF NAFTA

The international agreements that allowed nations to structure their business with each other started with the 1944 Bretton Woods Conference dealing with currency valuation and continuing through the establishment of the GATT (General Agreement on Tariffs and Trade) and finally the World Trade Organization. Along the way there were specific trade negotiations and agreements that began to shape the current U.S. trade strategy.

That strategy is, by now, a demonstrated failure. And there is enough blame to go around. The first Bush presidency began to negotiate the North American Free Trade Agreement, but it was President Bill Clinton who pushed it through the Congress.

Corporations, economists, newspapers, and others argued that all of this was a net benefit for our country because even though we would lose some lower-skilled jobs, our consumers would be able to purchase cheaper goods produced from foreign labor. Even better, we were promised it would also create new jobs here in the United States. Who could be against such a win/win deal?

I strongly disagreed with NAFTA (North American Free Trade Agreement) in speech after speech in the U.S. Senate, saying it would drain our country of good-paying jobs. And, unfortunately, I was proved right. We've suffered massive job losses because of NAFTA: 750,000 jobs lost at the minimum. In fact, contrary to the argument that the imports from Mexico would be the result of low-skill, low-wage jobs, the three largest imports from Mexico are now automobiles, automobile parts, and electronics—all the product of high-skilled jobs, displacing American jobs.

Have these new jobs significantly bolstered the Mexican workforce? No. Things haven't improved much in Mexico. In fact, Mexicans are now shocked to see some of their jobs migrating to China because even low-paid Mexican workers can't work cheaply enough to compete with lower-paid Chinese workers. And through it all, the United States is still losing substantial jobs. Ross Perot warned of a "giant sucking sound" as jobs left our country. Well, he was right. The relentless drain of jobs continues.

Need more proof? In 1994 the United States had a 1.3-billion-dollar trade surplus with Mexico. Ten years later it has become a 45-billion-dollar trade deficit. And still, some argue it is a success. Not for us it isn't!

There are many ways to sink a great ship—or an economy. You might strike an iceberg like the *Titanic* did, or a reef like the *Exxon Valdez*. The iceberg took down the *Titanic*, and the *Exxon Valdez* fouled Alaskan waters with crude oil and threatened the ecosystem. In one case, the captain was asleep; in the other case, the captain had been drinking and was not on the bridge. Now, let me be quick to point out I am not suggesting that the president is either asleep or drinking, but I do say the ultimate responsibility rests with the captain of the ship. This captain doesn't feel the pain of the millions of workers whose jobs are leaving our country, devastating families, even whole regions.

Wealth is a great insulator.

History tells us that the majority of the victims lost in the sinking of the *Titanic* were second- and third-class passengers, and immigrants and workers in steerage below. And so it is today as the giant corporations gather up profits through the outsourcing of American jobs. The wealthy grab the lifeboats, and the rest flounder. "Sink or swim," workers are told. "Compete with thirty-cent-an-hour labor or lose your job, that's just the new reality of the global economy," they say.

"Tough luck."

It's ironic. American jobs exit to China, where many workers slave away for pennies on the dollar when compared to American wages. What's the result of all of that? Lower prices for American consumers, you say? Sure, but don't forget who the American consumer is. It's you and me. It's Middle Americans. American workers—the same people under attack by outsourcing. Cut our paychecks; we cut our spending. It's astonishing. Corporate America is slowly but surely devouring its own customers.

It doesn't take a Ph.D. in economics to figure out that the unemployed or the underemployed—those formerly unemployed who have reentered the workforce at a much lower wage—have little disposable income. The buying will stop. Who steps up to the cash register then? Our friends in China who make a couple of dollars a day? I don't think so.

Economists were startled during the Christmas season of 2004 when Wal-Mart, the largest contributor to the U.S. trade deficit with China, reported lower than expected sales in what was supposed to be a strengthening economy. Why? I believe it is because lower-income and middle-income families who shop at Wal-Mart had less money to spend. That Wall Street recovery didn't show up in middle-income wallets. Upscale retailers were showing dramatically increased sales, while American workers under stress from lost jobs and lower-paying jobs had less money to spend.

DEBT EQUALS VULNERABILITY

So here we are, as a nation, up to our neck in debt. Our bankers abroad in China and Japan now hold about 40 percent of our debt. The problem is that debt equals vulnerability.

I don't know about you, but I know how it is in small-town America. No farmer in debt up to his eyeballs will engage his banker in any argument, be it religion or politics, at the risk of offending his lender. The lender is always the master. If China and America were not so intertwined economically, would we not press harder on the issue of human rights and workers' rights? Good question.

For years now, there has been only one consistent and thoughtless view about international trade being expressed in the United States by most corporations, politicians, and news outlets. That view says that "free trade" is good, and anyone who opposes it is some sort of xenophobic isolationist stooge who must want to build walls around our country and set the clock back a century.

Even in the face of all the evidence that this so-called "free trade" strategy is a bankrupt strategy, one that shortchanges our workers and cripples our manufacturing industries, American corporations and this administration continue to push the free trade myth.

After several decades of this trade strategy by both Republican and Democratic administrations, the results are in. We have become the biggest debtor nation on earth. Virtually every day's newspaper carries a dismal report of another company closing its U.S. manufacturing plant and moving jobs overseas to become "more competitive." In most cases, these companies export jobs overseas to produce products they will ship back to the United States. That's because there is no substitute for the American marketplace. It's the only one like it on the face of the earth. And the cornerstone of this marketplace has been a vibrant middle class.

So, let's gaze down the tracks into the future. Imagine the continued erosion of the middle class through the outsourcing of jobs. Can the wealthy, the upper 2 percent, possibly consume enough to drive the economy? *Of course not.* The broad middle class is the backbone of the American economy, and the American economy is the backbone of the global economy. The American worker is the most crucial cog in global commerce.

I believe in capitalism. Without it, society sinks into a malaise. The quest for profit, be it in the guise of efficiency, an improved standard of living, or cold, hard cash, is an engine that drives progress, but every engine must be monitored. It must be operated sensibly. Run the RPMs too high, and it blows up. Operate it carelessly, and it is ruined. That was clear in the nineteenth century, and clear in 1929.

THE CONTEST FOR THE SOUL OF THE COUNTRY

One school of thought sees our form of capitalism as one that should preclude *any* government involvement or regulation that would "tie the hands of business." They don't want any social interventions to aid the less fortunate. They don't want any government regulation of corporations. It's the Law of the Jungle: Eat or be eaten. Profit at all costs.

There's another school of thought that believes there is a marked difference between man and animal. That it is proper and noble that labors be rewarded, but also that the weak and defenseless not be exploited.

We are engaged in more than an academic debate over philosophy. I believe this to be a contest for the soul of a great nation, with immense ramifications for the entire world. It is about values. With all the talk about values in the 2004 election, why do government officials who develop our trade agreements care so little about the "value" of a good job? Do they really think it is fair for an American breadwinner to be forced, now, at the beginning of this new century, to compete with a twelve-year-old worker, working twelve hours a day, seven days a week for twelve cents an hour in some foreign country? It's happening! Every day. American workers cannot compete with that and shouldn't have to. Not after we've fought for a century for fair wages, safe workplaces, and the right to organize.

But corporate strategists set up no-win competitive comparisons between American workers and foreign workers, then tell U.S. workers they just don't cut it so they're moving their jobs to China, failing to take into account the ultimate devastation it will deliver to the American way of life. Sound crazy? Well, it is. In fact, it is unpatriotic. When corporations set up offshore subsidiaries in tax-haven countries to sell back to the company they own in the United States in order to show a paper loss, thereby avoiding U.S. tax liabilities, it is not only unpatriotic, it's also dishonest.

When hard work can't produce a living wage, I think it's immoral—in any country. In our finest hours, America has been generous, lifting up our neighbors. Now, the government is turning a blind eye to the exploitation of workers, both here and abroad.

FOR SOME, CORPORATE PATRIOTISM IS
JUST A DISTANT MEMORY

There are many business leaders in our country who are patriotic Americans and want our country to do well. And they make decisions reflecting that priority. I salute them and their corporations.

But there are an increasing number of corporations that move their jobs overseas and don't give a second thought to basing their decisions on factors that completely ignore the impact on our country or its workers. They deal in cold, hard cash. They've abandoned any pretense of patriotism. They've decided over several decades that they are no longer American corporations—they're international enterprises owing no allegiance to the country in which they were chartered. Their strategy is to define globalization pragmatically in their corporate self-interest. They salute dollars and cents. If they can hire cheap foreign labor for their production, they can fatten their profits, and, not coincidentally, their bonuses.

The influence that many of these corporations have over our government is enormous—and that may be the largest understatement of this book. Big business develops, with the support of our government, a set of trade policies that create opportunities for them to hire foreign workers to do what American workers used to do. Uncle Sam is selling out the American worker and, in the process, allowing these corporations to pole-vault over standards such as safe workplaces, minimum wages, labor unions, child-labor laws, and environmental protection. Some of the biggest corporations and best-known brand names have been able to circumvent all of those worker protections by moving their production overseas.

American politicians thumb their suspenders and speak of freedom all the time. "Freedom is on the march," they say. Right? No. Economic shackles are still shackles, and we are witnessing the creation of an economy transcending national boundaries. Some manipulative, unethical corporations chew up workers and spit them out in sweatshops around the world, creating enormous profits for a few while millions suffer. We're creating a world in which there are two classes—the wealthy and the poor.

The American Dream was a vision so powerful and so real that people came from all over the world to share it. It was a dream of opportunity and hope. We became a country who rejected the phrase "God save the King" in favor of "God bless America."

Have the new kings—multinational corporations—become too powerful to stop? We'll see. Some of us in Congress are fighting against the dismantling of the middle class, the approaches that threaten to diminish America as the number one economy in the world, the policies that have taken us from being the world's banker to the world's biggest debtor.

In a historical blink of an eye, our economic fortunes and outlook have changed in a way that should cause all of us grave concern. In this book I intend to expose the culprits and I offer some commonsense solutions. Even as you read this book, new trade agreements are being negotiated. It's the same old menu. American workers are being sold out, backdoor deals are in the works, but we can change all that. The people are still in charge. We have to organize and decide what kind of a country we want. In the manner that Adam Krebs shaped iron in his blacksmith shop, I hope this book will contribute to the shaping of a new trade policy that puts America first.

Let us strike a match to the forge.

TWO

THE SELLING OF AMERICA, PIECE BY PIECE . . .

I PLEDGE ALLEGIANCE TO THE FLAG . . ." DO THOSE words mean anything anymore? With all of the self-serving political talk about "values" these days and the burst of patriotism following the terrorist attacks against our country on September 11, 2001, I have often wondered whether all that talk about values or patriotism ever plays any role in business decisions about jobs.

I know it does with some companies. Those that believe their employees play a major role in their success.

Marvin Windows is a family-owned window manufacturer in Warroad, Minnesota, making high-quality windows. In 2005 they won a 156-million-dollar award in a lawsuit they had filed against a vendor who had furnished a defective preservative product for their windows. They stood behind their products made with the defective preservative and it nearly brought the company down. But later, after they had won their lawsuit against the vendor, at an employees' Christmas gathering in 2005, CEO and Chairman Jake Marvin announced that the company would be giving $50 million of that court award in bonuses to the employees of the company. That averaged $14,000 per employee. This is a company that has manufacturing plants in Minnesota, North

Dakota, and Oregon. It doesn't outsource its jobs to foreign countries. It treats its employees well. And it understands that it is an American company and, judging by its actions last Christmas, is proud of those who work for it and who stuck with the company during tough times. Now it wants its employees to share in its success. That is an American value worth remembering and celebrating.

And I know there are many other companies who have the same instinct to do right by their employees and do right by our country. Good for them! I applaud them!

But the answer to the question of who says the Pledge of Allegiance in the boardroom comes in many other forms as well.

A story in the *Detroit Free Press* about a General Motors meeting is just a small sample.

On April 7, 2005, Bo Anderson, the top purchasing agent for General Motors, gathered executives from the top suppliers to GM. He told the 380 executives that GM wanted to cut costs and that they should consider building their automobile parts in China. The effect, of course, would be to send even more American jobs overseas.

Meanwhile, even as GM is telling its parts suppliers they should move their jobs overseas, their biggest-selling brand, Chevrolet, waves the American flag and sports the tag line: "An American Revolution." It's a revolution all right! It's dumping American jobs in favor of cheap foreign labor.

The report in the *Detroit Free Press*, which exposed the meeting between GM and its suppliers, contained no obligatory platitudes from GM or even the same tired old lip service about competitiveness and the scourge of unions. I wondered how GM executives felt about brazenly telling suppliers to move their jobs to China. Did it matter to them? Or is it just about money, with all other considerations deemed irrelevant?

In November 2005, GM announced plans to cut thirty thousand jobs by 2008 and, according to *USA Today*, "shut nine of their factories." That is about 25 percent of GM's remaining U.S. workforce. Since 2000, GM had already cut twenty-nine thousand jobs. By midsummer 2005, the official unemployment rate in Detroit was 8.1 percent.

Also in late 2005, Delphi, the auto parts giant with 185,000 employees (a spin-off from General Motors), filed for bankruptcy. They said that they are paying workers $26 to $30 an hour and they want to cut costs by cutting workers' wages, health care, and retirement. The CEO said he hoped to get wages down to the eight-to-ten-dollar-an-hour level. And he said he hoped to outsource the production of much of what they manufacture offshore to take advantage of cheap labor.

Of course there is no discussion from the Delphi brass about the role that management might have played in pushing this company toward bankruptcy. The worker becomes the fall guy for aspiring to earn a good wage and support his family.

Then there is General Electric and the "GE April Fool's Day layoffs of 2005." Nearly five hundred workers at the Bloomington, Indiana, GE refrigerator plant learned on that day that they were going to lose their jobs. GE told the workers that the company planned to "discontinue production of mid-line, side-by-side refrigerator models that are not competitive on cost or product features."

What GE didn't tell the workers was that they were, at the same time, planning to set up a new operation in Mexico that would facilitate the manufacturing of the same type of side-by-side refrigerators that were being produced in Indiana. In Mexico GE builds the side-by-side refrigerators in a joint venture plant called Mabe, and when they were closing the Indiana plant GE was also building a new start-up plant called Qualcore in Celaya, Mexico, to supply parts for the appliances made at the Mabe plant. Even more, GE got a 3-million-dollar loan guarantee from the Export-Import Bank (a U.S. government agency) to build their new Mexico facility because it would include components from California and Illinois.

So, the Indiana workers lose their jobs. GE gets a U.S. government subsidy to build a new plant in Mexico. And it's just the global economy at work, right? Well, not really. It looks to me like it works for the big shots, but not so well for the people who lost their jobs in Indiana.

Or, consider the case of Big Blue, IBM. In June of 2005, *The New York Times* obtained internal documents that talked about how IBM was laying off thirteen thousand workers in the United States and Europe and hiring more than fourteen thousand workers in India.

Here's an excerpt from a presentation by IBM officials Harry Newman and Tom Lynch. They said, "The good news is that we have not been cited in the press a lot for what we are doing here. A couple of years ago we went to Mexico with our PC business . . . as a cheap source of labor. Now Mexico doesn't look as cheap as . . . some other labor markets."

Other IBM documents advise managers how to break the news to employees who are being laid off. "Do not be transparent regarding the purpose/intent . . . the terms On-shore [*sic*] and Off-shore [*sic*] should never be used." In other words, IBM executives wanted to get rid of their American employees but didn't want anybody to talk straight to them. Oh yes, the managers suggest workers be told "this action . . . is in no way a comment on the excellent work you have done over the years." Well, that had to be a big relief to those whose jobs were being shipped to India.

You don't have to be an economist or a mathematician to know that shipping good-paying American manufacturing jobs overseas is bad for our country. If workers must take lower-paying jobs with less disposable income, they are not the same reliable consumers who have pushed this economy forward since WWII.

When you consider that the poverty level rose for *the fourth straight year* under the Bush administration to 12.7 percent in 2005—some of that directly attributed to outsourcing—it appears that these gigantic corporations are digging their own graves. After all, to whom do they plan to sell their cars or computers when the middle class is diminished? It is impossible for the wealthy to consume enough to keep industry going.

At thirty cents an hour, Chinese workers are not going to be in the market for a Chevy or a laptop computer anytime soon, either. It should be obvious to these companies. Good-paying jobs are good for GM, good for IBM and the country.

Yes, this book is tough on some of our corporations. For good reason—I'm more than a little tired of these behemoth organizations hiding their misbehavior behind a corporate charter when they try to explain actions that hurt the country that nurtured them. Actions of some major corporations these days raise real questions about whether they care much about the future of this country. Structuring a business so that it can avoid paying U.S. taxes, outsourcing the labor, and hypocritically taking advantage of the U.S. marketplace by selling here can hardly be considered patriotic. That's a corporation that wants all of the benefits and none of the responsibilities that come with U.S. citizenship. That won't get them a spot in the Fourth of July parade in my hometown.

I know there are many other fine corporations who do business globally but understand that they are chartered in America and they behave accordingly.

I understand that big is not always bad and small is not always beautiful. Some things can only be accomplished by the economies of scale that come with large corporations. So this is not a book designed to paint all corporations or corporate executives with the same brush.

But still, if the shoe fits, wear it. And it damn well better be American-made.

THE ATTACK ON WHITE-COLLAR WORKERS

The delusional economic theory fed to Americans is that outsourcing is merely a transition. Blue-collar jobs go overseas, but the white-collar tech-based jobs would remain here in America. Anyone in the unemployment line in Silicon Valley will tell you that didn't quite pencil out, either. Those jobs are going to India in droves. In 2003, *The Washington Post* reported that more than *half* of all Fortune 500 companies were outsourcing software development overseas. It was having a chilling effect on senior software engineers, whose salaries had been driven down by outsourcing from $130,000 to $100,000 in a few short years.

Natasha Humphries is an example that the outsourcing of jobs is not just a manufacturing problem. She is a young African-American woman who received her college degree from Stanford University in 1996. She then went to work for Apple Computer, Inc. As she took additional classes and seminars in technology, she moved on to become a senior software testing engineer with Palm Pilot. But after three years on the job at Palm One, she lost her job.

In early 2002, the management at Palm Pilot decided to move all product testing to India and China, where they could pay wages as low as $2 an hour, a fraction of what they were paying engineers in the United States. Palm's management decided that, in order to make the engineers from India more productive, they would send engineers like Natasha to India to conduct training.

They assured Natasha that she would not lose her job due to off-shoring. She spent two weeks in Bangalore, India, helping train the Indian workers, then spent the next six months mentoring them from the United States. Despite assurances she had received from the company, Natasha was laid off in August 2003, along with 40 percent of her U.S. coworkers on the testing team. Why? She and her coworkers couldn't work for $2 an hour. So they couldn't compete with the engineers from India. Natasha told her story to a U.S. House committee in October 2003.

The ultimate indignity is that she had trained her own replacement. Here's the last message Natasha should have left on her Palm Pilot at work: *"My job's gone to India."*

So, we are told that we need to train more engineers here in the United States. But at the same time we had better answer the question about what those engineers can expect when they graduate from college. Is their future job competition going to be engineers from India who will work for one-fifth the wages here in the United States? How is that going to work to persuade young men and women to study engineering in colleges?

Samuel C. Florman, author and engineer, tackles the issue head-on in the *Engineering Times*:

> My instinct . . . is to support the engineering societies which seek, by legitimate political means, to protect their members from excessive foreign competition. What is excessive? Well, John Kenneth Galbraith said that politics "consists in choosing between the disastrous and unpalatable," and in this instance I believe it would be disastrous to so disenchant a large number of American engineers that the profession's image would be damaged and its appeal to talented youngsters diminished.

Florman is right. America lives and dies by innovation. If the innovators are all overseas, America's position on the top rung of the economic ladder will not last long. As important as the service industry is, America cannot be great if most of its workers are in the service sector or cashiering at Wal-Mart.

Many CEOs will tell you in today's global marketplace, there is no room for economic nationalism. They owe loyalty and service to their stockholders, not to their country. And so they circle the globe to determine where they can produce goods at the least cost and sell those foreign-made goods in the United States, where they can make the greatest profit.

The result is an unprecedented exodus of American jobs by companies that, in most cases, don't think much about the Pledge of Allegiance. Their pledge is to maximize profits, the consequences to our country be damned. The underlying philosophy of the free trade movement is that in the long run, things will turn out for the best. But while the politicians, academicians, and corporate leaders continue to promote free trade, real people are losing their jobs, and our manufacturing base is shrinking.

The following are just a few stories of American companies that have left our country. Have they left for better workers? No. They've left to find cheaper labor. Oh, they still want to be connected to America, because that's where they want to sell most of the products they produce. They just don't hire Americans to make those products. For some companies, outsourcing is a last-gasp attempt to compete. For others, it is greed and a complete lack of loyalty to their workers and to this country.

HUFFY BICYCLES: REMOVE THE AMERICAN FLAG BEFORE YOU GO

It was the last day of work at the Huffy bicycle plant in Celina, Ohio. The century-old company had terminated all of its eighteen hundred workers from plants in Ohio, Missouri, and Mississippi.

More than nine hundred employees at the Celina, Ohio, plant got their walking papers. Their jobs were going to a factory in China, whose workers are paid thirty-three cents an hour to work twelve to fifteen hours a day, seven days a week. At the plant in Shenzhen they are housed in crowded barracks and fed only two meals a day. These workers have no health benefits. (Like more than 40 million other Americans.) When they get sick they lose their jobs.

The new Huffy plant is located in the very same Chinese city where Wal-Mart held its annual board meeting recently. That is ironic, since it is alleged that it was Wal-Mart who instigated the move by demanding cheaper and cheaper bikes from Huffy, and as the number one bike seller in the country, Wal-Mart had the clout to make that demand stick.

One laid-off employee told me that he had worked for Huffy for ten years. "I was proud of the work we do here," he said. "I was proud to build American-made Huffy bikes." Many employees worked there for a lifetime, just as their parents had before them. These were considered good, stable jobs in the community. This was a good American company producing quality bicycles for more than a century. At one point they were making more than nineteen thousand bicycles a day!

It was an American company with a proud history, and most folks were working for less than $25,000 a year. The pride the employees had in American workmanship was evident in the small American flag decal between the handlebars and the front wheel of every bike.

While all of the workers at Huffy were sent packing, the CEO was paid $871,000 for that year.

"We made about $11 an hour plus benefits," sixty-four-year-old Ruth Schumacher said in an interview in the local paper after the layoff. "We weren't getting rich, but they were good jobs."

Ruth Schumacher did what she had to do after she lost her job at Huffy. "Now I earn $7 an hour in a part-time job tending the breakfast bar at the Holiday Inn, and I have trouble making ends meet," she said.

Her story illustrates the reality behind the facts and figures of unemployment and jobs creation. When some workers run out of unemployment benefits or just give up trying to find a job, they are no longer included in unemployment statistics. For instance, the official June 2005 unemployment rate in the United States was 5 percent. But 1.6 million people—*and that's up one hundred thousand over 2004*—who wanted to work but could not find a job were not included in that 5 percent. The actual unemployment rate was 6.1 percent—that's more than *9 million* Americans out of work.

Here's the scary part. Manufacturing jobs, which have long been a barometer of economic health, fell by twenty-four thousand in June 2005 alone. The manufacturing sector to that point had lost jobs in *twenty-five of the last twenty-nine* months. That is not a trend. It is a crisis. Yet it does not even appear on the Bush administration's radar screen. The manufacturing sector alone has lost *nearly 3 million jobs* under this president.

If Ruth had been able to find a job making hamburgers at McDonald's, the Bush administration would have counted her as working in a manufacturing job. That's right. The Bush administration 2004 Economic Report of the President thinks that flipping hamburgers might be "manufacturing."

So that's how they concluded that another 2.6 million jobs would be created in the next year? It sounds humorous to all but those people whose lives are turned upside down by the pink slips that tell them their real manufacturing jobs are gone.

How did things work out for Ruth Schumacher, who took a 37 percent pay cut after Huffy left town? She died of cancer sometime later. Her daughter is convinced that the stress of losing her job contributed to her early death.

The last job these fired Huffy workers had to do was the ultimate indignity. They had to take the American flag decal off the bike and replace it with a decal of the globe. If ever there is a metaphor for these harsh times, that is it.

Here's another. As I pointed out in chapter 1, a former employee told me that on the last day of work for the fired Huffy employees, as they drove out of the plant parking lot, every employee left a pair of shoes sitting in their now-empty parking space. It was a poignant message from the employees, telling the company, "You can move our jobs to China, but you're not going to be able to fill our shoes."

The epilogue to this story is that Huffy has now announced to its former employees in the United States that it has filed for bankruptcy and reneged on its pension obligations. The former employees received a letter telling them that the Pension Benefit Guarantee Corporation will now assume the payment of the pension. In other words, the company is going to get Uncle Sam (us taxpayers) to pick up the tab for the pensions that they had promised their former workers. Suddenly, that Huffy bike at those low Wal-Mart prices doesn't seem like much of a bargain, does it?

Think about it. We bail out reckless savings and loans. We bail out companies who have long abandoned any sense of American citizenship. We shower the great instigator—Wal-Mart—with tax breaks, then, when their workers can't make ends meet, we foot the bill for food stamps. Hidden in the seams of this economy is a welfare system for the richest corporations, and that ought to make your blood boil.

And here's the topper. In 2005, Huffy announced plans to become a Chinese-owned company. But, you know, when you think about it, isn't that just a formality?

ETCH A SKETCH: DRAW YOURSELF A PINK SLIP

I remember my first Etch A Sketch. Since 1960, there are few kids in the United States who haven't tried Etch A Sketch. It was one of those rare toys that appeal to all children. It brought out the creativity in kids and was a kind of perpetual drawing machine.

For years it was proudly "Made in the USA." But that changed a week before Christmas in 2003. Now, when today's kids get an Etch A Sketch, it is a Chinese-made toy. That probably doesn't matter much to the kids. But it sure does to the two hundred people who used to have union jobs in Bryan, Ohio.

The town of eight thousand identified with Etch A Sketch. It was the town mascot. It marched in the town parades. "You tell people you're from Bryan, and they look at you blankly," Carolyn Miller, a longtime assembly line worker at Ohio Art, told *The New York Times*. "You tell them it's the home of Etch A Sketch, and they smile." The sixty-four-year-old Miller continued, "Everyone knows the reason these jobs move to China. But when it happens to you, I can tell you, it hurts."

So, why *did* Etch A Sketch leave? It's a familiar story. When Wal-Mart, the largest toy seller in America, told Ohio Art Company, the manufacturer of Etch A Sketch, that it had to produce a product that sold under $10 to keep crucial Wal-Mart business, the owner of Ohio Art moved the production to China.

China now makes 80 percent of the toys sold in America in an estimated eight thousand toy factories. Conditions are often grim, and it is ironic that hardship is the price that must be paid to bring joy to American children.

Workers at Kin Ki, a toy company in Shenzhen, China, where Etch A Sketch is now manufactured, are paid twenty-four cents an hour with no health-care, retirement, or other benefits. *The New York Times* reported, "Kin Ki employees, mostly teenage migrants from internal provinces, say they work many more hours and earn about 40 percent less than the company claims. They sleep head to toe in tiny rooms . . . Most do not have pensions, medical insurance or work contracts."

Things are pretty tough in Bryan, Ohio, too. *The New York Times* reports, "Bryan's tax base is eroding from the loss of manufacturing and a population drain. The *Bryan Times* is full of notices of home foreclosures and auctions."

And as much as it was an economic blow to lose Etch A Sketch, the loss seemed to take a piece of Bryan's heart as well. "I could look at someone's face in the morning and see that something was wrong," said Nancy Bible, a lifetime employee. "Before the day was out, we all knew what it was."

The New York Times interviewed William C. Killgallon, Ohio Art Company's chief executive. "It tore our hearts out," he said tearfully in an interview in his office. "We ate with these people. We went to church with them. For some of them, this was the only job they ever had." Welcome to the brave new world of globalization, where even decent companies are forced to make heart-wrenching decisions. Most CEOs don't exhibit Killgallon's conscience.

FIG NEWTON COOKIES LEAVE A BAD TASTE IN MY MOUTH

If you have a hankering for Mexican food, it might surprise you if a clerk pointed you to the cookie aisle in the grocery store. That's right. Fig Newton, the cookie your grandmother kept around because they were about as healthy as a cookie could get, is now made in Monterrey, Mexico. And, as cookies go, maybe they are good for you. But they are not doing much for the American economy.

The story of Fig Newton mirrors thousands of other former American brands. Kraft Foods pragmatically decided to save money on labor costs. That's a nice way of saying they didn't think Americans were working cheap enough.

Why Mexico? Corporations can hire Mexican workers for much lower wages than they have to pay U.S. workers. And they don't have to worry about all of the other nuisances of labor law enforcement, environmental regulations, and more. While workers in New Jersey made $20 an hour, a Mexican employee gets $1.27.

Fig Newton first appeared on the grocery store shelves in America in 1892. It was a good year for figs. The cookies were produced by the Kennedy Biscuit Work in Massachusetts and named for Newton, Massachusetts. Through a number of mergers, the company became Nabisco, which was bought by Kraft Foods. And then it skipped town. Two hundred forty workers in Fair Lawn, New Jersey, were laid off.

"We ask our workers to absorb all the risk of trade, and they're not the ones who see the benefits," said Josh Bivens of the Economic Policy Institute, who was quoted in a *New Jersey Herald* story about the job loss.

Here's the impact NAFTA has had. According to the report, "In 1994, about 600,000 people were employed by *maquiladoras*—factories near the U.S. border making goods sold in the U.S. In July 2004, those factories employed about 1.1 million workers."

Before the North American Free Trade Agreement, which opened the doors to labor exploitation, Mexican manufacturing for export made up 11 percent of the country's gross domestic product in 1994. By 2003, it had *doubled* to 22 percent of the GDP, or just over one-fifth of the overall economy.

I don't take issue with Mexico's economic successes, or even China's, but their gains have largely come at the expense of the American worker—and the American economy. Exploiting labor forces in America and abroad by pitting them against one another is a flawed strategy and just plain wrong. You can't blame Mexico. They're playing the game created by global corporations, but the only ones winning are corporations. One of the basic rules for long-term successful trade is *everyone has to win*. Global corporations are making up the rules as they go along, but rule number one remains constant: Profit matters, people don't.

It can all work, but if international corporations continue to exploit the seams in this new global market in a way that weakens our economy, the U.S. government will have to force them to do the right thing. Every game needs referees. But don't expect this administration or their buddies in Congress to blow the whistle.

Mark Twain once said, "When there's no place left to spit, you either have to swallow your tobacco juice, or change with the times." Don't expect this administration to change with the times. They like this big-business strategy of "offshoring" or "outsourcing." So they'll just thumb their suspenders, swallow their tobacco juice, and ruminate how well things are going for them. But, then, they are not losing their jobs.

Okay. They're taking our cars, toys, and cookies. So help me God, if they take our beer, we'll organize a march on Milwaukee.

PENNSYLVANIA HOUSE FURNITURE WITH AN ORIENTAL TOUCH

Pennsylvania House Furniture dates back over a hundred years to Lewisburg, Pennsylvania. It was an old-line company that made some of the finest high-end furniture pieces in America in its heyday. If you had Pennsylvania House furniture in the house, then, that was saying something.

In 2000, Pennsylvania House was purchased by La-Z-Boy. Four years later, La-Z-Boy announced that it was going to close the Lewisburg plant and move the production to China, eliminating 425 jobs.

To say Pennsylvanians were surprised would be an understatement. How can you move a Pennsylvania company that uses special Pennsylvania wood to make furniture to China? It turns out it's easy. You just fire the workers and ship the wood to China. Then you ship the finished product back to the United States to be cynically advertised as Pennsylvania furniture.

But it's not as if some people didn't fight hard to keep those jobs in America. When La-Z-Boy announced they were moving the company, Pennsylvania governor Ed Rendell sprang into action and set up an action team of local investors to buy the plant from La-Z-Boy and keep the jobs in Pennsylvania.

They worked their tails off and put together a 37-million-dollar of-fer, but the La-Z-Boy management said no. They didn't want competi-tors in the United States. So they refused even to take the offer to their board of directors.

"It's agonizing," Rendell told a local newspaper when the deal fell through. He added: "We have to draw the line somewhere. We can't lose everything to China."

La-Z-Boy still promotes the Pennsylvania "legacy" on its Web site: "Deep in the lush green hills of Pennsylvania, in the heart of one of America's most beautiful natural forests, the legacy of Pennsylvania House began . . ."

Well, let me tell you how it all ended.

The *Daily Item* told the story of the last day at the factory:

> Robert Zechman's Christmas gift from the company to which he dedicated 29 years of his life was a severance package granting him just over $92 for each year he spent working at the plant.
>
> He got the letter outlining his severance on Dec. 21.
>
> It was the latest blow in a string of blows La-Z-Boy delivered this holiday season as it moved to close three local Pennsylvania House facilities and ship 425 jobs off to China.
>
> "I do not know how all the workers feel," said Zechman, 56. "But to me this is another slap in the face after spending 29 years working for this company."

When the last authentic piece of Pennsylvania House furniture rolled off the line, a few workers gathered to autograph the underside before it was crated for shipping. "Some lucky customer will buy the last piece that was ever made at Pennsylvania House with all our signa-tures on it," Zechman said. To the end, the craftsmen at Pennsylvania House showed the sort of pride that made the furniture great. God bless 'em.

LEVI LEAVES TOWN

Nothing seems more all-American than a pair of "Levi's." The brand conjures up images of both the Old West and Manhattan chic. But did you know that there isn't one pair of Levi's made in America anymore? The company—which held out long after other garment makers fled the country for cheap labor—now outsources production to fifty countries, including Mexico, Bangladesh, and China.

Brenda Pope was part of the grand Levi Strauss American tradition. She worked for Levi Strauss at the Blue Ridge, Georgia, plant with about four hundred friends and neighbors. But when the plant was closed in 2002, all she got for twenty years of service was $15,000 and a commemorative denim bag "made out of the same damn scraps I threw in a basket." Oh, she still has reminders of the job. On one wrist she has a purple scar that runs nearly to her elbow from the carpal tunnel surgery that was a result of two decades of sewing.

This is how Fred Dickey of the *Los Angeles Times* described her plight:

Measured against what most of us feel we need, the 44-year-old single mother asked little. She wanted to live among familiar pines and trustworthy people, create value with her hands and raise her child in the old ways. She did not think she needed a college degree to do these things. She was right, until she made the mistake of pricing herself out of the labor market—a feat accomplished by earning $14 per hour putting zippers in Levi's famous blue jeans.

Brenda Pope's job went to Mexico to a worker willing to settle for $1 an hour. Now, Brenda worries about how she will afford to pay the mortgage and care for her eleven-year-old son, Brian, who has lupus, which can be deadly if not treated. Treatments are expensive. "Lots of kids give him a hard time," Brenda said. "They call him pizza face and stuff like that. It just breaks my heart. He once asked me, 'Momma, are you ashamed of how I look?' When the doctor told him about the lupus, the only question he had was, 'Am I gonna die?'"

Brenda is divorced. And now, she is paying a steep price for mistakes made long ago. "I dropped out of school; figured I could live on love. I was stupid, I reckon," she said.

The reporter observes: "It's an old pattern. There are millions of people in this country like her who want to be productive workers and who are content to live marginally middle-class lives; instead, they become dependent on society because large corporations tromp on them chasing more profits from sweatshop foreign workers."

That's just one lost job and one hard-luck story. Now, let us measure the death of an industry and multiply Brenda Pope's story by half a million. In 1950, the U.S. garment industry employed 1.2 million, according to the *Los Angeles Times*. By 2001, that figure had fallen to 566,000. That same year, *83 percent* of all apparel sold in this country was imported.

Levi Strauss closed its last two American plants in San Antonio, Texas, in 2004.

AND THEN WE LOST OUR SHORTS—THE FRUIT OF THE LOOM STORY

You remember the commercials with two guys dressed as grapes (one bunch of red grapes and the other green grapes) dancing and singing odes to underwear? They were pretty jolly fellows as grapes go. Well, they didn't exactly sing out the news that the company was leaving Campbellsville, Kentucky, when the factory doors closed in 1998.

One former employee of the company recalled how the employees found out about the closing of the factory. "A company manager made an announcement over the P.A. system right before lunchtime. It was a thirty-second announcement."

In the time it takes for a heart to beat thirty times, a tradition half a century old ended. Some of the thirty-two hundred workers cried. Others became hysterical. In its heyday, the plant employed four thousand people who made $10–12 an hour. The company once employed as many as ten thousand workers in various Kentucky plants.

When I heard that Fruit of the Loom announced they were leaving, I said, "It's one thing to lose your shirt; it's another to lose your shorts!" Gallows humor, perhaps, but it wasn't funny to all of those who worked for the underwear company and lost their jobs to Mexico, El Salvador, then China.

The local newspaper, *The Courier Journal*, said:

> When Fruit of the Loom was king here, a job at 'The Factory' equated to a lifetime of well-paid security. High school class-mates, neighbors, brothers, sisters, parents and extended relatives spent entire careers working side by side, sewing, cutting and bleaching underwear for a household name. "It was a way of life," said Lana Wright, a Campbellsville native and 15-year Fruit of the Loom worker. "My mother was there; my brother was there, my husband worked there. My whole family." Opened in 1952, Fruit of the Loom's Campbellsville plant had so little turnover that about the only way to get a job there was when a relative re-tired.

Lana Wright and her family all found other jobs—for less money. She works for a collections firm, and her husband works for a company that manufactures travel trailers. Her mother retired, and her brother is in the lawn-care business and works for a plumber.

The company has had rough sledding, too. Fruit of the Loom filed for bankruptcy at the close of 1999.

The Fruit of the Loom Web site still emphasizes its all-American reputation: "For more than 150 years, Fruit of the Loom has fulfilled a promise to its consumers. . . . a promise of quality, value and trust." But for those thirty-two hundred workers whose lives were changed with a terse thirty-second announcement, forgiveness does not come easy. One former worker told me, "Nobody in the area buys Fruit of the Loom underwear anymore."

RADIO FLYER LITTLE RED (CHINA) WAGON

On the west side of Chicago, there are ninety workers who have been making the little red wagons named Radio Flyer for decades. In fact, the company has been in business since Woodrow Wilson was president, making the wagons that nearly every American child recognizes. But those ninety people were told recently that their jobs were moving. Sure enough! To China!

This is a company with such a great history. In 1917, a young Italian immigrant named Antonio Pasin started the company in a one-room workshop. The trained cabinetmaker had no luck finding a woodworking job, so, despite enduring long working days hauling water for a sewer-digging crew, he spent his evenings making handmade, wooden wagons he called Liberty Coasters—named after the Statute of Liberty. The man loved his adopted home. Later, he decided to name his wagons Radio Flyers in honor of Guglielmo Marconi, who invented the radio. The "flyer" part of the name was a reflection of his fascination with airplanes.

In 2003, Antonio Pasin was inducted into the Toy Industry Hall of Fame.

In my mind, I can imagine the young craftsman so filled with pride in his new home and the opportunity he found in America, and I wonder what he would think of his grandson's decision to abandon the country that was Antonio's salvation. Robert Pasin, the third generation CEO, said the move to China was to "keep pace with the toy industry."

Let me tell you, I took it hard when I heard the news. I wasn't the only one. Jack Zaleski, an editor at the *Fargo Forum*, spoke for many Americans when he wrote the following piece about Radio Flyer:

> I inherited my first Radio Flyer wagon. I discovered it buried beneath a heap of dusty burlap sacks in my grandparents' garage. It had been there for years, forgotten when my father and his brothers grew out of toys.

The little red wagon was packed and pitted with rust. The paint was faded and stained by coal dust. My father said he and his brothers used the wagon to carry coal they'd picked up along the railroad tracks during the Depression.

The wagon was dented and scratched, and the rubber wheels worn smooth, testifying to the hard use it had gotten in the 1920's and 1930's. 'Take it,' my grandmother said.

I used it until the wheels fell off.

When my kids were young, they had a Radio Flyer—the wood sided model—in which they flew down the sloping gravel drive to our rural home. They beat the hell out of it, but it held together until they left childhood things behind.

A couple of years ago, I bought a new Radio Flyer—the standard model—for our grandchildren. As I assembled the sturdy, steel classic, it took me back to that first rusted, coal stained treasure in my grandparents' garage. The uniquely American continuity of the Flyer struck me.

Uniquely American? No more, I guess . . .

The fate of the Radio Flyer Company is a symptom of the erosion of the nation's traditional manufacturing sector. Free traders and globalists say the change is a positive economic evolution that eventually will lead to better U.S. jobs and stability among developing nations. Better jobs in nations like China will result in more Chinese consumers who want to buy products to improve their lives. So the market expands and everybody wins.

But if the goods Chinese consumers want are made in China, the Chinese consumer with money to spend will buy things made—*where?*—in China. Little red wagons, for example.

It's all beginning to look like a business-driven transfer of America's once-unchallenged industrial dominance to any foreign country that delivers cheap labor.

I'd rather pay a few bucks more for a Radio Flyer knowing it was made by an American worker supporting an American family.

Yeah, yeah, I know that smarter-than-me economists and corporate board room gurus would classify me as a modern-day Luddite. But surely there is something morally suspect and ethically challenged about American corporations putting Americans out of work and justifying the damage by crowing about stabilizing China's economy . . .

Fact is it's about the bottom line. Move it to China and the profit margins fatten. Move it to China and stockholders grin. Hitch your little red wagon to the amoral sweep of unfettered globalized capitalism, and there's money to be made.

Not me. As long as Radio Flyers are made in China, I'll never buy another one.

OUTSOURCING AIRLINE MAINTENANCE

In October 2005, an Airbus 320 owned by Jet Blue was flying in circles near the Los Angeles International Airport, dumping fuel in anticipation of a potential crash landing. The television networks were covering it live as this plane with 145 passengers aboard prepared to attempt a landing with its nosewheel stuck, pointed in the wrong direction. When the plane finally touched down, the nosewheel hit the runway with a cloud of smoke and a fireball. It looked for a moment like it would end in tragedy. But, fortunately, the nosewheel did not collapse, and the plane rolled safely to a stop.

As I watched that scene unfold, I was thinking of a news story I had read months before.

An article in *The Wall Street Journal* reported that JetBlue Airlines was flying some of its Airbus airplanes to El Salvador for maintenance. That's right; to save money they had outsourced the maintenance of their planes. It is less expensive to have Salvadoran mechanics do the maintenance than to have it done by U.S. workers.

Airplane mechanics in El Salvador are paid from $300 to $1,000 per month. Only about one-third of them have passed the FAA certification for airplane mechanics that all U.S. mechanics are required to pass. In El Salvador, only the supervisors in the work group must have passed the FAA exam—in fact, that is the case whenever the mainte-nance is outsourced.

For the record, I found through an inquiry that the plane with the nosewheel problem had not had its maintenance done in El Salvador. But I wonder how many passengers on U.S. airlines know that close to one-half of the maintenance work on U.S. airplanes has now been out-sourced both to outside companies in the United States and to compa-nies in foreign countries. I wonder how airline passengers feel about farming out airplane maintenance to the lowest bidder here and abroad?

The thing is, this is not just about airlines. It is about a new business strategy in the United States to "outsource" nearly everything. In most cases the root of the decision is to get rid of American workers, espe-cially those that have a union contract and are making a good income with pension and health benefits, and replace them with lower-paid workers here and overseas.

I read recently about a worker whose job had been outsourced who decided to go back to school to become a mortician. "They can't out-source that," she said.

I'll guarantee you the "suits" on the top floor aren't losing their jobs. They are being *rewarded* for their cold-blooded calculations. According to *Forbes* magazine, as a group, the top five hundred CEOs in America received a 54 percent pay raise in 2004—of course, much of that can be attributed to the value of stock options. But if wages are the big issue, a Fortune 500 company could look to CEOs' salaries ($11.8 million was the average CEO salary in 2004) for some savings.

According to United for a Fair Economy and the Institute for Policy Studies, the ratio of average CEO pay to worker pay (now $27,460) in-creased from 301-to-1 in 2003 to 431-to-1 in 2004. Let's break that down a bit further. If the $5.15 minimum wage had risen as fast as CEO pay since 1990, the lowest-paid workers in the country would make $23.03 an hour.

So why don't CEOs get outsourced? The short answer is because they look out for themselves. It is just the employees that are treated like a worn-out machine. Use it and discard it when you are through. It's a hell of a poor way to run a company, but it has, regrettably, become commonplace in too many companies.

How did we get to this great divide? What changed? Wasn't there a time when a worker could sign on with a company and make it a lifetime's vocation and retire with a solid pension and a gold watch? Wasn't there a time when bosses were as loyal to their workers as their workers were to them? One answer as to what happened is bad trade negotiations. After multiple trade agreements called GATT, NAFTA, CAFTA, WTO, and more, things have gotten worse. Much worse.

When we signed an agreement after WWII, called the General Agreement on Tariffs and Trade (GATT), our trade deficit began to grow. We negotiated a trade agreement with Canada and a modest deficit with Canada turned into a huge trade deficit. The agreement called NAFTA (North American Free Trade Agreement) occurred when we had a small trade surplus with Mexico, and it has turned into a huge deficit. How is that bilateral trade agreement with China working out? Well, our trade deficit with China has increased to over *$200 billion a year* since we negotiated that one.

And the World Trade Organization . . . This one actually creates a new governing body. You hear a lot of discussion about the WTO, which was launched in 1995, and there is plenty of reason for concern. Our membership has cost this country sovereignty on some very important matters.

The WTO is essentially an extension and expansion of the old GATT treaty. What the WTO does is subject a democratic country to taking orders from those with a corporate mind-set. There's no Constitution or Bill of Rights to protect the vulnerable in this country or others. The WTO would not allow a ban of products made by child labor and makes no allowance for bans against goods produced under ruthless dictatorships.

Rather than being a means to save the world's rapidly disappearing resources, the WTO—again, with the best interests of corporations in mind—threatens to worsen the problem. Environmental protections are often viewed as trade barriers. For instance, the WTO once ruled that the U.S. Clean Air Act, which demanded that domestic *and* foreign producers market cleaner-burning gasoline, was illegal. More recently, the Endangered Species Act, which requires shrimp sold in the United States to be caught with nets that allows sea turtles to escape, was ruled illegal.

The WTO has opened the door wider to companies willing to exploit cheap labor and lax environmental standards, around the world. The pollution still floats back to America, and the pressure of outsourcing drags down wages of those still employed. By underpaying and overworking the global workforce, we're not doing impoverished nations any favors, either.

Global Exchange, a world-trade watchdog, says:

> By creating a supranational court system that has the power to economically sanction countries to force them to comply with its rulings, the WTO has essentially replaced national governments with an unelected, unaccountable corporate-backed government . . .
>
> The World Trade Organization is the most powerful legislative and judicial body in the world. By promoting the "free trade" agenda of multinational corporations above the interests of local communities, working families, and the environment, the WTO has systematically undermined democracy around the world.

EXPLOITATION IS NOT COMPARATIVE ADVANTAGE

Time and time again, companies decide that they can move their jobs to Mexico, China, Indonesia, or other countries to save costs and boost profits. It's bad for labor in both countries in the long run, but it's good for the company bottom line in the short run.

The economists say it is just something called "comparative advantage" in action. Those economists, puffing on their pipes, doubtless sitting in their sunrooms wearing their sweaters with leather-patched sleeves, are meditating on the theory developed by David Ricardo in 1815. In Ricardo's Theory of Comparative Advantage, he used an example of trade between England and Portugal.

England had a climate that made raising sheep advantageous. Portugal, on the other hand, had a climate more hospitable to growing grapes. So the English would raise sheep and shear them for the wool. The Portuguese would grow grapes and turn them into wine. Then they would trade. English wool for Portuguese wine.

As the theory goes, the productivity of both nations would increase. Each was doing what was most efficient for them, then trading with the other. That's the simple description of "comparative advantage."

The English-Portuguese example describes a *natural* comparative advantage each has with respect to the raising of sheep and the growing of grapes. It has to do with the climate and the soil, etc. Wine makers made a good living as did English shepherds. However, Ricardo's theory was developed two centuries ago when trade was largely country to country. That is no longer the case. Now, most of the international trade is trade between companies—and as we shall see later, often between companies that are essentially the same entity.

Let's look at the way trade is today. We'll call it "Dorgan's Doctrine of Manipulated Advantage." Say a Chinese manufacturing company sells the toys it produces to a U.S. retailer. While there is an advantage to producing toys in China, it is not a "comparative advantage." *Governments* create the advantage. One allows its labor force to be exploited for low wages. The other turns a blind eye as jobs are sucked from its workforce. It is not some natural "comparative" advantage. It is a *manipulated* trade advantage. Neither labor force wins.

For example, the Chinese government decides the conditions of production in China. When they decide it is okay for children to work, or for workers to be put in unsafe workplaces, or for companies to pollute the air and water, or to fire or jail those who try to start a union, those are political decisions made by a government. Yes, they can create an economic advantage. But it is not a *natural* comparative advantage. Manufacturing is less expensive in China precisely because workers are exploited. Trying to compete with that is to engage in a race to the bottom. And it is a race our trade agreements should prohibit.

When the political system of a country creates the artificial advantage for gain, say, through repressed labor rights, it has nothing to do with Ricardo's theory. And yet those economists who are employed by the corporations that benefit, continue to connect it to Ricardo's theory.

As I researched trade issues and theories I came across an interesting case—it is something David Ricardo would never have imagined. I'm not sure if this qualifies as comparative advantage or not. Did you know that under the NAFTA trade agreement, Canada under the special visa provisions allowed 622 Mexican exotic dancers to come to work in Canada?

The Canadians said the strippers were allowed in under the "special skills" category in NAFTA. So, there is a shortage of naked people in Canada? And what are those special skills? The *Toronto Sun* reported that in order to qualify for the "special skills" designation, exotic dancers had to send a videotape of their "special skills," which were then reviewed by Canadian Customs officials. Customs officials denied watching such videos. The *Toronto Sun* sticks by its story. And Ricardo is rolling over in his grave.

Okay, back to serious issues. The truth is, Ricardo described comparative advantage at a time when multinational corporations really didn't exist. Now, both capital and technology are transportable, so those who want to produce abroad can search the globe for billions of desperate low-wage workers and governments willing to exploit them. And it is happening at a breakneck pace.

Those of us who dare question any of these government trade policies or the actions of the global corporations are vilified as xenophobic, isolationist Luddites who just don't understand the modern world. They suggest we want to put up walls around our country and retreat into a protected shell safe from the rest of the world.

At least that is the uninformed rant from the blind who preach to the deaf about the virtues of our current trade debacle. They are preaching this nonsense to the ones who haven't lost their jobs yet. Once you've been laid off, your attention span gets real good—but by then it is too late.

The propaganda continues. Corporations, economists, and even our government tell us how wonderful it is that American workers can buy cheaper goods at Wal-Mart at a discount the day after they get their pink slips telling them their jobs have been outsourced.

A few years ago, I responded to *The Washington Post* columnist James Glassman's gushing commentary about the "success" of NAFTA after we had lost hundreds of thousands of jobs. His hubris reflected the blind confidence of so many "pro-business" politicians in Washington.

I wrote, "Glassman would've been perfect as a scout for General Custer. I can almost hear him say, 'Things look mighty good at the Little Big Horn, General.'"

THREE

EXPORTING MISERY

THE SHORT, CHUBBY MAN WITH THE MUSTACHE AND the ruddy red cheeks walked to the podium in the chamber of the U.S. House of Representatives. He waited until the lengthy standing ovation had ended; then he told his powerful story. . . .

It was a Saturday morning in a shipyard in Gdansk, Poland, and he was there to lead a group of workers in a strike against the communist government. He was an electrician who had already been fired from his job at the shipyard for his previous actions to organize workers.

On that morning, he was grabbed by the communist secret police, and they began to beat him severely. Then they hoisted him up and threw him over the barbed wire at the top of the fence surrounding the shipyard.

The man continued his story with every eye, including mine, riveted upon him.

He told us that he lay there, facedown in the dirt, bleeding, wondering what to do next. Our history books tell us what he did. He picked himself up and climbed right back over the fence into that shipyard again.

Ten years later, he was introduced to the U.S. Congress as the president of the country of Poland. That is when I heard Lech Walesa's story.

Lech Walesa was not an intellectual, a military leader, a business leader, or a politician. He was an unemployed electrician who believed that workers should be able to organize and should be free to choose their own destiny.

He said, "We didn't have any guns. The communist government had all the guns. We didn't have any bullets. The communist government had all of the bullets. We were armed only with an idea . . . *and ideas are more powerful than guns.*"

It was a speech I will never forget. Its simplicity and power was explosive. This ordinary man, Lech Walessa, lit the fuse that caused the explosion that brought down the communist government of Poland. And then Romania, Bulgaria, East Germany, and others. One by one, the communist governments fell in Eastern Europe. Freedom won. Their weapon was called "Solidarity." With it, they defeated communism.

The uncommon courage by a common man who knew the power of an idea—the idea that workers should be free to form labor unions and to choose their own destiny—was widely admired in America. Our country cheered for the brave members of the Solidarity labor movement who were willing to take on a much more powerful and dangerous foe, the communist government, at great personal risk.

But in more recent years that lesson has been lost on President Bush and on some in Congress. Now unions are often seen as a threat to maximum corporate profits.

At every opportunity the Bush administration tries to prevent labor from gaining ground. Even following Hurricane Katrina, President Bush announced that he would repeal the federal contracting provision that requires contractors to pay "prevailing wages" to their workers. This provision is called Davis/Bacon and was put in place to prevent contractors from competing for federal contracts by exploiting workers with sub par wages. Businesses have been trying to get rid of that requirement for years. In the days following Hurricane Katrina, President Bush announced he would waive the Davis/Bacon requirements for reconstruction contracts. In other words the president didn't want businesses that got contracts for gulf reconstruction to have to pay prevailing wages. Some weeks later, the president retracted his order after he was embarrassed by the bad publicity and pressured by Congress.

There's an irony in all of this. It was the support of Ronald Reagan for Solidarity and the labor movement that opened the door to freedom. In comments after Reagan's death in 2004, Walesa eulogized the fortieth president of the United States:

> I distinguish between two kinds of politicians. There are those who view politics as a tactical game, a game in which they do not reveal any individuality, in which they lose their own face. There are, however, leaders for whom politics is a means of defending and furthering values. For them, it is a moral pursuit. They do so because the values they cherish are endangered. They're convinced that there are values worth living for, and even values worth dying for. Otherwise, they would consider their life and work pointless. Only such politicians are great politicians, and Ronald Reagan was one of them.

So while Ronald Reagan set the stage to bring Republicans back into power in Washington, and has become a GOP deity, many in his party have forgotten the principles he stood for. And while I think some of Ronald Reagan's domestic policies were misguided (and there were times he showed a callousness to workers and labor unions here in America), I do not believe for a moment that he *intended* to be the enemy of common working Americans.

The waiving of Davis/Bacon for hurricane reconstruction is just one of many actions taken by the current administration to undercut unions and organized labor. When, in 2004, the president signed a bill cutting 6 million workers' overtime pay, Harry Kelber, a commentator on union issues, said, "President George Bush handed Corporate America a gift worth billions of dollars, for which it had lobbied unsuccessfully for 66 years—the elimination of overtime pay for hours worked beyond 40 in a given week." It was a direct attack on the 1938 Fair Labor Standards Act.

This sort of thing has been going on for a long while in our country. Now, with the advent of the global economy, American businesses can undermine workers and labor unions by moving the jobs overseas to countries that will fire or jail those who want to organize.

With all of the discussion about freedom these days (President Bush's second inaugural address was almost solely about freedom), it is fair to point out that this so-called free trade is actually allowing those who don't like labor unions in the United States to weaken them by sending their jobs to foreign countries where, in many cases, there is no such thing as a free labor movement.

We have a short memory.

It wasn't so long ago that the battles for workers' rights occurred right here in the United States.

THE FORGOTTEN FIGHT FOR FAIRNESS

You might not know about James Fyler. He died of acute lead poisoning.

He was shot fifty-four times.

He wasn't a gang member or a terrorist. He was a member of a labor union. And he was killed at what was called the Ludlow Massacre. Now, this happened nearly a hundred years ago, and probably isn't mentioned in most school history books, but that doesn't mean James Fyler and what he stood for isn't important.

It was April 20, 1914. In Ludlow, Colorado, nine thousand mineworkers were on strike for better working conditions and higher wages. John D. Rockefeller's Colorado Fuel and Iron Company

(CF&I) and other smaller companies refused to meet with the miners to discuss things such as union recognition, an eight-hour workday, abolition of armed guards, a pay increase, and enforcement of Colorado's mining laws.

By April the dispute had escalated and a troop of National Guardsmen were camped in the hills above Ludlow station. It was no ordinary National Guard unit. It included mine owners, mine guards, pit bosses, and assorted ruffians. One publication called them a "force of professional gunmen and thugs subservient to the will of the mine owners."

On Monday morning, April 20, 1914, the National Guardsmen in the hills overlooking the tent colony opened fire with a machine gun and rifles. The miners shot back, but when the gun battle was done at the end of the day, the guardsmen overran the tent city. They used kerosene to set the tents on fire. Over forty striking miners and their families were killed, including eleven children and two women. James Fyler, the union secretary, was shot fifty-four times simply because he believed that some of the fruits of a worker's labor ought to go to the worker.

LABOR STANDARDS HELP BUILD THE FOUNDATION OF THE COUNTRY

While "globalization" has galloped along at lightning speed in recent years, the rules for globalization have not kept pace. I believe that by helping create a broad middle class, the labor movement in America was a crucial key to opening the door of greatness for this nation. And can be for underdeveloped countries as well. Reasonable workplace standards and fair wages built a strong working class that became the backbone of America. But it has not been easy, and there have been great sacrifices along the way.

- In 1835, children working in the silk mills in Paterson, New Jersey, went on strike. Their demand? An eleven-hour day and a six-day workweek.

- In 1877, ten coal-mining labor activists were hanged in Pennsylvania. Also that year, U.S. rail workers struck to protest wage cuts, resulting in thirty deaths at the hands of federal troops.
- In 1884, the Federation of Organized Trades and Labor Unions—a forerunner to the AFL—passed a resolution in support of the eight-hour workday that began to transform thinking about labor standards in America.
- In 1903, the famous Mary Harris "Mother" Jones led child workers in a demand for a fifty-five-hour workweek.
- In 1911, a fire at the Triangle Shirtwaist Company killed 147, mostly women and young girls, who were locked in the ten-story building in sweatshop conditions. Company owners were indicted for manslaughter.
- In 1919, in the wake of the steelworkers' strike, 250 so-called "anarchists, communists, and labor agitators" were deported to Russia.
- In 1920, U.S. Bureau of Investigation officers targeted labor leaders, who were prosecuted as anarchists.
- In 1932, five auto workers were killed and dozens beaten by Dearborn, Michigan, police and Ford goons in the Hunger March against Ford Motor Company. While Henry Ford should be credited for his support of a minimum wage, he was no friend of unions.
- In 1934, two workers were killed in the "Battle of Toledo" during a 1934 strike against the Electric Autolite Company. The conflict led to the organization of the United Auto Workers International Union. Also in 1934, in an incident known as "Bloody Thursday," a California coast shipyard strike ended with six dead strikers, hundreds beaten and gassed.

THE SACRIFICE OF FANNIE SELLINS

I want to tell you about an exceptional woman named Fannie Sellins, a widowed garment worker who helped organize the United Garment

Workers of America in 1911 to clean up the horrid sweatshop conditions. In that experience, she discovered her calling, and soon thereafter helped organize the United Mine Workers of America, whose members worked in more dangerous and dismal conditions than did women and children in sweatshops. Her reward was six months in a West Virginia prison for "inciting to riot." President Woodrow Wilson pardoned her, and she was released.

The details of her death at forty-seven are foggy, but some say that during the Allegheny mine strike of 1919 she was rushing to move some children out of danger when drunken deputy sheriffs led by a mine official rushed the picket line, brutally clubbing and killing miner Joseph Starzeleski. When Fannie Sellins attempted to intervene, she was clubbed to the ground. As she tried to drag herself away, she was shot three times. A deputy then stepped up and fired another shot into the motionless body, as her false teeth lay nearby in a pool of blood.

Before the body was hauled away in the back of the truck, a deputy crushed her skull with a club. One of the deputies picked up the dead woman's hat, put it on, and danced around exclaiming, "I'm Mrs. Sellins now!"

No one was ever convicted of the murders.

Fannie Sellins's story is important because, today, her work is being undone by corporate mind-sets that are pitting American workers against those in third-world countries, and American workers are losing their jobs. In some of the sweatshops in dark corners of the world, many workers are losing their lives.

THEY TOOK THE FREEDOM OUT OF FREE TRADE

While our society is still not perfect, we have since made a lot of progress by developing rules and standards that give workers the power and ability to organize and push for humane standards like reasonable hours, wages, safe workplaces, and child-labor laws.

But that was before the "global economy" made U.S. labor laws obsolete.

In the new world order, if corporations find the labor laws in the United States too stifling, they can just move their operations abroad, where they are not inconvenienced by them.

The clock is being turned back. So much for worker rights.

"Free Trade! Free Trade!" It has become the mantra of the global corporations and their cheerleaders, suggesting all of the virtues of freedom. But is this "free trade" a practice that is mislabeled? Is it really about freedom? If so, for whom? And more important, is this free-trade strategy of the United States exporting freedom or misery?

At the end of 2005 the World Bank released a book that pulled the rug out from under those who have been selling the notion of free trade as the cure-all to help the poor people in the world. For many years the World Bank has been cited by the experts as claiming that eliminating all tariffs in world trade would lift many of the world's poor out of poverty.

Just three years ago the estimate by the Bank was that eliminating all subsidies and barriers, including tariffs, would lift 320 million people above the two-dollars-a-day poverty level by 2015. However, their new estimates suggest that from 6 to 12 million people would be lifted from that poverty level. That's quite a change. In 2003, the free-trade advocates were boasting that there would be close to a trillion dollars of benefits from their plan. Now, the new study claims no more than one-eighth of that gain.

It is unbelievable that American workers are being burned at the stake by a trade strategy that moves their jobs overseas and lowers their income, for what? There is no significant benefit to poor people. It is the excuse the corporate beneficiaries used to justify their strategy. But it's now clear. This is about corporate profits, not about helping poor people.

I'm sure there are examples around the world where the new strategy of global trade has provided opportunities for those who have never had it before. But, for every inspiring story of opportunity, there are countless horror stories both here at home and abroad.

WORKED TO DEATH IN A TOY FACTORY

One of those stories is the account of a young Chinese woman named Li Chunmei. It is too late for her to tell her own story. I read about her death in *The Washington Post*, a newspaper that supported the very trade policies that created the type of jobs resulting in this young woman's death. But to the newspaper's credit, it is also exposing some of the worker abuses with stories like this.

The editorial pages of our major newspapers continue to preach the virtue of this so-called "free trade" without telling the American people the real cost of that trade. So let me describe some of the costs. Every U.S. consumer should know what has happened to this young woman and many others like her.

According to *The Washington Post*:

On the night she died, Li Chunmei must have been exhausted. Coworkers said she had been on her feet for nearly 16 hours, running back and forth inside the Bainan Toy Factory, carrying toy parts from machine to machine. When the quitting bell finally rang shortly after midnight, her young face was covered with sweat.

This was the busy season before Christmas, when orders peaked from Japan and the U.S. for the factory's stuffed animals. Long hours were mandatory, and at least two months had passed since Li and the other workers had enjoyed even a Sunday off.

Lying on her bed that night, staring at the bunk above her, the slight 19 year old complained she felt worn out, her roommates recalled. She was massaging her aching legs, and coughing, and she told them she was hungry. The factory food was so bad, she said, she felt as if she had not eaten at all . . .

Finally, the lights went out. Her roommates had already fallen asleep when Li started coughing up blood. They found her in the bathroom a few hours later, curled up on the floor, moaning softly in the dark, bleeding from her nose and mouth. Someone called an ambulance, but she died before it arrived.

The exact cause of Li's death remains unknown. But what happened to her . . . in this industrial town in southestern Guangdong province is described by family and friends and coworkers as an example of what China's more daring newspapers call "guolaosi." The phrase means "over-work death" and usually applies to young workers who suddenly collapse and die after working exceedingly long hours, day after day.

Li came from a poor, remote village in the mountains seven hundred miles from the factory town where she died. She left school in third grade and was put to work farming and feeding the livestock. Then, at age fifteen, she was sent to work in the toy factories in the city. I've seen a picture of the pretty young woman, and she would have been even more beautiful had the strain of her hard life not been so evident on her young face.

She died working in conditions that we, long ago in America, decided we would not tolerate. She died making stuffed animals. Perhaps one of them lies on your child's bed.

The minimum wage for workers like Li was thirty cents per hour. And overtime is limited to no more than thirty-six hours a month and it must be voluntary. But according to those who have investigated working conditions in China, these restrictions are largely ignored. Workers like Li are forced to work up to sixteen hours a day in polluted plants without air-conditioning and in temperatures reaching near ninety degrees. Workers are housed in cramped company dormitories, twelve to a room. And so, a young woman named Li dies. Worked to death. But who cares?

The profits on those stuffed toys were great.

I'm sure the stockholders were pleased.

THE CHINA GRIND

A worker in China, as documented by a National Labor Committee report, may work for literally pennies per hour. Or less. When the workers are done for the day, they often have to pay the factory for food and shelter.

The 1998 NLC report discovered that warehouse workers making the handbags marketed by Wal-Mart earned as little as ten cents an hour. The workweek in the Qin Shi Factory, where Kathie Lee handbags were manufactured, was as long as ninety-eight hours. The report continued, "At the end of the day, the workers return 'home' to a cramped dorm room sharing metal bunk beds with 16 other people. At most, workers are allowed outside the factory for just one and a half hours a day. Otherwise, they are locked in."

The report said, "The workers are charged $67.47 for dorm and living expenses, which is an enormous amount given that the highest take-home wage our researchers found in the factory was just 10 cents an hour. There were others who earned just 36 cents for more than a month's work, earning just 8/100th of a cent an hour. Many workers earned nothing and owed money to the company." When Tennessee Ernie Ford lamented, "I owe my soul to the company store," it was nothing like this.

According to the same 1998 research, workers in Kmart factories made twenty-eight cents an hour. Garment makers for JCPenney were paid eighteen cents. Women making Ralph Lauren blouses, which sold for $88 in the United States, pocketed twenty-three cents an hour. Young women making just fourteen cents an hour sewed two-hundred-dollar Ann Taylor jackets and skirts.

It was the National Labor Committee's research that first brought the issue to the forefront in 1996, when NLC director Charles Kernaghan testified to Congress that child laborers in Honduras were making Kathie-Lee-Gifford-brand garments. In the decade since sweatshop labor had become a scandal, and Kathie Lee cried her public tears, change has come slowly, as evidenced by the NLC's subsequent investigation of Chinese factories. A few companies have been shamed into improving conditions since the initial uproar.

The NCL report from 1998 called Wal-Mart's inspection and subsequent approval of the infamous Qin Shi factory "a farce." But, since then, the megaretailer appears to have budged. According to a 2005 story in the *San Francisco Chronicle*, Wal-Mart terminated one hundred factories for child-labor violations. Another twelve hundred were put on notice. Is Wal-Mart making an earnest effort to clean up conditions? Time will tell.

Another company on the hot seat, Gap, Inc., has released its second corporate report detailing working conditions in the supply chain. Nike, too, has kept a sharper eye on worker conditions, publishing details of conditions at seven hundred factories. As the *San Francisco Chronicle* story pointed out, we still don't know about JCPenney, Target, Macy's, Sears, and others.

The Investor Responsibility Research Center says a mere *12 percent* of S&P 500 companies have formal codes to address labor issues. Yet they should, for very pragmatic reasons. Protests and public scrutiny hurt business, as Nike and The Gap discovered when stock prices took a hit. Nike executive Sarah Severn said in a public forum that the reason other companies had not reacted was, *there simply was not enough public pressure on other corporations.*

"I DON'T HAVE TIME FOR MY CHILDREN"

Once in a while there will be a news story about the working conditions of those who are making products for the American marketplace. It's big news when celebrities are involved. It happened to Sean Combs. Better known as Puff Daddy. Actually you might recognize him as P. Diddy. He changes his name as often as he changes outfits. And this just in . . . He now wants to be known simply as "Diddy." I don't know what that's all about, but as columnist Dave Barry might say, Simply Diddy would be a good name for a rock band.

Anyway, Mr. Diddy wanted to produce his own line of men's clothing. He's into fashion and likes to wear white because, he says, "Deep down inside, I'm an angel."

The companies producing his line of clothing were contracting production with small shops in countries like Honduras. In 2003, I held hearings in the U.S. Senate on the subject of these global sweatshops and heard testimony from several young women who worked in a plant in Honduras making Sean-John-brand shirts.

One of the witnesses was Lydda Eli Gonzales, a young woman from Honduras who testified that she had worked under appalling conditions. Lydda was seventeen when she was hired and she worked in the factory for a year before being fired for union activity. She and others had decided to try to organize their fellow workers to protest what they considered to be intolerable working conditions.

Lydda said workers in the company were forced to work overtime to meet unreasonable quotas. Sometimes the days were eleven and a half hours long. "It is forbidden to talk, and you have to get permission to use the bathroom. We have to get a pass from the supervisor and give it to the guard in front of the bathroom, who also searches us before we go in," she said.

They were limited to one bathroom break in the morning and another in the afternoon. A production line of twenty workers had a quota of 2,288 shirts per day, "but it is impossible," she added.

"You can't move or stretch, or even look to the side. You have to focus and work as fast as you can to complete the production goal, always under pressure. By the end of the day your whole body aches, your back, arms, shoulders—everything—and one feels exhausted."

Female employees were required to take pregnancy tests because a pregnancy means the loss of the job. "Older workers also suffer a lot of harassment and discrimination because the management prefers workers between seventeen and twenty-five years old," Lydda said. "If a woman gets to be thirty, she can't work in the *maquila* factories [the factories on the Mexican side of the U.S./Mexican border], and if she is working, often she is harassed and sent to worse positions to make her quit." For enduring this, a young Honduran woman can expect to make less than $50 a week. Meanwhile, one Sean John shirt sells for $40 or more.

When she was working at the factory, Lydda's workday started with a 5:00 A.M. bus trip, which cost nearly a dollar a day. She arrived at 6:45 A.M. The cheapest breakfast and lunch cost another $1.80. The daily expenses for transportation and food amount to nearly four hours of labor.

"You cannot live on these wages," she said. "Really, you work just to eat. It is impossible to save. You can't buy anything; it's just to survive."

Another witness at the hearing was Martha Iris Alberto, a single mother of three children. She began working at age seven, selling bread in the street to buy her school books, and went to work for the "AAA *maquila* company" when she was seventeen.

Before she was fired for helping organize a work stoppage, Martha was paid about seventy-five cents per hour to produce Gildan and Fruit of the Loom T-shirts. The factory has also produced shirts for Nike, Adidas, and Hanes, she said. Each production line of fifteen workers had a quota of three thousand shirts a day. Because quotas are not met, workers must toil six days a week. "I get up at 5:00 A.M. and I get home at seven-thirty at night," Martha testified. "I am even more tired than hungry, and I just want to go to sleep. I don't have time for my children." Martha and other union organizers have been blacklisted, she said. "We need these jobs. But we also want them to respect our rights and be treated like human beings."

Lydda Gonzales appealed to the Angel Diddy in her testimony. "I want to ask Mr. Sean Combs for his help so we can win our rights and be treated with dignity and not in a humiliating manner, because we are human beings. We do not want him to take his work from the factory. On the contrary, we need these jobs, and are willing to work very hard. But the maltreatment and abuses are too much."

To his credit, after the exposure and arm-twisting, Combs did make improvements at the factory, and he did not pull his work orders, which would have put many people out of work.

Are these just unusual cases? No. They are far from the most heinous examples of mistreatment. The evidence of the exploitation of children and of workers is compelling.

The dividend from all of that exploitation is that here in America our children wear the newest fashions at bargain-bin prices and the American garment industry has been reduced to tatters. Since President Bush took office in 2001, 350,000 textile jobs have gone overseas—nearly one-third of the entire U.S. garment industry. At the rate we are going, another 400,000 textile jobs will disappear before the end of the decade, and the demise of our textile industry will be complete. All to save a couple of bucks on that "designer" shirt or pair of jeans.

CONSUMERS IN DENIAL

The American consumer is in denial. One of the eternal truths of this world is "There is no free lunch." So the next time you are at your local Mega-Mart checkout counter with those cheap T-shirts for your children, ask yourself, "Who is really paying the price for these low-priced shirts?" As American consumers rush to the new big-box department stores in their neighborhood to pay lower prices for their purchases of nearly everything from textiles to electronics, no one stops to ask how the products were made.

Well, it's long past the time to ask.

As your youngsters slip these brightly colored new shirts over their heads, imagine for a moment having them transported thousands of miles away to a dimly lit, dangerous factory floor where they will work from dawn to dusk for pennies, often while breathing dangerous fumes. It's happening to children every day. The International Labor Organization, the labor arm of the United Nations, estimates there are more than 250 million child laborers in a hundred countries between the ages five and fourteen. That number is nearly equal to the population of the United States.

A decade ago, Robert Sensor wrote in *The Christian Science Monitor* about a shocking photograph of a bedraggled eight-year-old in Bangladesh gripping the bars of a factory's iron gate: "My friend Rosaline Costa (who took the photograph), a staff member of the Catholic Commission for Justice and Peace, caught sight of the little boy peering out from behind the locked gate of a garment factory. Kneeling there in ragged clothes, apparently on the verge of tears, he was asking to go home. Instead, the nearby security guard ordered the boy to return to his workplace."

We don't know what happened to the boy in that haunting photograph. Like millions who have suffered his fate and worse, he was disposable. Global trade agreements created the world economy where corporations rush to exploit vulnerable laborers like that nameless child.

DISPOSABLE CHILDREN

Children are easy to control.

Children don't form labor unions.

Child laborers in undeveloped countries—some of them slaves—pay a horrific toll. Slavery? An exaggeration, you think? The International Labor Union reported in 2005 that *at least* 12.3 million people "work as slaves or in other forms of forced labor." Other estimates more than double that number. UNICEF reported in 2005 that one in twelve children in the world is forced into child labor.

Kevin Bales, antislavery activist and author of the book *Disposable People*, says that in 1850 a slave would have cost the equivalent of $40,000 in today's dollars. Today, a slave working the coffee or cocoa plantations on the Ivory Coast—some as young as nine—will set you back as little as $30, Bales says.

Work them until they drop.

They are considered disposable. Shame on those who traffic in this ugliness!

According to CorpWatch.org, "The [U.S.] State Department's year 2000 human rights report concluded that some 15,000 children between the ages of 9 and 12 from poorer neighboring countries of Mali, Burkina Faso, Benin and Togo have been sold into forced labor on northern Ivory Coast plantations in recent years."

In 2001, some of the biggest names in the chocolate industry were discovered to have purchased cocoa harvested by child slave labor in the Ivory Coast. If not directly guilty of using forced labor, they were certainly enablers.

Michel Larouche, the West Africa regional director for Save the Children of Canada, was quoted in the Knight-Ridder exposé: "If your products are this cheap, it's because of this situation," he said. "Every time one closes his eyes and buys a product made by children, then he is also responsible. He becomes an accomplice."

In 2001, the 13-billion-dollar chocolate industry was forced to adopt a four-year program to combat child slavery or face legislation that would assure consumers by label that slave labor was not used in the production of the sweets. A start, but there is much more to be done.

According to Anti-Slavery International and the Bonded Liberation Front, the Indian hand-knotted carpet industry has three hundred thousand child slaves at work on the looms, with a similar number estimated in neighboring Pakistan. Nepal may have one hundred thousand to two hundred thousand child slaves making carpets.

These carpets were once produced in Iran, but when the Shah of Iran outlawed child labor in the early 1970s, the demand for the carpets did not abate, so the door to exploitation opened wide in other countries. Today, India is estimated to have seventy thousand small "factories" in the carpet-making region of Uttar Pradesh, most too small and remote to monitor for abuses. Yet, combined, these small shops translate into big business.

Children of the lower castes often become slaves to pay off family loans. Some are put to work as early as four or five. An iAbolish report says that some children are chained to their looms. And there is this story from that Web site:

A total of 27 child slaves between the ages of 5 and 12, released with the help of the Bonded Liberation Front, told the following story. The boys, on the promise of being taken to a film, went with the village barber, Shiv Kumar Thakur. They did not tell their parents, as the trip was to be a secret. From their village of Chichoria, Palamau, they were taken on a two-day journey to the remote village of Bilwaria in the Mirzapur district of Uttar Pradesh. They were told that they would receive 10 rupees and 3 meals a day and then given to the loom owner, Panna Lal. It is believed that the barber received 7,000 rupees—he was saving for a motorbike.

The new child slaves were introduced to the intricacies of the trade by being locked up and beaten for the first few days. Requests for food were met with blows from iron rods and yardsticks and woundings by the sheers [sic] used in carpet making. Mistakes in weaving or slow work received the same treatment. The boys' day began at 4 a.m. when Panna Lal poured cold water over them to wake them up. They worked until their lunch break of a half an hour at 2 p.m. According to Suraj, who was 7 years old when he was rescued, they often worked until midnight and only then received their second inadequate meal of the day. They were all locked in at night. Suraj said, "We wept and pleaded with Panna Lal to let us go back to our parents." When these young boys cried, they were beaten with a stone wrapped in a cloth. The loom owner said they would each have to pay him 500 rupees before they could go, but the boys were never paid any wages. Suraj also said that they were branded with hot iron rods as his fellow slave, Bhola, silently displayed brand marks under his right armpit. He also had bruises on his temple caused by a blow from a bamboo staff—punishment for a weaving mistake. Many of the children fell ill and were denied medical treatment. Despair caused seven of the boys to try to run away. They were caught, slung upside down from trees, and branded.

The youngest of the children, Suresh Mochi, recalls, "I was tied to a jackfruit tree and beaten daily with a bamboo stick because I was all the time weeping and wanting to go back home. The marks of my beatings can still be seen on my arms and legs.

When the police came some were hidden in a well or other locked up in a small back room. Once we tried to run away, but were caught and given a severe beating."

The iAbolish Web site also speaks of children being branded with hot irons, and "If they cut their fingers (which happens often on the sharp cutting tools), the loom masters are known to shave match heads into the cut and set the sulfur on fire so that the blood will not stain the carpet."

A good third of the carpets produced under these conditions come to American homes to consumers who haven't an inkling of the misery involved.

Like it or not, we are global citizens. As consumers, should we be asking more questions about the origins of our products? You know the answer.

If this were happening in our hometown, we would stop it immediately. If we knew the company down the block was employing twelve-year-olds and working them twelve hours a day, seven days a week in an unsafe workplace, most people would refuse to purchase the merchandise made under such conditions. But, because it is far from here and out of sight, most Americans seem content to pretend it doesn't exist.

A RECIPE FOR DISASTER

The global economy is one big vicious circle, and don't think for a moment that all the gains of the labor movement can't be rolled back in a historical blink of an eye. The corporate and political power structure in place today is doing everything it can to fragment the basic human protections Franklin Delano Roosevelt promised with the New Deal.

Common men were empowered when FDR signed the Fair Labor Standards Act (FLSA) in 1938, which set a minimum wage—twenty-five cents—and overtime requirements, both of which are under assault these days by the same conservatives who embrace outsourcing.

Under the FLSA, the workweek was shortened to forty-four hours. It required employers to keep time and payroll records and did away with child labor.

It was, of course, denounced as socialism and a tremendous burden on free enterprise, an example of "Big Government" at its worst. But that's far from true. In fact after the FLSA, the economy took off.

Today, thanks also to the vision of FDR, workers have at least a modest Social Security income when they retire. But that is under assault, too, by President Bush, who wants to take it apart and "privatize" it. He is offering a wonderful gift to his Wall Street friends. It is one more fight American workers can't afford to lose.

And when tax breaks go to the wealthy, the burden falls on the rest of us. So when the federal government slashes tax dollars to our schools because the rich need their tax breaks, those least able to afford it are stuck with higher local taxes. Education suffers. Students in those districts are less able to compete in the global marketplace and will be forced to work for less, perpetuating a downward spiral of poverty.

LET US NOT FORGET THE PAST, FOR IT COULD BE OUR FUTURE

Winston Churchill said, "The farther backward you can look, the farther forward you are likely to see." That is why it is important to remember the hard-fought history of the labor movement. Unlike Franklin Delano Roosevelt, the heroes of the labor movement such as Fannie Sellins and James Fyler may never take their rightful places among those honored in America. We remember what Lincoln did when he signed the Emancipation Proclamation. We remember Rosa Parks and Martin Luther King. We honor Susan B. Anthony for leading the way for women's rights.

Still, those fights are not over. Bigotry still plagues black Americans and other minorities. Because of the loss of so many manufacturing jobs under this administration, the jobless rate among African-

Americans is rising twice as fast as it is for whites, according to the AFL-CIO. Women are still paid less—seventy-six cents to a man's dollar in 2002—despite the fact that John F. Kennedy signed the Equal Pay Act in 1963.

But, just as the fight must continue for true fairness for minorities and women, the fight for fair labor conditions is an ongoing battle. Opening the floodgates to global trade has put workers in the fight for their lives. Labor forces have been pitted against each other on a scale never seen before. It is splintering unions, stagnating and lowering wages, and, worst of all, weakening the manufacturing infrastructure of this country.

These days free trade means that the protections for American workers are a stumbling block for companies that say they must employ less expensive labor in order to compete. So, they go abroad and hire workers who come cheap. No labor protections for these workers. You are free to fire them if they decide they want to organize. Or have the host country throw them in jail and make an example of them.

Do you doubt that? If so, try to track down Yue Tianxiang. He is in prison, sentenced to ten years for helping workers demand unpaid wages from Tuanshui Auto Transport Co. and for publishing the newsletter *Chinese Workers Monitor*.

Or look up Yao Fuxin. You'll find him in prison, too. He got a seven-year sentence for leading two thousand workers from the Ferroalloy Factory along with fifteen thousand other workers from five other factories in Liaoyang in a protest against corruption and unpaid wages and pensions. These are not isolated instances. Chinese prisons are now home to many courageous men and women who stood up for better working conditions for Chinese workers.

These stories are important—important in a moral sense, because I believe most Americans have good hearts, and when they begin to understand the direct connection between lost jobs in America and brutality in other countries, they will demand change.

YOU DON'T HAVE TO LOSE YOUR JOB
TO LOSE THE OUTSOURCING GAME

Even the rosiest predictions suggest that, if this continues, America will lose 10 percent of its manufacturing jobs and millions more white-collar jobs in the next decade to cheaper overseas labor. I believe at the pace we are going it will be much worse, and if you check the record, I predicted the enormous job loss due to NAFTA when so many others considered the idea outrageous. I was right then, and I believe I am right now.

But for a moment, let's operate on the premise that the economists with the rose-colored glasses are right. If we only lose 10 percent of the manufacturing jobs, heck, that's not so terrible, you might say. But consider this. Labor has become an unregulated commodity. *You don't have to lose your job to lose in this equation.*

Like it or not, you are competing with global slave labor. You are a commodity, not a person. Your value is based on your production versus your cost. Even if you are the most dependable and most productive employee, if a manufacturer can hire fifty Chinese, Indian, or Mexican workers at the same total wage, there is no way you can compete with that.

Even if your employer *wants* to hire Americans, in some form or another, he or she is competing with other companies around the world. If your company's competitor uses child labor, it can sell its products cheaper and for a higher profit margin. Thus, even good companies are forced to make the move to China.

Even if you don't lose your job, the best-case scenario is that you don't get raises or benefits. Or the employer, citing increased competition from abroad, will strip health-care and pension benefits. While wages stagnate, the cost of living certainly will not. Just look at the prices at the gas pump. And the home-heating bill is getting so large that you can almost see the envelope bulging.

Think back. Most typical Americans probably came from a family in which the father worked while the mother stayed home with the children. You probably enjoyed a good standard of living, had plenty to eat, and your parents had enough time to raise you right.

Now look at your life. You've got two cars. The kids are in day care. Both spouses work. And work longer hours. On your block there are smaller families and bigger houses. The mortgage is a backbreaker. The credit cards are maxed out. Your employer can no longer afford Blue Cross, so you have to pay for your own health insurance, too. And that defined-benefit pension plan you used to have? Forget it! What happened to the American family? How did we lose ground? And why? Some of it is born of our own materialism. But the economic pressures from around the world have played a major role and will play even a larger part in the future.

CORPORATIONS MORE POWERFUL THAN COUNTRIES

The history in this chapter is important because so much of what has happened before serves as a cautionary tale. Even though times have changed, greed and black hearts remain prevalent, and the stakes are even higher. Cornelius Vanderbilt, one of the plutocrats of the Gilded Age, once snorted, "The public be damned. I am working for my stockholders." Vanderbilt's sentiment is alive and well, and corporations have gotten more powerful.

In 2000, the Global Policy Forum, which monitors and consults with the UN on policy, consolidated information from them and a host of other reputable sources to compile some astounding findings:

- *Of the world's largest one hundred economies, fifty-one are global corporations.* Forty-nine are countries. That is an incredible amount of power unregulated by the higher ideals of constitutions and justice. I had a constituent tell me once, "I don't fear big government nearly as much as I fear big corporations." His fears are well-founded. While a country like America is governed by a Constitution and Bill of Rights, many corporations have but one rule: *Profit above all else.*

• *Combined sales of the top two hundred corporations are larger than all the combined economies of all countries with the exception of the largest nine.* These two hundred surpass the combined economies of 182 countries. ExxonMobil reported $10 billion in profits in the second quarter of 2005 alone! When it finished the year, it reported profits of $36.1 billion, the highest profits ever for a U.S. corporation.

With $258 billion in sales ($10 billion in reported profits) in 2005, Wal-Mart is economically more powerful than 161 countries. That is an enormous amount of power, and it is wielded every day by shipping jobs overseas.

So where is this all going? As power is consolidated, small businesses are being eaten alive. Up and down America's Main Streets, in struggling mom-and-pop shops, owners will tell you that often big-box stores sell cheaper at retail than the mom-and-pop shops can buy at wholesale.

The mom-and-pops can't pay the wages their workers deserve, they can't afford the outrageous cost of employee health care, and so workers must leave or settle for jobs that produce little disposable income. This rips entire communities apart. There is an exodus from the heartland of America—from the small towns that are the trademark of this land— that is truly disheartening. As illustrated by some of the stories of factory closings in the previous chapter, entire regions may be decimated by job loss.

LABOR UNDER ASSAULT

Along with destroying communities—and ultimately our infrastructure— outsourcing serves the dual purpose of diminishing, dismantling, and destroying unions and the workers they protect right here in America. Even if you are a nonunion worker, that should concern you.

Nonunion workers have always benefited from the collective bargaining of unions. The unions set a standard that all employers were forced to meet, or at least approach. As the unions of this country go, so go the working conditions they fought to improve.

The gains of the American labor movement will unravel if we force our citizens to compete with exploited foreign labor. While the president talks about bringing democracy to other nations, I say why not bring *basic human rights* to the oppressed workers in other nations through our trade agreements? Why don't we use our economic muscle to ensure that those with whom we trade raise their workplace standards to meet our own? In saving others, we save ourselves.

America attained greatness on the shoulders of the middle-class worker. When workers demanded to be treated fairly, our economy rewrote the history books. The world had never seen such an economically empowered middle class. The Greatest Generation bought houses, cars, and millions of other products that had the factories humming. This was all the result of treating workers fairly.

Workers with less disposable income will stagnate the marketplace and ultimately send the very same companies, who are profiting wildly in the short term, into a death spiral. While I remain astonished at the selfish, shortsighted thinking that is shipping good American jobs overseas, I suppose I should not be surprised.

And the truth is, without government intervention, it will continue.

THE NEED FOR BALANCE

The struggle for balance between labor and industry is eternal. If unions are unreasonable, they can sink companies. If enough big companies are unreasonable and myopic, they can sink entire economies. I believe that is exactly what is happening today.

My good friend national radio talk-show host Ed Schultz calls outsourcing "union-busting by another name." It is. And it is working. Labor unions are at a low point in America, with union membership at only 12.5 percent of the labor force, according to the Voice of America (down from 20 percent in 1983).

The Party of Big Business has embraced the mantra of outsourcing. The White House and Congress continue to do little to stem illegal immigration, which further degrades the pay of American workers.

According to research in 2004 by Harvard professor George J. Borjas, the increasing supply of labor via illegal immigration between 1980 and 2000 had shrunk the wages of native-born American men by an average $1,700 in annual wages.

Industry has made a brilliant strategic move. Divide and conquer. But the victory will be short-lived if the erosion of the middle class is allowed to continue. The consolidation of immense wealth, as illustrated a few paragraphs earlier, is a warning sign of a growing economic imbalance. This is a simple observation. All things require balance. An economically top-heavy society will topple.

THE GIANT SHELL GAME

There is a giant shell game going on in global economics. Corporate welfare is disguised to look like economic development, while those put out of work by outsourcing are made to look like welfare slackers. Americans will continue to lose jobs and industries under today's trade strategy. Even in a measured, managed approach to global trade, there will be some displacement of workers And that means those workers will have to be retrained and reeducated. Yet the dollars for those programs are going in the form of tax breaks to the culprits who helped cause the problem. There will always be winners and losers, but right now the deck is stacked against the workingman. Like Roosevelt's New Deal, workers need a *Fair Deal.*

Let me repeat what I said in the opening chapter of this book about the way things used to be: *Work was valued. There was no social program as important as a good job that paid well.* The issue is as simple as that. Good jobs make a society great. Yet we are shipping our good jobs over-

seas in a radical form of economic hari-kari. Worse yet, we are bas-
tardizing these jobs by exploiting the desperate workers who must accept them to survive. Labor just to provide meager sustenance is
immoral. Labor that provides a fair wage allows a worker to live in dignity. It is both moral and a means to elevate society.

YOU CAN MAKE A DIFFERENCE

We are in a transition as a country.

This transition has the potential to enlighten or enslave.

We are curiously conflicted. If you are one of the lucky ones, you
have a 401(k) or some other investment in companies that may be
bringing you dividends in the short run, but in the long haul are under-
mining your security by outsourcing American jobs. So we send mixed
messages to Corporate America in much the way we send mixed messages to the media. We moan and pitch fits until veins in our foreheads
pop about ambulance-chasing, celebrity-fawning no-content news, and
then we ignore substantive reporting to watch *Survivor*.

We can point fingers all day at corporate bogeymen and clueless
politicians, but real change always needs strong roots. Until Americans
start paying attention and asking questions, nothing will happen. When
consumers begin to question the origin and ethics behind some business practices, we will have an opportunity to effect positive change.

I believe that will happen, because I have faith in the decency, common sense, and resiliency of the American worker. One person and one
voice can make a difference. James Fyler made a difference. Fannie Sellins made a difference. Cesar Chavez, who fought and won rights for
migrant farm workers, made a difference.

All regular citizens . . . No politicians . . . Not a John Wayne among
them . . . Heroes come in all sizes, shapes, and colors. My heroes are
the working man and woman of America. They have been carrying the
load for a mighty long time, and now they need us to stand up for them
and their rights.

FOUR

HOGS AT THE TROUGH: HOW COMPANIES CUT THEIR TAXES BY SHIPPING JOBS OVERSEAS

Dear God, we had to decide between health insurance and a tax cut, and we took all the money as a tax cut. We hope this pleases you.
—*A grateful nation*

THAT WAS HOW PROFESSOR UWE REINHART OF PRINCE-ton University describes the priorities coming from the Bush administration and the Congress his party controls. To hear them describe it, tax cuts for the well-off will cure everything from a sluggish economy to hiccups and the gout.

There are good tax cuts, and then there are tax cuts that seem downright loony. Helping working families by relieving some of their burden makes sense. But offering up another ladle of tax-cut gravy for those who already fail to pay their fair share is bizarre. In fact, a few of the tax breaks border on insane.

For example, did you know that our tax code actually gives tax breaks to those who move their U.S. jobs overseas? It's true. Companies fire their American workers, move their jobs abroad, then collect a big fat tax break, with hardworking families and others having to make up the difference.

It's a little like being fired by your boss at a lunch meeting, *then getting stuck with the check*. Most Americans would react with outrage if they were stuck with some fat cat's dinner check. That is, *if they realized it.* I am here to tell you it is happening every day. It is happening to *you.* While U.S. corporations send American jobs overseas every day—possibly yours—they are rewarded with tax breaks that force hardworking Americans and hometown businesses to shoulder more of the tax load.

That's nothing new. America's workforce has always carried the tax burden, but these days, an American worker is being asked to do even more. Forget the window dressing of paltry tax cuts that the president boasted went to working Americans. Here's the real story. From 1945 to the year 2000, the share of total income taxes paid by corporations dropped from 35 percent to 10 percent, a 71 percent decline. Big shots have created an entire industry to avoid paying taxes, and it appears they have been remarkably successful.

Corporations use our roads to transport merchandise. Their children and employees are educated in American schools. They want their interests protected by our courts and armies at home and abroad. More and more, they just don't want to pay for it. These days, tax avoidance is the entitlement program for the wealthy and their corporations.

A congressional study, cited in a report by Cheryl Woodard, executive director of AskQuestions.org, found that *63 percent* of U.S. corporations paid no income taxes in 2000 while collecting some $2.7 trillion in gross receipts. This was a time when corporate profits were escalating. I'm no mathematician, but that just doesn't add up. Think about the fairness of that. Your average McWorker pays more income taxes than six out of ten corporations.

According to Woodard's research, between 1990 and 2000, corporate profits rose by 93 percent while the average CEO pay increased 571 percent. Meanwhile, according to the Census Bureau data, in President George W. Bush's first term in office, the median income of the public at large *declined* by more than $1,600—3.6 percent—and the middle class shrank. Fueled by corporate greed, we are quickly evolving into a country of haves and have-nots.

THE FINE ART OF THE TAX DODGE

I served as a state tax commissioner before I became a congressman, but I never saw anything like the shenanigans I see corporations trying to pull off today.

The lengths to which some corporations will go to avoid paying their fair share of taxes belong in the theater of the absurd.

Here's the hood ornament on the outrage of tax avoidance!

In 2004, David Evans, a reporter for Bloomberg News, disclosed that in the capital of the Cayman Islands there is a white, five-story office building on Church Street that is called the Ugland House. It is the official address for 12,748 companies. Digest that for a moment. More than 12,000 companies doing business out of one modest building? I've never seen a college frat party that was that overcrowded. Call the fire marshal! I'd love to see *that* floor plan.

But of course, it isn't really home to all of those businesses. It's just a convenient address they can use to cut their U.S. tax bills. It is corporate make-believe. A sham! And we wouldn't even know about it if it were not for some first-rate reporting by David Evans.

Many of the largest U.S. companies use tax havens such as the Cayman Islands to escape paying billions of dollars of U.S. taxes. Of course, they aren't really doing business there. They are just pretending to by setting up a mailbox address.

"We don't pay taxes," hotel magnate Leona Helmsley famously sniffed. "Only the little people pay taxes." What she said was close to the truth. Helmsley simply had the poor taste to say it out loud. A lot of big shots really do think they should just be allowed to do business in America—in a marketplace built and supported by *all* Americans—and not have to pay taxes.

In the new global economy, some of our best-known corporations take that attitude every day as they set up tax-haven subsidiaries to try to avoid paying taxes to Uncle Sam. No matter how hard the IRS looks for a true accounting of profits, the corporations remain a step ahead.

The nearly impossible task for the IRS is to sift through the maze of confusion the corporations create to avoid showing their true profit to the tax agency. One tax man described the job of following transactions between wholly owned corporate subsidiaries, offshore and onshore, as "trying to connect the ends of two plates of spaghetti." So the IRS is often outgunned and outsmarted by the new, clever schemes some companies construct to avoid paying taxes.

WE WON THE COLD WAR BUT ARE LOSING THE TRADE WAR

This exploitation of tax laws is a result of an entirely new paradigm in global trade. In many ways, it is the Wild West out there. Before the end of the Cold War between the Soviet Union and the United States, each bloc traded and dutifully sent aid to the countries within its sphere of influence. While having thousands of nuclear missiles aimed across the ocean was not comfortable, the stakes were so high that each bloc had a vested interest in the welfare of its protectorates. They were more inclined to send aid and trade fairly with more vulnerable nations within the bloc. Now, that has changed. Everyone is trading at breakneck speed, but we are headed for an economic disaster, and, in some weaker countries, living conditions have declined. It has become a free-for-all.

Almost overnight the whole world has become capitalists. It is an astonishing time in history, the ramifications of which can only loosely be predicted. Governments have struggled with the lightning changes in global trade. Corporations, whose decision-making processes move much faster than democracies', have been much quicker to exploit this evolving global economy. More succinctly, they are exploiting the system. They are exploiting people. They are exploiting *you*. You get the bill while they get dessert.

How we manage this global transition will determine the direction of this country and, ultimately, the world. Will global corporations supersede nations as the dominant powers? I believe we are headed in that direction.

A NOVEL PERSPECTIVE ON TAXES—AN INVESTMENT IN AMERICA

According to the Citizens for Tax Justice, 275 of the largest profitable American corporations paid a tax rate of 17.2 percent in 2003—less than half of the top statutory corporate rate of 35 percent. Today in America, companies are rewarded for destroying America's vital manufacturing base and crucial middle class with immense tax breaks.

Most corporations are shortsighted. They see taxes as an incursion on the bottom line.

And the bottom line is what they need to show Wall Street and their stockholders. It determines the capability to pay dividends. It relates to executive salary. And it has a major impact on stock price.

But these days, with the global economy allowing corporations to hide income from the IRS, there has not been a real public debate about the responsibility the corporation has to maximize profit for the stockholders as opposed to their responsibility to pay their fair share of taxes to the U.S. government.

Bill Gates has another perspective. He says the dollars that support the transportation grid, public utilities, research programs, and public schools and universities have created the very vibrant marketplace companies need to thrive. So Bill Gates considers taxes an *investment.*

He's dead right. Taxes, fairly administered and wisely spent, are an *investment* in a better country. But as you will see later in this chapter, even Bill Gates's company has found it necessary to join the herd in using foreign tax shelters to lower the tax bill they would be required to pay the U.S. government.

"We hope our taxes continue to rise in the future," Warren Buffett said in a letter to Berkshire Hathaway shareholders. "It will mean we are prospering—but we also hope that the rest of corporate America antes up along with us." He understands that higher profits mean success. And, yes, paying a portion of that success to the government to cover the common costs of our country that make that success possible (schools, courts, roads, defense, homeland security, help for the poor, and much more) is the right thing to do.

Contrast Buffet's patriotic attitude with the owner of the flag-waving Fox News Network, Rupert Murdoch. According to the *Economist* newspaper and the BBC, from 1994 to 1998, Murdoch's News Corporation and subsidiaries paid an estimated *6 percent* on $5.4 billion in profits. A *Washington Post* article said that the News Corp.'s average tax rate for most of the 1990s was 5.7 percent while certain competitors paid 27.2 percent to 32.5 percent tax rates. His media empire operates primarily in three countries—Australia, Great Britain, and the United States—with respective statutory tax rates of 30, 35, and 30 percent. So how can all of us get a 6 percent tax rate? What ever happened to being Fair and Balanced when it comes to paying taxes?

CROCODILE TEARS OVER OUTSOURCING

While the global economy has provided corporations new opportunities to avoid paying taxes in the United States, they've had plenty of accomplices in our government. You might file this under the "believe it or not" category, but there is actually a provision in our tax laws that will *reward* U.S. companies that move their manufacturing jobs overseas.

But why would a country that is drowning in trade deficits and watching its good jobs move overseas actually encourage the export of these jobs in its tax code? Ask the politicians who support it. The majority of politicians in Washington, D.C., who cast votes to support this practice publicly mourn the loss of jobs that are moving overseas. The American worker, whose family suffers when good jobs go to China, gets crocodile tears and lip service while the politicians get "campaign contributions."

The fact is this is dangerous. No society, no government, no business enterprise can long survive in a society without a vibrant middle class. AskQuestion.org's Cheryl Woodard nailed it when she observed, "Middle class spending is the growth engine in a free market economy, and when taxes rob the middle class in favor of the rich, the economy shuts down. Huge fortunes also produce political power that is hard to control."

I am not against wealth. I do not oppose responsible megacorporations. I simply seek a fair deal for the working people of America.

In this country we have real citizens (you and me) and we have artificial citizens (corporations). Corporations are chartered as artificial citizens that can enter into contracts, sue and be sued, and do business in a way that limits the liability of the owners and investors. So, we've made them artificial citizens of the United States. But many of them want to shirk their responsibility to pay taxes to support those things we do together through our government.

HOW TO SHIP JOBS OVERSEAS AND
GET A TAX BREAK, TOO

Even as you are trudging to the post office on April 15 to pay your taxes, big business is hatching new plots to avoid taxes.

Steve Liesman, in an article for *The Wall Street Journal*, illustrated how this insidious tax break works:

> Don't go looking in the tax code for a chapter titled *Tax Break for Hiring Foreign Workers*. It doesn't exist. The way it works is more complicated. One of the most important is through the ability to defer and often never pay taxes on foreign-earned profits. The result: foreign profits of U.S. companies end up taxed at a lower rate than their U.S. income, creating an incentive to invest overseas in factories. The jobs are where the factories are. . . .
>
> The tax code is written in a way that allows companies not to pay the full 35 percent U.S. corporate tax rate on foreign income

when that money remains invested overseas. . . . Backing up a step, here's how it works before the loophole:

A company earns $100 million abroad in "Lowtaxistan" where the corporate tax rate is 20 percent. The foreign subsidiary pays that money to the U.S. parent. The parent then pays the $35 million to the U.S. government and takes a credit for the 20 percent (or $20 million) payment to the "Lowtaxistan" government. So the net to the U.S. Internal Revenue Service is $15 million.

But here's how it works with the loophole. The U.S. subsidiary simply keeps the money offshore and certifies to its accountants that the money is invested overseas. It never remits the money to the parent and so never pays the $15 million extra to Uncle Sam. Do the math yourself. Which is better—a factory in Lowell, Massachusetts, that will generate $100 million in pretax profit that nets $65 million, or a factory in "Lowtaxistan" that will generate $100 million in pretax profit that nets $80 million?

The bottom line? The Lowtaxistan-based company brings an extra $15 million to the bottom line as a reward for firing all its American workers. Yes, it's complicated, but you can bet the high-priced accountants working for the big corporations understand it. And they use it for all it is worth.

Corporations that move their U.S. jobs out of our country always talk about doing so to be more competitive. Really? Competitive with whom, I wonder—other companies that have moved their jobs overseas? The fact is, with this tax break for leaving the United States, they gain a competitive advantage over those loyal corporations that stay here and continue to hire Americans. It wouldn't be good public relations for these rascals to tell us straight out that they move these jobs in order to boost their profits by having foreign workers create products they hope to sell to American customers. But that is what is happening.

I know that the tax rate isn't the only reason for a corporation to close its U.S. plant and move overseas. The ability to exploit workers for low wages, the absence of child-labor laws and unions, and loose environmental regulations are all attractive incentives to corporations willing to fatten their profits in the absence of ethics.

But taxes do matter, and I can't for the life of me understand how, as we've galloped toward globalization, anyone can justify giving those who move American jobs overseas a tax break for doing it.

WHOSE SIDE ARE THEY ON? THE VOTES AGAINST CLOSING THE TAX LOOPHOLE

Even more bizarre than the corporate demand for outrageous tax breaks is the votes that have been taken in the U.S. Senate on my amendment to shut down this absurdity. Four times I have offered amendments to shut down this tax loophole that encourages corporations to move jobs overseas.

Four times I have failed.

On March 17, 2005, a majority of the senators—fifty-nine to forty—voted to continue the tax break by opposing my amendment to the budget act to close the loophole. (How did your senator vote? You can check at www.Senate.gov/legislative/LIS/roll_call_lists/vote_menu_1.8_2.htm.)

Why would anyone vote for this tax break? In fishing terms, some of them just swallowed the hook, line, and sinker thrown out by the corporate interests and the White House, which insisted that outsourcing is good for trade and good for America. I'm kidding, right? No, I think for many who voted to continue supporting moving jobs overseas it was just blind support of the corporate interests. Maybe some think it is good policy, but they are just dead wrong.

In fact, the most recent estimate of the cost of this tax break is that it will drain $12 billion in revenue out of our treasury over the next decade. Put another way, we are spending $1.2 billion a year to subsidize those who move U.S. jobs overseas. Do you think that this loophole might have contributed to the loss of our 3 million manufacturing jobs in the past four years? I do!

On February 10, 2004, the *Los Angeles Times* ran a story entitled

"Bush Supports Shift of Jobs Overseas." The story quoted Greg Mankiw, Chairman of the President's Council of Economic Advisors, who was the principal author of the annual economic report the president signs and sends to Congress. He said, "Outsourcing is just a new way of doing international trade . . . more things are tradable than were tradable in the past. And that's a good thing."

Oops. Mankiw made the egregious mistake of revealing White House policy.

Iowa Republican senator Chuck Grassley blustered, "That's not the policy of the president and the economic advisor of the president had no business saying that." Grassley said that if that were the president's policy, "he would have no business being president."

Well, Senator Grassley and I find ourselves on opposite sides of the fence from time to time, but I can't argue with that last statement.

You just cannot argue the fact that jobs are fleeing this country as a result of bad trade agreements and special corporate tax breaks supported by the Bush administration. Good jobs are leaving while President Bush and some members of Congress are driving the getaway car. Most of those fifty-nine senators who voted recently to continue rewarding these corporations who are spiriting jobs away didn't want to cross the president, corporate lobbyists, or the U.S. Chamber of Commerce, which was pushing to continue the tax break. It is still my hope that some of them just didn't understand it and will come around to support closing this loophole in the future. I am always an optimist.

The next time a major layoff hits your community, and good jobs are sent overseas, remember to ask those who represent you in Congress how they voted on our attempts to shut down this perverse tax loophole. It is the only way anything will change.

A SWEETHEART DEAL GETS SWEETER

There is another side note to this saga about sweetheart tax breaks for those who move our jobs overseas. I described the tax break on the income corporations earn from their factories abroad when they don't bring the profits back here. The story doesn't end there. That tax break is called "deferral." It means that someday the corporations will have to pay U.S. taxes when they bring the earnings back. *Theoretically.* But until then they can avoid paying the taxes on those earnings abroad. Or they can wait for another Republican-dominated Congress to offer up a jackpot deal.

Grab a migraine pill—if you can afford one. Have you taken your blood-pressure medicine? I'll wait . . . because there is a new twist to this scam I want you to know about.

In 2005, the Republican-controlled Congress decided to sweeten the deal for these corporate job exporters. Congress passed a special law to lower the tax rate to $5^1/4$ percent for those corporations that wanted to bring their earnings home. Holy Cow—even Rupert Murdoch pays more! Remember, the top corporate tax rate is 35 percent! In other words, they told these corporations that they could pay a tax rate that is just a small fraction of the income-tax rate paid by every other American. A major daily newspaper called it "Hitting the Tax-Break Jackpot." Not even in Vegas do you hit it this big.

The pharmaceutical industry alone was on track to repatriate as much as $75 billion at bargain-basement tax rates according to published reports. This is the same bunch that tells Americans to pony up the highest prices in the world for their medicines because they claim they can't make any money overseas. But when it is convenient, suddenly they find $75 billion they earned overseas, where they charged lower prices for their products. Eli Lilly claimed nearly $3 billion in profits in 2004 yet paid a *mere 1 percent* of its worldwide pretax profits in U.S. taxes according to a *New York Times* report.

The Tax Holiday provision was slipped into a piece of legislation called the JOBS (Jumpstart Our Business Strength) Act. It is ironic that they stuck a provision that *encourages the loss of jobs* in a bill that advertises itself as *creating jobs.* You have to hand it to the White House. While they are short on good public policy programs, they are geniuses at naming them. They call a bill that will cut down forests the Healthy Forest Act and a bill that will pollute the air the Clear Skies Act. But most of us recognize it for what it is—we use a manure spreader to distribute it back home. The term *Orwellian* is overused, but entirely appropriate when it comes to this outfit.

Curiously, the very day he signed the JOBS Act that included the special breaks for offshore tax scofflaws—*less than two weeks before the election*—President George Bush was on the stump in Wilkes-Barre, Pennsylvania, complaining about tax avoidance.

Republicans who pushed this nutty idea of a Corporate Tax Holiday claimed it would create new jobs in the United States. Nonsense!

On May 11, 2004, there was a vote in the U.S. Senate on Senator Fritz Hollings's amendment to kill this special tax break that allowed corporations to pay a $5^1/4$ percent income-tax rate. The vote to continue this corporate plunder and several other favorable foreign tax provisions was a lopsided seventy-four to twenty-three. (If you are curious about who would have supported this clever bit of gifting, go to www.Senate.gov/legislative/LIS/roll_call_lists/vote_menu_1.8_2.htm.)

With hundreds of billions in profits stockpiled offshore on which U.S. taxes have not been paid, this little legislative gem cost the U.S. Treasury a massive amount of lost future tax revenue (because dollars are coming back earlier than they otherwise would, it raises some money in the first year, then loses about $104 billion that should have been paid to the U.S. Treasury).

It now appears that corporations brought home nearly $350 billion that they had stashed overseas in order to take advantage of the new $5^1/4$ percent tax rate. That is a big fat 104-billion-dollar tax break for them.

It is an unconscionable giveaway to Corporate America. Once again the message to those who are moving jobs overseas, "Go to it. We will give you a special sweetheart tax deal." Unbelievable!

By the way, in the months following the enactment of this special tax break the headlines disclosed that this is *not* going to create new jobs in the United States. If you've been following along with the news from this Republican-controlled White House and Congress, this should be no surprise.

How can so many working men and women continue to vote against their own economic interests? Where is the morality in firing loyal American workers? And didn't Jesus admonish citizens to "render unto Caesar what is Caesar's"? These days, corporations are not rendering much unto Caesar.

The biggest beneficiaries are the pharmaceutical and technology industries. They will use this windfall to pay down debt, buy back stock, buy up patents, or use it as offset funding for mergers and acquisitions.

The sponsors claimed the JOBS Act would create 660,000 new jobs, but some of the corporations that benefited most from the tax holiday are snatching the cash and moving even more jobs overseas. According to *The New York Times,* Hewlett-Packard, which has accumulated $14 billion in foreign profits and lobbied hard for the tax break, announced on January 10, 2005, that it would continue to reduce its U.S. workforce. In July, the California company announced plans to modify its pension benefits and eliminate 14,500 jobs, or nearly 10 percent of its (global) workforce, *BusinessWeek* reported. The story noted, "U.S. corporations announced plans in June to cut 110,996 jobs—the highest monthly total in 17 months. Overall job cuts are on the rise in 2005, reaching 538,274 through June."

The Oracle Corporation, a leading technology company, had nearly $3 billion in foreign profits that could be brought back to the United States under the special tax rate. According to *The New York Times,* analysts expected Oracle to use that money to help pay off its recent takeover of PeopleSoft. In the meantime, the company plans to reduce its combined workforce by some five thousand or more people.

If anyone needs real proof that this was an expensive boondoggle, here it is. In January 2006, the Ford Motor Company announced that it was laying off thirty thousand workers and closing fourteen manufacturing plants. According to *The Washington Post,* the Ford news release announcing the layoffs also said on page 2 that "repatriation of foreign earnings pursuant to the American Jobs Creation Act of 2004 resulted in a permanent tax savings of about $250 million."

So, Ford announces that they have gained a quarter of a billion dollars under the "Jobs Creation Act," then says, "By the way, we are laying off thirty thousand workers."

This is job creation? I don't think so!

CORPORATIONS RENOUNCE AMERICAN CITIZENSHIP TO EXPLOIT THE U.S. MARKETPLACE

Is all of this making your blood boil? Well, there's more. Here is another, even more brazen strategy.

It is something called *inversion*, which is a fancy way of saying that a corporation renounces its U.S. citizenship to avoid taxes.

I think the most sordid example of excess in this area is a company called Tyco. You may be familiar with that name because the CEO of Tyco, L. Dennis Kozlowski, was prosecuted on criminal charges for stealing corporate assets for personal expense. Among other things, he purchased (with company money) a six-thousand-dollar shower curtain for his apartment, a fifteen-thousand-dollar umbrella stand, and much more. The corporation paid $1 million for a birthday party in Italy for his wife that among other things featured Stoli vodka being poured from the penis of an ice statue of David while guests were serenaded by Jimmy Buffett. Or was David strumming a guitar while Jimmy Buffett . . . *Never mind!* You get the point that this is not a CEO concerned about interests other than his own, or those of his company. As one reporter put it, this was just the "tip of the ice statue."

Kozlowski and fellow executive Mark Swartz were convicted on twenty-two counts of stealing $542 million (from stockholders) through unauthorized cash bonuses, secretly forgiven loans, and stock deals.

It won't stun you to learn that the folks at Tyco structured a reverse merger, which moved Tyco's headquarters—on paper—to Bermuda. Because of its Bermuda base, Tyco no longer pays U.S. income taxes on its growing overseas income. And through a variety of other schemes, it also minimizes its taxes on U.S. income. For instance, Tyco set up a Luxembourg-based subsidiary to finance most of their debt in a manner designed to reduce their U.S. income-tax bill. Good gravy, we can't be frittering away Tyco money on things like taxes when there are 5-million-dollar wedding rings to be purchased with Tyco money (*The New York Times*) and nearly a million dollars in hush money to be paid to Kozlowski's secretary, with whom he allegedly had an affair, as reported by the New York *Daily News*.

Tyco reported that by relocating to Bermuda the company "saved" about $400 million in U.S. taxes in 2001. That ought to cover the next birthday party.

Bill Allison, the senior editor at the Washington-based Center for Public Integrity, described Kozlowski as a "Benedict Arnold billionaire" for moving offshore and renouncing his company's citizenship. But Tyco is not the only company to have done this.

They are the most notorious example, but there are many more:

- Triton Energy became a Cayman company.
- Fruit of the Loom reincorporated in the Cayman Islands.
- TransOcean Offshore became a Cayman company.
- Xoma became a Bermuda company.

These are just a few of the companies that decided they no longer wanted to claim American citizenship. But, because their main offices remain in the United States, they know that they would receive American protection if a rogue interest were to try to expropriate their assets overseas. I personally think that if they run into trouble, they should call the Bermudan Navy. I'm told they have an imposing force of twenty-seven men (but don't hold me to that).

In 2004, during House negotiations over an appropriations bill, Representative Rosa DeLauro, a Connecticut Democrat, offered an amendment that would have banned expatriated companies from contracting with the U.S. Department of Transportation and Treasury departments and agencies. "Tell these companies that if they are going to not pay taxes in this country, then, they will no longer reap the benefit of government contracts," she said. Her amendment lost 189 to 211, with 196 Republicans making up the majority of the no votes. Call it Business as Usual.

In 2005, the Congress did enact a provision that prohibits "inverted" companies from contracting with selected government agencies.

While corporations ultimately make the decision to avoid paying U.S. taxes, their accountants are the ones preaching the Gospel of Off-shoring. An Internet broadcast to clients by Ernst & Young in 2001 offered a clear picture of what the accounting firms were pushing. Kate Barton, a partner at Ernst & Young, was discussing the pros and cons of corporate inversions with other Ernst & Young officials. Speaking of inversion (renouncing a corporation's citizenship) she said, "The improvement in earnings is powerful enough to say that maybe the patriotism issue should take a back seat [*sic*]."

Patriotism should take a backseat? Unreal.

These are the people your Congress supports?

Price Waterhouse Coopers is another accounting firm that aggressively touted its expertise with inversions on their Web site. They should know. They actually were planning an inversion for themselves until public pressure made them back off.

With the exposure of an almost unbelievable amount of corporate fraud and avarice in the cases of Enron, Tyco, MCI WorldCom, and many others, it appears that the line between intelligent business decisions and sleazy, irresponsible corporate greed has become unrecognizable. And it is apparent that at least in some corporate boardrooms the Pledge of Allegiance is out of date.

DOING BUSINESS THROUGH A MAILBOX

A study by *Tax Notes* found that subsidiaries of U.S. corporations operating in the four major tax havens—the Netherlands, Ireland, Bermuda, and Luxembourg—claimed 46 percent of their profits in those countries in a recent year, with the support of only 9 percent of their employees and 12 percent of their plants and equipment. Incredible efficiency, eh? Wink.

In a recent year the General Accountability Office (GAO) found that fifty-nine of the one hundred largest publicly traded federal contractors who benefit from federal contracts had established hundreds of subsidiaries in offshore tax havens. In other words, the same large companies that improve their profits by doing business directly with the federal government are trying to shift their profits overseas to avoid paying taxes to the government that employs them.

Remember Enron—the poster child for fraud and greed? Enron's ownership structure included thirteen hundred different foreign entities. Published reports suggest that Enron used *nearly nine hundred* offshore entities in an effort to avoid paying taxes. The Joint Committee on Taxation of the Congress found that Enron had 441 entities formed in the Cayman Islands alone (a country without an income tax). Four hundred forty-one!

According to recent information from the GAO, ExxonMobil now has eleven tax-haven subsidiaries in the Bahamas.

Dick Cheney's old company, Halliburton, has reportedly set up seventeen tax-haven subsidiaries, including thirteen in the Cayman Islands as well as two in Liechtenstein and two in Panama. Xerox reportedly has twenty-four tax-haven subsidiaries, including ten in Bermuda and four in Barbados.

Had enough? Take a deep breath. There's more. Another tactic used by international corporations to avoid paying their taxes to the United States is called *transfer pricing*. If you thought ice statues urinating booze was outrageous, follow along. Here's how it works:

A U.S. corporation sets up a wholly owned foreign subsidiary and either overprices or underprices products that it buys or sells to itself in order to show whatever profit or loss it chooses in any country. In that manner they are able to avoid paying American taxes. The Pied Pipers at Ernst & Young proudly offer a Transfer Pricing Global Reference Guide, *"based on the vast knowledge of the firm's leading global transfer pricing professionals."*

Florida International University professor John Zdanowicz and Penn State University professor Simon Pak, both experts in finance, have been studying this type of tax avoidance. They believe our government lost $53 billion in 2001 alone from this scam. I helped secure $2 million in funding to expand this study—no small amount, to be sure, but a wise investment if our government has the will to act on its findings. What we're talking about is almost unbelievable tax avoidance.

Examples of the over- and underpricing scam Zdanowicz and Pak have found in transactions a parent corporation does with its wholly owned subsidiaries include the following.

OVERPRICED IMPORTS

- Tweezers from Japan, $4,896 each (*You'd have to work at Tyco to afford one!*)
- Battery-powered smoke detectors from Germany, $3,500 (*A testament to fine German engineering.*)
- Lawn mower blades from Australia, $2,326
- Toothbrushes from India, $171

UNDERPRICED EXPORTS

- Bulldozers to Colombia, $1,741 apiece (*I'll take one. I'll never be cut off again in my commute to the Capitol.*)
- Radial truck tires to the UK, $11.74

- Missile and rocket launchers to Israel, $52 each (*I rarely shop for such things, but this strikes me as a bargain.*)
- Bicycles to Mexico, $11.00

Here's how the scam works. If you are an American corporation that has a wholly owned foreign subsidiary, you can underprice your exports to your subsidiary and make the claim that you are not making any money. Of course, you claim that because you are underpricing your exports to a company you own. The reverse is true for overpricing imports, once again to claim you aren't making any money in the United States. Presto. You have avoided paying U.S. taxes.

Okay, now you're asking what can you do about this? Simple! Start demanding that your senator or congressman put an end to this blatant, unethical behavior by changing the laws that allow this to happen. U.S. citizenship should be accompanied by some responsibilities, too. Let's stop giving a pass to these corporations who want all America has to offer but are unwilling to do what we expect of other citizens. And stop electing politicians who cave in to corporate interests. You deserve better.

Nobody likes taxes. But taxes are necessary. As Bill Gates pointed out, taxes are an investment in America.

But even Microsoft's tax planners are busy. *The Wall Street Journal* pointed to Microsoft and other companies employing a new approach to reducing their U.S. tax bill.

Microsoft and other technology companies are now transferring their "intellectual property" to a low-tax country like Ireland so that they can license the use of it from Ireland and run the income from it to that low-tax country. *The Wall Street Journal* reports that Microsoft has set up an office on a quiet downtown street in Dublin and from there it controls $16 billion in Microsoft assets and, on paper, it had gross profits of about $9 billion in 2004.

The result is to shave their U.S. tax bill by hundreds of millions of dollars.

How do they do it? They transfer their intellectual property rights in their software to their Ireland subsidiary, then license it to users from there. That way they run the income from their product through this low-tax country. It is designed only for one purpose. It's estimated that Microsoft is saving at least $500 million a year on their tax bill.

It's not just Microsoft. Oracle is doing it. So is Google. And so are most of the drug companies. It's a gold rush. A century ago, Irish immigrants were finding their way to the United States. Now companies are exporting their intellectual property to Ireland to avoid paying U.S. taxes.

We are told by the experts that our future is not in manufacturing. Those jobs are gone. Our future, they tell us, is in innovation, invention, and technology. But if those very companies that are the innovators, the creators, and the inventors are sending their intellectual property abroad to avoid paying U.S. taxes, what next?

It's way past the time to stamp out tax loopholes for those who travel abroad or ship their patents and intellectual property abroad simply to avoid paying what they owe back here at home. Requiring everyone and every corporation to pay a fair share of taxes is a basic requirement of citizenship. Cracking down on tax evasion isn't just a matter of fairness. It is vital. Some estimate that the cost of tax fraud and tax avoidance is more than $300 billion a year.

In his excellent book, *Perfectly Legal*, David Clay, a *New York Times* reporter, notes that from 1970 to 2000, the average income of the top 13,400 households leapt from $3.6 million to nearly $24 million—a 538 percent increase. Clay says that during that same time frame, the average income for 90 percent of American families actually decreased slightly. The disparity in wealth in America is the largest of any industrialized nation.

According to data from the IRS, in 2000—*before* the president's tax cuts for the wealthiest Americans—the richest four hundred taxpayers, most of them big-business owners, paid 27 percent of their income in total federal, state, and local taxes. All other taxpayers paid about 40 percent. My friend Warren Buffett once said, "If there is class warfare in America, my side is winning."

But this isn't hopeless. It isn't rocket science to fix these problems. There are three simple steps that would do away with these outrageous abuses.

First, repeal the tax break that is now given to those who move U.S. jobs overseas.

Second, change the law to treat U.S. companies that set up foreign subsidiaries in tax-haven countries as if they had never left the United States. That way, there will be no tax advantages to U.S. companies who try to do business through a mailbox in a low-tax country. It's time to nail the door shut on these tax cheats who take advantage of all that America has to offer them but do not want to pay their fair share of U.S. taxes.

Third, tax U.S. corporations and their foreign subsidiaries on a fair share of their combined worldwide income. That would eliminate the opportunity for transfer pricing to avoid their taxes.

These steps are simple and direct and by themselves would largely prohibit the tax avoidance that I have described in this chapter. I have introduced legislation in the Congress to accomplish these changes. At this point both the president and the majority party in the Congress oppose these changes.

But this fight is far from over.

It's time for our side to get a turn at bat.

FIVE

SUCKING THE BLOSSOM— PHARMACEUTICAL COMPANIES PERVERT TRADE FOR PROFIT

Little bee sucks the blossom big bee gets the honey.
Poor man picks the cotton rich man gets the money.
—*Bob Wills and the Texas Playboys, "Take Me Back to Tulsa,"*
Wills/Duncan, Peer International, 1941

I DON'T KNOW IF BOB WILLS EVER CONTEMPLATED THE pros and cons of global trade, but he sure could sing, and when it came down to human nature, he had it pegged.

Every absurdity benefits from a poster child, and the poster child for absurd trade deals is the sweetheart arrangement for the prescription drug industry. So it deserves and gets special attention in this book.

The big bee still gets the honey, and the little guy gets stung, and nowhere is it more apparent than with the lucrative deal the pharmaceutical industry has with the U. S. government.

Sure, the drug industry does some good things. They do some excellent research and produce some lifesaving drugs. And I know there are some good people working for the industry who are dedicated to serving the public good. But their drug-pricing policies undermine the good intentions of those who work in that industry. Their pricing policies are an outrage. Miracle drugs offer no miracles to those who can't afford them.

The fact is, the drug companies charge the U.S. consumers the highest prices in the world for prescription drugs even though a substantial portion of their drugs comes from taxpayer-funded research. But there's more. They are able to charge those high prices because they hide behind a sweet little nugget in federal law that prohibits anyone from importing prescription drugs into the United States except the manufacturer.

In other words, a licensed pharmacist in the United States cannot buy and import identical FDA-approved drugs from Canada, where they are priced at a fraction of the U.S. cost. In fact, many of the overpriced drugs are made in the United States, then exported where they are sold for lower prices. But American consumers cannot have access to those lower prices.

In short, trade with respect to prescription drugs is a one-way street. The special deal benefits the drug industry but prevents American consumers from benefiting from trade.

How can this happen?

When you follow the money, it all makes perfect sense.

Elected officials aren't serving you.

They are serving the pharmaceutical industry.

According to *USA Today*, drug companies contributed at least $17 million to federal candidates in the 2004 election. Seventeen million? Sounds like they made a lot of friends.

According to government records, the drug industry eclipses all others in lobbying dollars as well, with $758 million spent since 1998. So what does all this money buy Big Pharma?

For starters, they have historically had the highest profit margins in all major industries. But even more, they get the protection of the government allowing them to charge the U.S. consumers the highest prices in the world for prescription drugs.

But back to the contributions . . . President Bush alone received nearly $1 million in campaign funds from America's drug companies. According to *USA Today*, in the 2004 election, eighteen congressmen collected more than $100,000, favoring Republicans two to one. Direct from a *USA Today* report, here is the list of the top recipients in the House and Senate and their positions of influence.

U.S. SENATE:

- Richard Burr, R-NC: $288,684 Health, Education, Labor and Pensions
- Arlen Specter, R-PA: $235,712 Appropriations; Health subcommittee chair
- Judd Gregg, R-NH: $171,000 Appropriations; Budget chair; Health, Education, Labor and Pensions

U.S. HOUSE OF REPRESENTATIVES:

- Mike Ferguson, R-N.J: $264,560 Energy and Commerce
- Nancy Johnson, R-CT: $154,512 Ways and Means; Health subcommittee chair
- Dennis Hastert, R-IL: $153,500 Speaker of the House

It is possible that 2004 was a *down* year in election spending by pharmaceutical industry standards. According to *USA Today*, "In 2002, drug makers spent *$20 million* on congressional races, four-fifths of it to help Republicans. That doesn't count a 17-million-dollar television ad campaign that the industry funded to boost Republican members of Congress in close races. Those ads featured, among others, once funnyman now turned dour right-winger, Art Linkletter, defending Republicans who support the drug industry." (Republicans say the darnedest things!)

"They [the ads] helped the GOP solidify its grip on Congress," *USA Today* concluded. No kidding.

There are 1,274 people in Washington working for the drug companies—two for each member of Congress. My colleague Senator Chuck Grassley, R-IA, said, "You can hardly swing a cat by the tail in that town without hitting a pharmaceutical lobbyist." Not only is it hard on cats and pharmaceutical lobbyists, it is damn hard on consumers. What do American citizens derive from this arrangement? Here's a hint, Bob Wills. It ain't the honey. It's a financial nosebleed caused by paying the highest drug prices in the world.

THE COAST IS CLEAR—LET'S JACK UP PRICES!

With the 2004 election behind them, even as Senate Majority Leader Bill Frist, R-TN, was making a victory tour of the South, makers of thirty-one of the top-selling fifty drugs were rolling out price increases—most of which are far more than inflationary adjustments. In the five years from 2000 to 2005, the prices of commonly prescribed brand-name drugs rose at more than twice the rate of inflation—a 35 percent increase (inflation during that same time was 13.5 percent).

According to *The Wall Street Journal,* Pfizer's prices went up about 5 percent across the board after the election. Sounds almost reasonable, doesn't it? Reasonable, until you consider that Americans who take Pfizer's cholesterol-lowering drug, Lipitor, must pay 40 percent more than their neighbors in Canada. Americans spend $318 for a ninety-day prescription while Canadians pay $192. It's astonishing. The pharmaceutical industry has somehow created a business model in which a company can ship products—apparently, at no cost—and sell them in other countries far cheaper than it can in its own. It must be magic. Maybe David Copperfield is a consultant. If this crowd can accomplish that, time travel ought to be a walk in the park.

Here are some more comparisons for savvy shoppers. Prevacid, which treats John Elway's ulcers, costs him $401 for ninety doses. He can afford it. Meanwhile, a Canadian citizen pays just $199—half as much. The depression drug Zyprexa would cost the same Canadian a mere $167. An American pays $517. That's a difference of 68 percent. Now, *that's* depressing.

On June 19, 2003, I made a speech on the floor of the Senate to talk about the price disparity of Zocor, a drug endorsed by Elway's old coach, Dan Reeves. I held up two identical bottles of the cholesterol-lowering medication, one from Canada, one from the United States. "It's the same FDA-approved pill, put in the same bottle and manufactured in the same place by the same company. The only difference is that when the medicine is sold in the United States to U.S. consumers, it costs $3.03 a tablet. In Canada, the same pill in the same bottle made by the same company costs $1.12 per tablet."

Not only is there a price gap between the prices paid in Canada versus the United States, it is growing rapidly despite a weakening U.S. dollar. The price gap of the arthritis medication Celebrex rose from 39 percent to 55 percent from 2002 to 2005. Perhaps these growing profit margins *are* magic. Then again, it smells like price gouging. The same price gap exists between the United States and nearly every industrialized nation. Real people are getting hurt. Real people are paying the price—sometimes at the risk of their own lives.

Yes, there are some good people working in the pharmaceutical industry, and the drug companies do some good things. And sure, they produce some lifesaving drugs. But their pricing policies are preventing many Americans from having access to the drugs they need. They claim to need these prices to raise the revenue necessary for the research and development they do. But the fact is they spend more on promotion, marketing, and advertising than they do on research and development. Oops! We aren't supposed to know that!

"I WILL JUST HAVE TO TAKE MY CHANCES"

Dr. James Baumgartner told me about a patient of his with breast cancer. After surgery to remove her tumor, the doctor told her she should take a certain prescription medicine to reduce the chances of a recurrence of her breast cancer. When she found out what the cost of the drug was, she said, "I can't afford to take this drug. I will just have to take my chances."

Then there is the letter I got from Laudie J. Chorne of Bismarck, North Dakota, in which he recounted an incident that brought tears to his eyes:

> Standing in front of me, at a drug counter, was an elderly gentleman, approximately 80 years of age. He handed two prescriptions

to the pharmacist. He said, "Before you fill those, I need to know the price first." The pharmacist checked the prices with her computer and told the elderly man, "The first prescription is $94.76. The other one is $49.88. Do you want me to fill them?"

The old man looked around, deep in thought, and replied, "No, I guess not. I haven't bought my wife's Christmas present yet nor my grandchildren's. I guess I'll just have to put up with the pain." Using his cane, he sadly walked away.

So how has our government responded? By tightening the screws on these poor people. By letting the profiteers run wild. While I and some other senators have led the fight to make drug reimportation legal in order to drive down drug prices, the Bush administration and the drug companies have fought tooth and nail against it. The Food and Drug Administration, which is supposed to protect the American public, has become an accomplice in one of the great injustices of our time. And the majority party in Congress continues to do the drug companies' bidding by blocking legislation that would bring drug prices down.

The drug industry even has the Canadian government helping them. But it is under duress. The *Los Angeles Times* quoted Canadian Health Minister Ujjal Dosanjh as saying, "Canada cannot be the drugstore for the United States of America—280 million people cannot expect us to supply drugs to them on a continuous, uncontrolled basis."

Of course what he didn't say is that the American pharmaceutical companies have threatened to withhold drug shipments to Canada if the U.S. Congress allows its citizens to import the identical drugs from Canada at a fraction of the price they are sold for in the United States. It is raw corporate muscle. And sick Americans are caught between a rock and a hard place—as usual.

While senior citizens make up just 12 percent of the population, they consume more than one-third of the prescription drugs in the United States. I can't count the times I've had an elderly person tell me they have to buy their prescription drugs first, so that they know how much money they'll have left for food.

At the conclusion of a meeting in a small town one evening, a frail, elderly woman about eighty years old approached me and touched my elbow.

"Mr. Senator, can you help me?"

"I'll try," I said.

"My doctor tells me I have to take pills for my diabetes and heart trouble . . ." Her chin began to tremble, and her voice quivered. "I don't have the money to pay for the medicine I need," she said. Her eyes welled with tears, and she added, "Can you help me? I really need your help."

I put my arm around her and told her that I would. I helped arrange some assistance for her, and I have never forgotten the look in her eyes and her plaintive voice. She was speaking for millions more, millions of senior citizens—your grandparents and mine, our mothers and fathers—on fixed incomes, living from one Social Security check to another, struggling to pay for the necessities, let alone the highest drug prices in the world.

"Can you help me?" The words echo in my mind.

We live in a world of wonder drugs and medical advances, yet like a sea filled with drowning swimmers, the lifeline is out of reach for so many Americans.

Miracle drugs offer no miracles for those who can't afford them.

THE TRUTH ABOUT REIMPORTATION

It could be different. The drug companies don't need to overprice their drugs to sick Americans. They charge Americans the highest prices in the world for one simple reason—*they can*. Until something changes, *they will*. We've named their accomplices—the Bush administration, the FDA, the lobbyists, and their favorite congressmen—but it is the pharmaceutical industry's juggernaut disinformation campaign that keeps Americans back on their heels, confused and fearful.

"DRUGS FROM CANADA ARE NOT SAFE," the message blares.

Sure they are. The only danger is to the bulging bottom lines at the drug companies. But the pharmaceutical industry has made it its mission to convince people that there would be serious safety problems if they did anything to break the headlock the drug industry has on U.S. drug prices.

The importing of prescription drugs across international borders is an everyday occurrence in Europe. They've been doing it for decades. It's called parallel trading. If you live in Spain and need a prescription drug from Germany, it is no problem. If you are in Italy and want to buy a prescription drug from France, it is yours. Parallel trading works. The competition keeps the price of medicines lower. It is an excellent model of free trade that benefits all sides—including pharmaceutical corporations who claim to make most of their profit in that environment.

Free trade need not be a free-for-all. Every industrialized nation in the world except ours knows it makes sense to protect vital industries without allowing them to become monopolies. Yet our trade negotiators have been willing to trade away entire sectors of the American infrastructure in the name of free trade. Our manufacturing base is being gutted as corporations move overseas where they can dodge American taxes and operate unencumbered by labor laws and environmental restrictions. The technology sector is setting up shop in India.

And when it comes to the well-being of the American farmer, tough luck. Our borders are wide open to Canadian wheat and Australian cattle. Some days I feel like half the administration is ready to saddle up and have a Mad Cow cattle drive from Canada to the United States in the name of free trade. The problem is, these storefront cowboys are all hat.

But try to bring a bottle of Zocor from Winnipeg to Fargo? Oh my! That's worse than cattle rustling according to the government and the drug industry!

What's dangerous is millions of Americans going without lifesaving medicine because they cannot pay the 46 percent higher cost of Zocor in America. There is a small loophole that allows individual U.S. citizens to cross into Canada and bring a three-month personal supply of prescription drugs back into our country. But few senior citizens live close enough to the border to be able to do that. And for those who can it is a hardship.

I once arranged a bus trip with senior citizens from North Dakota to Emerson, Manitoba, to buy prescription drugs.

"I'm saving a lot of money," Sylvia Miller, a seventy-two-year-old grandmother from Fargo, said wistfully as she looked at the bottles of lifesaving medicine in her hands. We were standing in a simple one-room pharmacy in Emerson, which is just five miles from the border. "The problem is," she added, "I can't come to Canada every time I need to fill a prescription."

Sylvia was taking seven different medications each day for diabetes, heart problems, and emphysema. She told me that, the year before, she had received $4,700 in Social Security benefits and paid $4,900 for prescription drugs. "Things don't add up, do they?" she asked. By making the trip across the Canadian border to buy identical prescription drugs, she bought the same drugs for half the price.

FDA: CHEERLEADERS FOR THE DRUG INDUSTRY

Still, lawmakers, who have made their beds with major pharmaceutical companies, cynically insist that allowing citizens and U.S. drugstores to import the identical FDA-approved drugs from Canada at lower prices wouldn't work. That's complete rubbish! The Food and Drug Administration—particularly under Dr. Mark McClellen—was a cheerleader for the drug industry raising bogus safety issues. For that he got promoted in the government to run the Centers for Medicare and Medicaid Services agency (CMS).

The FDA relentlessly, mind-numbingly parrots the drug industry's propaganda that there is a safety problem with reimporting drugs. They know better. The FDA is supposed to be regulating the drug industry, not representing them.

Permit me a minor detour to tell you how the obsession at the FDA to support the drug industry price strategy has allowed it to ignore other, real issues. When they should be minding the store, and protecting consumers from dangerous drugs, the FDA has been playing it fast and loose.

For example, Dr. David Graham, the FDA associate safety director, accuses the agency of trying to suppress a study on COX-2 inhibitors, a controversial class of painkillers. Senator Charles Grassley, the Republican from Iowa, came to the same conclusion and called for an independent commission to review safety policies.

According to a study by Dr. Graham, Vioxx, a Merck product, led to thirty thousand to fifty-five thousand deaths in the United States alone and more globally. An estimated 80 million people took the drug.

Ironically, Graham told an FDA Advisory Committee that with other effective medicines on the market, "There doesn't really appear to be a need for COX-2."

Furthermore, he says, "The classic approach of industry and FDA has been to do studies that are too small to conclusively identify that a risk is real. They can conclude, therefore, that there is no risk." Graham charges that the division of the FDA that pursues drug testing and approval sees its mission as "reviewing and approving as many drugs as it can," with safety a "low priority."

The American Medical Association indicated alarm about FDA oversight by publishing a paper in 2002 that strongly urged physicians not to risk prescribing newer drugs when established and proven drugs are an option.

The pharmaceutical industry has politicians protecting their monopolistic enterprises. And it has the FDA protecting their race to shortcut safety issues to get new drugs to the market.

According to the CommonDreams report, "half of the FDA's human drug budget is met by the total fees generated by the 1992 Prescription Drug User Fees Act (PDUFA), in which companies pay millions of dollars to have their drugs evaluated by the agency."

Dr. Sheldon Krimsky of Tufts University in Boston, an ethicist who has studied corporate influence on science, says, "People [at the FDA] know that their salaries are dependent upon the companies that initiate drug testing. It has a certain effect on the consciousness of the reviewers. There shouldn't be this supporting role of government by multinationals.

"There's no other industry in which the manufacturer has such a tight control, and pays for most of the testing that goes on," says Krimsky, author of the book *Science in the Private Interest: Has the Lure of Profits Corrupted Biomedical Research?*

Given the recent public testimony of Dr. Graham and others, I think it is time for the Congress to decide that it will not be funding the evaluation of new drugs with money from the industry that will benefit from the evaluation. This is a public responsibility and should be done with public funds.

My point in this brief detour into drug testing and ethics is to show how intertwined the FDA is with the drug industry. Certainly, we cannot count on objectivity when the topic of reimportation arises.

ANOTHER BRAVE MAN SPEAKS OUT

One brave man at the highest levels of the pharmacy industry has told the truth about reimportation. Dr. Peter Rost, a vice president of marketing with Pfizer, testified before Congress, saying that he personally marketed prescription drugs in Europe and for many years observed the parallel trading system operating safely and efficiently.

Rost said, "During my time [in which] I was responsible for our region in northern Europe, I never once—not once—heard the drug industry, regulatory agencies, the government or anyone else saying that this practice is unsafe, and personally, I think it is outright derogatory to claim that Americans would not be able to handle the reimportation of drugs when the rest of the educated world can do this."

Rost became an instant pariah in his company and was subsequently interrogated by company lawyers, according to *The Washington Times.* Rost said, "People are dying, and if I can make a difference by speaking out, it is clearly worth it. I think it would be immoral for me not to continue to speak out."

When Tommy Thompson was the head of the Health and Human Services Department under President George W. Bush, I met with him on a number of occasions, pressing him to allow a pilot program to allow drug reimportation from Canada.

He wouldn't.

He *couldn't.*

But privately he told me he was sympathetic, and that "ultimately this is going to happen." But according to him the policy was being steered by the White House.

As Tommy Thompson was leaving his cabinet position, I ran into him in the Capitol, and he winked at me. "Keep pushing on that prescription drug issue," he said. "You are right."

The Republican-controlled Congress continues to stall legislation so the drug companies can continue their profiteering a while longer. "Make no mistake about what is going on right now," Dr. Rost has said. "Holding up a vote on reimportation, stopping good reimportation bills has a high cost—not just in money but in American lives. Every day Americans die because they cannot afford life-saving drugs."

According to *Time* magazine, global sales of Lipitor in 2002 were *$8 billion.* Zocor grossed $5.6 billion. It is doubtful that allowing reimportation of drugs from Canada will leave Pfizer or Merck destitute.

IMPORTING DRUGS AND EXPORTING JOBS

In the face of all of these facts, the drug industry insists there are safety problems with importing drugs. The thing is, Americans are already consuming billions of dollars of medicines made in Hungary, Slovakia, and the Czech Republic, as well as India, China, Pakistan, and many more. These drugs are made in FDA-inspected and -approved facilities, just like the medicines that would be imported under the legislation we've introduced in Congress.

In fact, according to *Time*, seventeen of the twenty largest drug companies worldwide now make drugs in Ireland because of tax incentives. Pretty great deal, huh? These pharmaceutical companies get to send good-paying American jobs overseas to dodge U.S. taxes. Then they get to jack up the price and sell these drugs to the very same Americans they put out of work.

This lays a greater burden on the struggling American taxpayer, who is paying the highest drug prices in the world—if he can afford them! Sometimes the toll it takes is hidden. One Minnesota resident recounted a conversation with a cabdriver in a southern American city. She was astounded to discover he was starting his second eight-hour shift of the day. "You work two eight-hour jobs a day?" she asked incredulously.

"Have to," he said. "My wife's waiting for a kidney transplant, and this is the only way we can afford the medication to keep her alive until then." Had he lived nearer to Canada, he might have been able to fill prescriptions more affordably. He might have actually had time to spend with the wife he was trying to keep alive.

But when the American consumer wants to experience the benefits of global trade, just like the drug makers do—oh no—there are drug company profits to protect.

ADDING TO THE TRADE DEFICIT

What it is doing to the trade deficit is alarming. The U.S. International Trade Commission says the balance of pharmaceutical imports and exports was nearly equal in the early 1990s. According to the Census Bureau, our deficit in pharmaceutical trade was $26 billion in 2004. We imported $52 billion (these imports were by the industry, not consumers) and exported $25 billion in pharmaceutical drugs.

Now, drug companies are being courted by Singapore; lured by tax breaks, Merck is investing $500 million for two plants which will manufacture Zocor and Eztrol, both cholesterol drugs. Oh my! But what of the dangers of shipping drugs from Asia to America?

The trade deficit—$700 billion and rising—is exacerbated by this outsourcing. We are gutting our tax structure, and we are gutting middle-class workers. The trade deficit marches lockstep with the national deficit, which, in turn, requires the government to cut services or raise taxes. The pharmaceutical industry has long abandoned any sense of economic nationalism. The only American icon they salute these days is the greenback.

It's curious. Those same members of Congress who claim messages from the Almighty on subjects like the estate tax and capital gains surely must be getting some messages about monopoly pricing of prescription drugs. But their silence is deafening. Consumers are being burned with the highest drug prices in the world and some of my colleagues in Congress are carrying the wood.

ACCOUNTING CHICANERY AND TAX CUTS

Astonishingly, not only is the Republican majority uninterested in investigating or putting an end to this drug-price scandal, it has the arrogance to reward these same corporations. As I discussed earlier, they've given the drug industry and others a 2005 tax holiday so they could move their huge profits from overseas tax havens back to the United States at a fraction of the normal tax rate—5.25 percent versus 35 percent (see chapter 4). I'm sure the average middle-class American worker would love a tax rate like that. It's a huge shell game. The administration touts toothpick-sized tax breaks for regular Americans while allowing redwood-sized tax breaks for its corporate friends.

The New York Times reported that six drug companies were on track to repatriate $75 billion in profits. The taxes due on that amount are less than $4 billion. According to the *Times*, some of the most impressive accounting wizardry took place at Eli Lilly, "which reported that it had about $200 million in profits from United States sales in 2004, compared with $2.8 billion in profits from sales everywhere else." Yet Wall

Street analysts estimate the percentage of profit derived from American sales is between 60 and 75 percent.

Okay, let's suppose the drug companies are being straight with us on pricing and profits (while we're at it, let us also suppose the moon is made of cheese, pigs can fly, and Michael Jackson has never had a nose job). So how does the industry explain *charging less* while *making more* money overseas? This astonishing business model will have them rewriting economic theory.

Let me summarize with this excerpt from *The New York Times* (May 8, 2005):

> Companies can hide profits from the IRS by moving their drug manufacturing overseas, said Martin A. Sullivan, contributing editor of *Tax Notes,* a nonprofit journal that examines tax issues. Companies transfer drug patents to their own foreign subsidiaries, he said. The subsidiary then helps pay for research on the drug. If the medicine is approved for sale in the United States, the subsidiary manufactures the drug for a few cents a pill. The pills are then shipped to the United States, where they are sold to a pharmacy or a wholesale company for several dollars each. But the parent company claims that almost all the profit should go to the subsidiary, not to the parent in the United States. "Then the name of the game is to have that foreign subsidiary pay as little as possible back to the United States for the rights to all that income," Mr. Sullivan said.

Even if the government wanted to make them pay their fair share, these powerful companies have the resources to hold the IRS at bay. They can stall through the legal system until the fight just isn't cost-effective for the IRS.

It's about power.

According to OneScience.com, Eli Lilly shut down its research and development operations in Philadelphia early in 2005, putting three hundred workers on the street. GlaxcoSmithKline cut 250 jobs—about half of them in Philadelphia's Research Triangle Park. Other drug makers have done the same, citing hard times. Yet these same companies are reaping the rewards of the new 5¼ percent tax rate and then running television ads telling us how great things are. I say can the ads and restore the jobs.

MARKETING VERSUS RESEARCH AND DEVELOPMENT

And what of the drug companies' claim that they need to charge high prices to fund research? I'd find that easier to believe if they were willing to open their books. For nine years, the industry battled against opening its books to the General Accounting Office, which is Congress's investigative arm. What are they afraid the American public might learn? That this is price gouging? We already know that!

Time magazine's 2004 cover story on the industry reports that 36 percent of medical research in America is already funded by the American taxpayer through the National Institutes of Health.

Bottom line? You're subsidizing the research. Shouldn't you get a price break?

Until these companies open their books, we should have no qualms about seeking a better deal for Americans who cannot afford the skyrocketing cost of health care. In 2002 alone, according to *Time,* healthcare spending rose 9.3 percent. Reimportation of drugs is only a temporary fix. In the meantime, lawmakers have to get aggressive about putting downward pressure on prices and saving lives.

We know drug companies are spending exorbitant amounts on market research and advertising. What happened to the good old days when Doc Smith made the diagnosis and not television commercials? The industry is making Americans paranoid.

Who needs to see a doctor? Just watch the early-morning television shows. The commercial will tell you "ask your doctor if the purple pill is right for you."

Even Dr. (Senator) Bill Frist demonstrated to America that you don't really need to see a doctor. He watched a brief videotape and then embarrassingly rushed to the Senate floor to diagnose Terry Schiavo as someone who was not in a persistent vegetative state. An autopsy on the poor woman proved he was wrong. But I digress.

According to a June 2005 story from *The Economist,* the drug industry spent about $19 billion on marketing in 2004. Novartis acknowledges spending one-third of its revenues on marketing—just 19 percent on research and development.

Pfizer, the world's largest drug company, employs thirty-eight thousand salespersons, but, like other pharmaceutical companies, is trimming its sales force by 5 percent. It isn't altogether altruistic on the part of the drug companies. The FDA is simply making more drugs available over the counter. Drug companies no longer have to sell the doctor. They just have to sell *you.* Pharmaceutical advertising did not become legal until 1997—New Zealand is the only other country to allow it—but it works, sort of. A Kaiser Family Foundation survey says 30 percent of respondents said they had talked to their doctor about an advertised medicine. That's not necessarily good news.

Do we need to return to the days when drug companies were kept off the airwaves? I believe in freedom of speech, but we limited the tobacco and liquor industries for the sake of the public health and welfare. Would it be so bad to put the decision-making process back in the hands of the patient and the doctor instead of the patient and a New York advertising director?

DESPITE THE PERILS OF HOCKEY, CANADIANS LIVE LONGER

It is often said that America has the best health-care system in the world. Well, Italy makes some of the finest high-performance cars in the world—Ferrari, Lamborghini, and Maserati—but not everyone can afford one. The same holds true with the American health-care system. As Pfizer's Dr. Rost told CBS's *60 Minutes,* "We're the wealthiest nation on earth, yet we have between 49 and 67 million Americans without any kind of insurance for drugs. And when they need drugs, they pay full price, cash . . . and they can't always afford them."

America's tepid life expectancy ranking may well be directly connected to the unaffordable cost of health care. According to CIA 2006 global statistics, the United States ranks forty-eighth in life span—77.85 years. Our neighbors to the north rank *twelfth*, and have miraculously managed to survive an average of 2.5 years longer (80.10) despite ingesting those dangerous drugs from Canadian pharmacies, enduring the ravages of socialized medicine, and playing hockey.

According to a 2004 *Time* magazine cover story, even in Japan, where prices are high enough to give you a nosebleed, life expectancy is eighty-one. Yet pharmaceutical sales per capita were only $421 compared to $654 in the USA in 2001. In Spain, life expectancy is seventy-nine, while the annual outlay for medicine is $190—less than half of what an American would pay for a three-month supply of Prevacid.

Republicans have made the issue of a national health-care program taboo, but when you check the long list of industrialized nations with healthier populations, most have some kind of national health care. Why should compassion and common decency be taboo? I believe we have a moral obligation to help those who need help—to heal those who can be healed. To leave proper health care in the hands of the highest bidder is shameful.

By the time insurance companies and health-care conglomerates have taken their cut, health care can cost an arm and a leg (that is, figuratively). A good 30 percent of each health-care dollar is spent on paperwork! On the other hand, Medicare spends less than four cents of each dollar on paperwork. It's proof that some government-run programs can be more efficient than Corporate America. Putting the burden on employers only quickens the pace of outsourcing. General Motors and Ford say health-care costs add $1,500 to the cost of a vehicle.

Why all the hysteria about national health care? We trust the government to attend to some mighty formidable tasks. We don't pluck generals from Wall Street desks to defend our nation. We trust the U.S. Army. Government-owned and -operated.

Our public education system—despite some well-deserved criticism—has been a key to making America a superpower, driven by an educated workforce. When the president didn't think things were going well with public education, he rolled out a government program, No Child Left Behind. If we can trust government to run national defense and fix education, why can't we get it more involved in cleaning up the health-care mess that is wounding our economy and costing lives? Medicare is a good example of a government program that, for the most part, works. But politicians have been working hard to mess that up, too.

A MIDNIGHT BOONDOGGLE

When the Congress passed the Medicare Prescription Drug bill, the Republicans inserted a little provision that expressly prohibited the federal government from negotiating lower drug prices with the drug industry. It is nearly unbelievable.

USA Today called it a victory for the drug makers. It is just one more handout to the pharmaceutical industry. *USA Today* summed it up neatly: "Pharmaceutical-makers already have averted what they feared most: a single new bloc of 40 million consumers with the market power to dramatically drive down prescription prices—and industry profits." A 2001 Health and Human Services report, quoted in *Time,* says Medicare reimbursements for two dozen medicines "exceeded actual wholesale prices by $761 million a year."

You want to trim the federal deficit? You want to cut entitlement spending? Opening a bid process on drug purchases would make a dent. Senate Majority Leader Dr. Bill Frist says he's opposed to "having the federal government set prices—fixed prices—for the American people." But he apparently is unconcerned about the pharmaceutical industry setting prices without any competition. *Oh yes, there would be riots in the streets if Americans were not allowed to continue paying the highest drug prices in the world!*

Senator Frist neglects to mention that there is a precedent. The Veterans Administration is allowed to negotiate prices on behalf of veterans. A 2002 General Accounting Office study reveals the VA managed to reduce the prices of some cholesterol medications by more than 70 percent.

So that's the dismal story about the pharmaceutical industry and the way it has perverted trade for its own benefit. From overpricing to tax dodging to false alarms about the safety of imported drugs, this industry, with the help of its friends in Congress and at the White House, is in hog heaven. But hang on.

Change is coming. The first step is exposure.

And now that you understand the problem, you can make a difference. Put pressure on the rascals. Write letters to the editor. Call your congressman or senator. When one of my constituents gives me an earful, believe me, I hear it! One voice *can* make a difference.

And this can be corrected simply and quickly with two law changes.

First, if the Congress will repeal the provision that prohibits the government from negotiating with the pharmaceutical companies for lower prices, the fleecing of the taxpayers will stop. The prices the government pays for the prescription drugs covered under Medicare will then be less expensive.

Second, if the Congress would repeal the law that prohibits the importation of less-expensive, FDA-approved prescription drugs from other countries, such as Canada, the prices of prescription drugs would drop here in the United States. Giving the American people the right to purchase FDA-approved prescription drugs from other countries will break the back of the monopoly pricing imposed on U.S. consumers by the drug industry.

Both of these solutions are made more difficult because President Bush and the Republican Congress oppose repealing this law.

But we can do this. "We the People" . . . those first three words of our Constitution are not just idle words. We're in charge and it's time to tell those who are siding with the drug industry that their time is up.

SIX

OIL—THE LUBRICANT OF TRADE AND TERRORISM

A T A FOUR-WAY STOP SIGN ON A COUNTRY ROAD IN North Dakota, I pulled up behind an old beat-up Chevrolet. Its back bumper was dented and hanging at an angle, and the car was pumping smoke out the tailpipe. But the bumper sticker caught my attention. It read, "We fought the gas war, and gas won!"

I suppose most of us feel that way these days.

We read that the big oil companies are racking up the highest profits in their history while Americans are being charged higher and higher prices for gasoline and home heating fuel.

It's as if there is a siphon that connects your pocketbook directly to the bank account of big oil!

It's the "free market system," the oil companies tell us. That's nonsense!

Here's the real story about oil prices and oil profits. It's about trade, rigged markets, and yes, terrorism, too. The simple story is the American consumers are getting fleeced while the big oil conglomerates are getting richer.

Here's how it works:

In January 2004, the price of a barrel of oil was $34.50. At that price, the big oil companies were piling up their largest profits. *Ever.* A year and a half later, the price they were getting for a barrel of oil was $65.

Now figure it out. We use 21 million barrels a day. Sixty percent of it comes from abroad and 40 percent comes from here at home. That means the oil companies and the oil-exporting countries were sharing about $17 billion a month more than they did just eighteen months previously. Put another way—Americans were *paying* $17 billion a month more for the energy they used. *That's about $200 billion at a yearly rate in excess charges, above the level at which the oil companies had already recorded their highest profits.*

OIL, THE FREE MARKET, MUD WRESTLING, AND THE PERFORMING ARTS

This pricing has nothing to do with a free market. The price of oil is to a free market like mud wrestling is to the performing arts. The price of oil is created by three major events, none of which represents a rational, competitive, and free market.

First, the OPEC oil ministers sit around a table and create production targets in order to affect prices. (Having a cartel set production and price targets is hardly a useful first step in setting a fair price!) For the record, OPEC (Outrageous Profits Easily Counted?) consists of eleven nations—Algeria, Indonesia, Iran, Iraq, Kuwait, Libya, Nigeria, Qatar, Saudi Arabia, the United Arab Emirates, and Venezuela. (Actually, OPEC stands for Organization of Petroleum Exporting Countries.)

Now, it is illegal for gas stations to "fix" prices, but OPEC does it all the time. And some of these countries are supposed to be our allies. We ought to be able to jawbone those prices right down, huh?

The second big impact on oil prices is the fact that the major oil companies, larger and stronger because of blockbuster mergers in recent years, apply their considerable muscle to affect the price of oil and oil products. An example of that is their decision to close refineries following their mergers. This restricts the amount of oil that can be refined, resulting in less supply and higher prices.

And third, the futures markets, which were intended to provide liquidity to facilitate market trades, have become an orgy of speculation. "Irrational exuberance," if you will.

So, in 2005, as consumers were finding it hard to pay the bill to fill the gas tank or heat the home, the news was full of the dramatically increased profits reported by the major integrated oil companies. Increased profits of 75 percent (ExxonMobil), 68 percent (Shell), 89 percent (Conoco-Phillips), 34 percent (British Petroleum), and more.

These behemoths were rolling in cash with oil prices above $60 a barrel. And the same companies that were reporting these record profits were also reporting *decreased production* of oil and natural gas. More money for the oil companies. Less oil for us. With a president and a vice president who came from the oil industry, this result doesn't seem so surprising. Upsetting, yes! But not surprising.

So when the majority party in Congress started to get some heat from home about energy prices, they finally took action. They held a hearing. When the Congress held a hearing on steroids in Major League Baseball, they required the witnesses to be sworn in. But when it came to big oil they said swearing in the witnesses was not important. Curious!

LIMITING REFINING CAPACITY KEEPS PROFITS HIGH

With all of these oil-company profits, there has not been a major U.S. refinery built since 1976, and while it is convenient to blame that on environmental standards, the reality is that oil companies are using this excuse to tighten supplies and ratchet up prices. In fact, you can find internal memos on the Web from Texaco, Chevron, and Mobil about *reducing* refining capacity (www.consumerwatchdog.org). Not only did mega oil companies purposely reduce their own refining capacity, they worked to drive small refiners out of business. In no way has refining capacity grown to meet consumption—and that's just the way oil companies like it.

According to a 2005 *New York Times* report, "Over the last quarter-century, the number of refineries in the United States dropped to 149, less than half the number in 1981. Because companies have upgraded and expanded their aging operations, refining capacity during that time period shrank only 10 percent from its peak of 18.6 million barrels a day. At the same time, gasoline consumption has risen by 45 percent." The Energy Information Administration says it is expected to rise *another 39 percent* by 2025.

When you consider those factors, you can see how Big Oil controls price and supply. There's some psychology involved here, too. After Hurricane Katrina, gas prices exceeded $3.00 a gallon in some parts of the country. However, *coincidentally*, after a growing outcry from consumers, the spotlight of Senate hearings, and my call for a Windfall Profits Rebate to consumers, the prices fell to just above $2.00 a gallon before starting a steep climb up again. Consumers breathed a sigh of relief, and the oil companies made off with billions. They got exactly what they wanted—a huge increase in profits that a Pavlovian public might now perceive as the status quo.

Their continuing windfall does not embarrass the oil companies. In fact, they claimed they needed the extra money to explore for more oil. Again it was a bogus claim. The major oil companies are doing *some* exploration, but they are also doing other things with their windfall profits. First, they are busy buying back their own stock. Second, they are hoarding cash in their corporate treasuries. And third, they are "drilling for oil on Wall Street" according to *BusinessWeek*. By the way, there is no oil on Wall Street—Big Oil is using its extraordinary profits to search for additional mergers and acquisitions. If they use their cash to acquire other companies that have oil reserves, they end up controlling more oil, but their investment has produced no new oil.

While the price of oil, gasoline, natural gas, and home heating fuel has been increasing, oil-company CEOs are hardly feeling the pinch. Take a look at the compensation:

Ray Irani, Occidental Petroleum $64 million a year
Lee Raymond, ExxonMobil $25 million a year

John Drosdick, Sunoco $33 million a year
David O'Reilly, Chevron-Texaco $8 million a year
(Give the guy a raise!)

In 2005, ExxonMobil announced a third-quarter increase in profits of 75 percent. Oh yes, and they also announced that they had a 4.7 percent reduction in oil and natural gas production. Part of that was attributable to the hurricanes, but even without the hurricanes they admitted their production would have dropped. Go figure.

While these companies and their executives count their cash, the American people are trying to figure out how to cope. Heating your home in the winter is not a luxury. It can be a matter of life and death. In most parts of the country the increased cost of natural gas and heating oil has been devastating for the elderly and people on fixed incomes who are living paycheck to paycheck.

These prices are also an especially heavy burden for family farmers who are big users of energy. They are struggling to pay the fuel bills and fertilizer bills (produced with petroleum) to plant and harvest the crops. Meanwhile, they continue to feel the pinch of imported grain and meat dumped on the market, which further erodes their ability to continue farming.

American families, who use their cars to drive to work, buy groceries, run errands, and drive their kids to soccer games, are having a tough time paying the gas bills, too. I'm sure they felt real good when Rush Limbaugh crowed about the booming economy and how gas prices were down to $2.50 a gallon. Don't you love it when rich guys tell you how good you've got it?

I tried to force the issue in 2005 with a proposed windfall profits tax on the record earnings of big oil companies, with rebates to go to American consumers. My bill called for a 50 percent tax on the profits earned by oil companies on crude oil sold above $40 a barrel, *unless* the companies invested those earnings in more domestic oil and natural gas production or to increase refinery capacity. It was defeated sixty-four to thirty-five.

Most people think that with a president and a vice president who came from the oil industry and a Republican-controlled Congress, it is a hopeless situation. It's an uphill struggle, for sure. But, this country belongs to all of us. And when things are unfair, we have a right to complain and a right to take action. If we let them get by with this now, it is just the beginning. These oil companies are getting bigger and stronger, and they are now holding the cards. But stay tuned. The American people have a way of imposing their will.

HELD HOSTAGE BY OUR APPETITE FOR OIL

Americans need to understand how we got to this place and where it is leading. We should understand that there are long-term, serious issues with the supply, the price, and the location of the oil we need for our economy that could pose serious risks for our country.

Some of these risks stem from the growth of the large oil companies, but there's more. The fact that we are dependent on foreign oil holds all of us hostage to the actions of others outside our country. So, you can't write a book about trade without describing the Byzantine twists and turns of the oil trade. Who has it. Who needs it. How much they pay for it. And who gets the money.

It is a strange and disturbing story.

The 21 million barrels of oil a day America consumes accounts for nearly $120 billion of our current annual trade deficit, which these days is around $60 billion a month and is over $700 billion a year! Over two centuries, as the U.S. economy grew, we developed a powerful thirst for oil. When automobiles began to roll off our factory floors and took to American roads, our addiction to oil, that black gold, became insatiable.

And through some strange quirk of nature the demand for oil exists *here* and the largest pools of oil are *over there* in a rather small region covered with sand called the Middle East.

So it turns out, for the kind of life we want to lead in the United States we need to turn to the people who control the oil in the Middle

East to sell it to us. Well, the countries that sit on top of all of that oil knew that, too, so in 1965 they decided to form a cartel called OPEC to establish production and price targets for their oil. Theirs isn't the only oil in the world. But they have the largest reserves, and it is easy and inexpensive to extract. Nothing else in the world compares to it. This really is the "comparative advantage" I described in chapter 2.

For a commodity that so dominates our lives, it is interesting that no one ever *sees* the oil. It is traded, transported, and used. And yet no one ever lays eyes on it. In places like Saudi Arabia, Kuwait, and Iran, the oil fields are dotted with pumping wells. Oil is pumped from those wells, moved through pipelines to seaports where it is loaded on ships, and transported to the United States. It is then offloaded, put in pipelines, sent to refineries that turn it into gasoline. Then it is transferred to trucks that haul it to the local gas station and put it in underground tanks. When you drive up to the gas pump and put the nozzle in your gas tank, you pump that gasoline from Saudi Arabia into your gas tank. And you never laid eyes on the product.

And your money goes straight back to Saudi Arabia.

And the Royal Family thanks you.

FACE IT, WE'RE OIL JUNKIES

The U.S. economy can't function without all of that foreign oil. We mainline oil like a junkie with a needle. If it were suddenly cut off, we would have serious withdrawal symptoms. So we keep buying it from the countries in the Middle East and elsewhere, and it drives up our trade deficit and feeds our dependence and addiction to an essential commodity that we must rely on others to provide.

We are in debt to the Saudis, the Kuwaitis, and other Middle East oil-producing countries. As they invest their profits, essentially we find ourselves selling our country, piece by piece, to foreigners to purchase the oil that we will use on American roads. Just like a junkie sells everything he owns to feed his habit.

As I've noted, nearly 60 percent of the oil Americans consume is imported, and it is true that if you look at the supply of foreign oil coming into the United States, we receive more from Canada than the Saudis. But that is just a function of regional access to an international market. Saudi Arabia and other Middle Eastern countries make the important decisions that determine the price of oil in the world market.

When you consider that production in the Middle East has likely peaked as the global appetite for oil increases, Caltech physicist David Goodstein, author of *Out of Gas: The End of the Age of Oil*, says, "We have created a trap for ourselves."

Of the 30 billion barrels of oil produced globally each year, America guzzles about 7 billion. In comparison, China consumed about 2.4 billion barrels in 2004. But if production remains stagnant and consumption jumps rapidly in places like China and India, with usage increases of 7.5 to 5.5 percent per year respectively, we have an enormous supply and demand problem.

OIL WARS

You see where this is headed, don't you? If we do not wean ourselves from oil imports, we face not only skyrocketing prices and a devastated economy but the potential for military misadventures as countries seek to secure oil supplies.

And let's face it: The unspoken agenda of America's military and political involvement in the Middle East is the oil supply. That is not to say that there are not other good reasons for our interest in the region, but oil is always a factor in our strategy.

Always. This supply of Middle East oil is so important to us that we go to war for it. The first Gulf War was a war about whether we would allow Saddam Hussein to gain control of Kuwait's oil reserves—the fifth largest in the world. I know, they said it was about freedom. But we all know better. If Kuwait had been a country in central Africa and without oil, do you think we would have sent a half a million American troops to reclaim it?

We even have a special foreign policy for those countries like Saudi Arabia that produce the oil we need. We are willing to ignore a multitude of sins as long as we can continue to nurture the relationship that feeds our habit.

Iraq has either the second- or third-largest oil reserves in the Middle East (depending on whose estimates you accept) and, before the second Gulf War, supplied about *one-fourth* of our Middle East imports.

The potential is much greater. The 1991 Gulf War and the subsequent sanctions wreaked havoc on the Iraqi oil fields. Necessary parts to repair and maintain the oil fields were denied Saddam Hussein in an effort to handcuff and topple his regime economically. A revived Iraq oil economy would provide some breathing room, but not for long.

The reality—setting aside Monday morning quarterbacking—is that American troops are in Iraq, at least in part, because of the strategic importance of Iraq oil. Yes, there are other reasons as well, such as international terrorism (and because we were told our intelligence experts thought Saddam Hussein possessed weapons of mass destruction), but without oil, Iraq is of far less consequence to America's future.

I think many Americans are beginning to see the true cost of a barrel of oil. We pay in blood. Our addiction to foreign oil puts our country at great risk from a security standpoint and contributes to our growing trade deficit. Year after year we buy their oil in exchange for foreign claims against American assets in the form of stocks, bonds, American dollars, and property.

But there is an even more sinister and dangerous facet to our oil trade. It contributes to the growth of terrorism. The oil wealth has spilled far enough from the barrel to help finance the terrorist groups that threaten our country and the rest of the free world.

If you think that our oil trade is just another commercial activity, consider this. On September 11, 2001, a Saudi Arabian citizen named Mohammed Atta was at the controls of American Airlines Flight 11 aiming for the north tower of the World Trade Center in New York City.

He was just one of the nineteen terrorists who hijacked four commercial airliners that day with the intention of killing American citizens. Fifteen of the nineteen hijackers were citizens of Saudi Arabia. (One was from Egypt, another from Lebanon, and two from the United Arab Emirates.) It is estimated that about 70 percent of al Qaeda recruits are Saudis. One Gallup poll found that nearly half of the Saudis polled had a very unfavorable opinion about the United States. Many claim they are offended by the presence of "infidels" in a country that hosts the two holiest cities in Islam, Mecca and Medina.

HOW WE HELPED FINANCE SEPTEMBER 11

Would it surprise you to learn that the terrorist plot against America was financed, at least in part, by oil money? Money that American drivers paid to fill up their tanks at the gas pumps?

The relationship between the United States and the Saudis has been a special and an unusual one. That has been true under Democrat and Republican presidents, but it is especially true with the two Bush presidencies.

George W. Bush and his father have a very close personal friendship with the Saudi Royal Family. Never was that more evident than in the meeting President Bush had with Prince Bandar, the Saudi ambassador to the United States, in the Oval Office of the White House on January 13, 2002.

The day before, Vice President Cheney had invited Prince Bandar to the West Wing of the White House to meet with him and Secretary of Defense Donald Rumsfeld. According to Bob Woodward's book *Bush at War,* President Bush had decided to go to war with Iraq, and he wanted the Saudi Crown Prince to be informed of his decision. So he asked Cheney and Rumsfeld to tell the prince.

Cheney and Rumsfeld delivered the message.

"You can take this to the bank," Rumsfeld is said to have told Prince Bandar about the certainty of the attack against Iraq. But Bandar said he would need to hear it directly from the president. So the very next day, January 13, he was invited to a meeting with the president in the Oval Office, where he heard the same message from President Bush.

In one of the strangest twists, the president's own secretary of state, Colin Powell, had not yet been informed that we were going to war. It wasn't until later that day that the president informed Powell of his decision. Ever the good soldier, it was Powell who was sent out to the United Nations to make the case for weapons of mass destruction as the reason for invading Iraq. As we all know, the WMDs remain MIA.

It is not inconsequential that the president of the United States had notified his close personal friend Prince Bandar of Saudi Arabia that he was going to go to war with Iraq before he informed his own secretary of state. It is almost unbelievable, but it describes and underscores the kind of relationship the Bushes have with the Saudi Royal Family, and it describes how important our government thinks our relationship with the Saudis is.

Another curious and largely unexplored event that exemplifies the cozy relationship between this president and the Saudis was the secret flights out of the United States in the days following the terrorist attacks of 9/11. Private charter flights were allowed to spirit Saudi citizens out of the United States and back to Saudi Arabia in the days following the attack. The passengers included Bin Laden family members who had been living in the United States at the time.

Who gave the order allowing such flights? Did the FBI have the opportunity properly to interrogate all of the Saudi citizens who were allowed to leave? There is plenty of evidence that these secret charter flights that spirited 142 Saudi citizens out of the United States took place without the full approval of the FBI or any other agencies that should have been carefully interrogating these people for any suspected connection to the terrorists.

And even more curious is the fact that in December 2002, a year after the terrorist attacks, the House and Senate Intelligence Committees did a joint report on 9/11. That lengthy published report contains twenty-eight pages that are completely redacted. They are the pages of the report that the president labeled "TOP SECRET" so that they would not be available to the public. It has been widely reported that these redacted pages deal with Saudi Arabia and the relationship of the Saudis to the hijackers.

When some in Congress pushed for the declassification of this material, the president refused, saying it could compromise the work of the 9/11 Commission. But both Senator Bob Graham, chairman of the Senate Intelligence Committee, and Senator Richard Shelby of Alabama, the ranking Republican, called for its release as well. Both agreed that it *would not* compromise sources and felt the information should be available to the public. Even Saudi Arabian officials finally called for its release. But the president refused, and those twenty-eight pages are still unavailable to the American people.

What are they hiding? Every American should be outraged that they aren't allowed to read these twenty-eight pages.

I have grave concerns about this administration's unprecedented penchant for secrecy and am reminded of a 1960 quote from the House Committee on Government Operations, which said, "Secrecy—the first refuge of incompetents—must be at a bare minimum in a democratic society, for a fully informed public is the basis of self-government. Those elected or appointed to positions of executive authority must recognize that government, in a democracy, cannot be wiser than the people."

No matter how they would like to dance around it, there is a long and mutually satisfying relationship between the United States, the Bush family, and the House of Saud. It's about close friendships, sure, but the foundation of the relationship is oil.

Author Craig Unger, who documented the forty-year relationship between the Saudis and the Bushes in his book, *House of Bush, House of Saud*, said in an interview:

Without the Saudis, you don't have 9/11. And we haven't focused on that. It's not just that 15 out of 19 of the hijackers were Saudis, that it was master minded by Osama bin Laden who, of course, is Saudi. If you look at the roots of Al-Qaeda, it was largely funded by Saudi Arabia and that includes members of the House of Saud, the Saudi merchant elite, great billionaire bankers who do lots of work with the United States, and have had relationships with the Bush family itself.

Saudi Arabia is supposedly our friend, our ally. The entire United States has benefited from this relationship, we all fill up our tanks with cheap gas (and this dates back to the 1940's when Franklin Roosevelt made an alliance with Saudi Arabia). The Bush family in particular has played a huge, huge role in all of this; they've been the architects of the policy for the last generation. The elder George Bush, James Baker, his close friend, ally and secretary of state, and the younger George Bush. They've been active in this, in the private sector and the public sector, back and forth as they've been in and out of power.

The connections between the Saudis and both Presidents Bush are well documented. When the current President Bush was the head of the floundering Harkin Oil, in the late 1980s, "it was losing money hand over fist," Unger explains. "There were enormous accounting irregularities. At the time, the price of oil was plummeting. Now I ask you, why would Saudis, who have all the oil in the world, journey around the globe to invest in this pathetic, failing company?"

The easy answer is probably because George W. Bush's father was president at the time.

There are some who might say there was a case for taking some strong action against the Saudis following the 9/11 attacks. But whoa! Saudi Arabia pumps about 10.5 million of the roughly 84.5 million barrels produced every day to meet the world's need for oil. They have what the world needs.

Their estimated reserves are 263 billion barrels, but for the want of an independent assessment, no one knows for sure. But if that figure is accurate, it is more than 20 percent of the known oil reserves on earth.

The fact is the terrorist threats that we face today are financed, at least in part, by the oil money that has poured into Saudi Arabia and other Middle East countries. I know the Saudis dispute it, but the evidence is abundant. The Saudis and their supporters point to the 9/11 Commission report as evidence that the Saudis are not financing terrorism. The report says the Commission "found no evidence that the Saudi government as an institution or senior Saudi officials individually funded [al Qaeda]."

But the report also states that Saudi Arabia "was a place where al Qaeda raised money directly from individuals and through charities," and indicates that "charities with significant Saudi government sponsorship may have diverted funding to al Qaeda."

The Council on Foreign Relations sponsored an independent task force to look into terrorist financing by Saudis. In October 2002, the task force issued a report that was very critical of Saudi support for financing international terrorist groups. "For years, individuals and charities based in Saudi Arabia have been the most important source of funds for al Qaeda. And for years Saudi officials have turned a blind eye to this problem."

In 2004, the second report from the task force welcomed steps the Saudis had made to tighten controls over "modalities of terrorist financing." But that report also calls for the Saudis to do more "because of the fundamental reality that persons and organizations based in Saudi Arabia have had in financing militant Islamist groups on a global basis."

TERRORISM FROM TEHRAN

The use of oil money to finance terrorism extends beyond Saudi Arabia, as other countries are using the accumulated wealth from oil sales to finance terrorism as well.

Iran, with the third-largest reserves of oil in the world, sells that oil on the world market and cashes in handsomely, and the evidence tells us that some of that money is used to finance terrorism against the United States.

In 1996 terrorists carried out an attack on a dormitory that housed

U.S. Air Force pilots and staff in Saudi Arabia, killing nineteen Americans. Former FBI director Louis Freeh told a federal judge in December 2003 that the blame for the murder of those Americans in the Khobar Towers bombing rested with Iran. "My own conclusion . . . was that the attack was planned, funded, and sponsored by the senior leadership of the government of Iran," Freeh testified.

The former FBI director and another former FBI official said they formed their opinions based on interviews with six men detained in Saudi Arabia. Freeh said the six admitted involvement in the bombing plot and provided details about planning, money, and training.

A November 2004 Associated Press story about suicide bombers described the murky, deadly world of terrorism inside Iran. "The 300 men filling out forms in the offices of an Iranian aid group were offered three choices: Train for suicide attacks against U.S. troops in Iraq, for suicide attacks against Israel or to assassinate British author Salman Rushdie (author of *Satanic Verses*)."

The AP story continues: "The presence of two key figures—a prominent Iranian lawmaker and a member of the country's elite Revolutionary Guards—lent the meeting more legitimacy and was a clear indication of at least tacit support from some within Iran's government." The U.S. State Department's report on state sponsors of terrorism concluded: "Iran remained the most active state sponsor of terrorism in 2004."

TRADING WITH THE ENEMY

Because Iran is on a list of rogue nations that support terrorism, we don't buy their oil, and U.S. law bans American companies from doing business with Iran.

But there is a loophole, and some American companies, more interested in profits than patriotism, have found a way around the ban on trading with Iran. Halliburton, General Electric, Conoco-Phillips are among those that have exploited the loophole. The law banning American companies from doing business in Iran does not apply to their foreign or offshore subsidiaries as long as non-Americans conduct operations.

The result, unbeknownst to you, is that your 401(k) might be helping fund terrorism. A CBS *60 Minutes* news report in August 2004 quoted William Thompson, the New York City comptroller, who invests the $80 billion in pension funds for city workers. He said, "The revenue that is generated from the work that these companies (Halliburton, General Electric, Conoco-Phillips, etc.) are doing, we believe, helps to underwrite and support terrorism." Of course, he was outraged, and he had a right to be. Anyone who watched the Twin Towers crumble on 9/11 would be aghast to discover that American companies are sleeping with the enemy.

Halliburton's practices are a model case study in violating the spirit of the law.

According to the CBS report, "Halliburton is the company that Vice President Dick Cheney used to run. He was the CEO from 1995 to 2000, during which time Halliburton Products and Services set up shop in Iran. Today it sells about $40 million a year worth of oil-field services to the Iranian government."

Halliburton Products and Services is wholly owned by the U.S.-based parent and is registered in a building in the capital of the Cayman Islands. When the CBS reporters decided to ask Halliburton's subsidiary about its work in Iran, they went into the building in the Cayman Islands with a hidden camera. It turned out that there was no one there who worked for Halliburton.

In a letter to the New York City comptroller, Halliburton said its Cayman Island subsidiary was actually run out of Dubai, halfway around the world. Curious! So, the *60 Minutes* crew went to Dubai and found that the Halliburton foreign subsidiary there "shares office space, phone, and fax lines with a division of its U.S.-based parent company."

And, despite all this, it continues to receive lucrative government contracts here at home.

But it is not Halliburton alone. Roger Robinson, who runs the Investor Responsibility Research Center in Washington, D.C., has identified *nearly four hundred companies* that are doing business in terrorist-sponsoring states. The state treasurer in Arizona, who is also tracking this information, says "there's about 11 to 14 companies that are on the S&P 500 that are involved in some substantial projects with some of these countries."

SHEDDING OUR ADDICTION TO FOREIGN OIL

How do we overcome this dangerous addiction to foreign oil and investiture in rogue regimes? How do we become independent, or at least much less dependent on countries like Saudi Arabia for our long-term economic health?

If you look at the demand for oil in the United States, the fastest-rising area of demand is for the gasoline to power our transportation system. The fuel to run our cars and trucks is the line on the demand side that is increasing rapidly. At some point we have to stop running gasoline through our carburetors or fuel injectors to decrease our dependence.

My first car was an antique. I bought a 1924 Model T Ford for $25 when I was sixteen years old and I restored it over a two-year period. It was a car that had sat in an old shed on an abandoned farm for over forty years. It was rusted, and the rats had eaten all of the wiring and seats. I worked hard to restore it, and I was so excited when I got that engine to run.

Do you know how I put gasoline in a Model T Ford? The same way you fuel a 2006 Ford. Put the hose in the tank and begin pumping. Almost everything else on a new car is changed. In fact, there is now more computing power on a new car than existed on the Lunar Lander when Neil Armstrong and Buzz Aldrin landed on the moon. These cars are technological marvels. One new car model even parallel parks for you. But for all of the changes, we've done nothing that would allow us to end our addiction to Middle East oil.

The fact is we have to change. I believe we should adopt a crash program called "Energy Independence" to make us independent of foreign oil by 2020. We can't continue to have our economy held hostage by the oil ministers of the OPEC countries. I know what the doubters will say.

"It can't be done." Well, we went to the moon in less than ten years. We can do this. It ought to be our national goal.

In the meantime we need to take some interim steps that can make us much less reliant on foreign oil even as we move toward a goal of independence.

I want us to develop a future that powers our vehicles with hydrogen and fuel cells. Hydrogen is everywhere. And using hydrogen to power fuel cells means that you put water vapor out the tailpipe even as you have twice the efficiency of power to the wheel. A transition to hydrogen production and hydrogen filling stations will take time. But there is some hope.

The 2005 Energy Bill passed by the Congress included a 3.7-billion-dollar hydrogen title that I and a few others pushed to include. It has the support of President Bush and I believe will be the first step in converting to a different energy future for our transportation needs. And even some of the large energy companies now understand the current predicament leads only to trouble and are now aggressively involved in hydrogen/fuel cell research and development. And hydrogen fuel can be produced using many different kinds of domestic energy sources, including renewables. That is a hopeful sign for the future.

But something exciting that is happening right now is the production and distribution of biofuels—especially ethanol and biodiesel. The Congress has finally made a big commitment to the production of renewable fuels such as ethanol and biodiesel. We can *grow* energy in our farm fields! The key is that this is *renewable energy* that can be reseeded year after year. That solution is not only one that contributes to less dependence on foreign oil, but it also helps our family farmers with a new market for their crops. Biofuels cannot completely replace oil, but they can have a huge impact and allow us to transition away from dependence on foreign oil.

According to an extensive 2004 study by the Natural Resources Defense Council, biofuels could be produced for less than a dollar a gallon and by 2050 could save Americans $20 billion at the pump while giving farmers $5 billion in profits. They say that more efficient vehicles combined with high-tech biofuel plants could cut America's energy dependency on foreign oil by two-thirds by 2050. At the rate we are going, by 2050, America's thirst for oil could grow to 30 million barrels of oil per day. By 2050, if we have the will to invest in the research and development, biofuels could contribute about 8 million barrels a day.

We can also take the energy from the wind and turn it into electricity. That, too, is renewable energy that can replace some of our need for oil or natural gas. According to the American Wind Energy Association, wind towers are producing about ninety-two hundred megawatts of energy, reducing the amount of natural gas burned for energy by 4–5 percent. The Global Wind Energy Council believes 12 percent of the worlds' electrical power can be supplied by wind by 2020.

These are clean energy sources, which will cut greenhouse gases dramatically.

It's just common sense.

Fifty years from now, if our grandkids are still pumping gas into their automobile tanks—*if the supply lasts that long*—we still lose. This isn't about the health of the big oil companies. It is about our country's future.

In the 1990s, the blockbuster mergers created an oil industry that is much more concentrated and more powerful. And for the most part they don't want things to change. Those interests that control markets like things the way they are.

It is hard to change energy policy. When a country changes a primary fuel source, there are all kinds of issues surrounding production, transportation, storage, and infrastructure. But we can do it if we decide that is what we want for our future. And don't we owe something to the next generation?

We surely can't continue a relationship to oil that has us financing terrorism when we fill up at the gas pumps. And we must understand that having our future standard of living and economic growth hinging on our ability to get sufficient oil from the Middle East is a dangerous course.

The American people deserve better than that.

SEVEN

WAL-MART AND CHINA—DANCING IN THE DARK!

No MORE BULLSHIT!" THAT WAS THE UNORTHODOX campaign slogan for author Norman Mailer when he ran for mayor of New York City in 1969. I suppose it wouldn't be politically correct to use that slogan today. The bulls would sue. But *bullshit* would be the perfect description of the inane defense of our current trade policy by those who can't seem to understand the difference between success and failure, winning and losing.

So, I admit I'm tempted to adopt Mailer's slogan. How could we have allowed Corporate America and their outsourcing cheerleaders to turn truth on its head?

Deficits are good.

Job loss is fine.

It will all work out in the end for us.

Don't file those theories under economics. Put them in the fiction section.

BEING PLAYED FOR A SUCKER

P. T. Barnum used to say, "There's a sucker born every minute." Sure, but we don't want a sucker in charge of our trade policy.

And the fact is that the American people are being played for suckers. The story can most easily be illustrated by describing the recent marriage between Wal-Mart and China. Didn't know they were dating? Well, it surprised us all. All of a sudden this behemoth American retailer, which had its roots in a small town in Arkansas, fell head over heels for the Chinese. Actually, their affection is for the low-wage Chinese workers. It is a simple marriage, really:

Wal-Mart gets to sell products that are made by cheap labor from China.

China inherits the jobs that used to belong to American workers.

And the unemployed and underemployed American workers get to buy cut-rate imported Chinese shirts, shoes, and electronics at an American Wal-Mart. *Seventy percent* of the products on its shelves come from China.

Everybody wins. Right? Well, hardly. There is no "happily ever after" here.

Okay, you say with a heavy sigh, is this going to be the same old obligatory beating up on Wal-Mart? You can't have a book about the backward slide of the middle class, outsourcing, and the trade deficit without hammering Wal-Mart, right?

Well, the fact is Wal-Mart is important because, in the blink of an eye, the world economy and workplace is changing—and not necessarily for the better. And with all due respect to Sam Walton, I think Wal-Mart is the poster child for what has gone so terribly wrong in this global economy.

Let me be quick to say that Wal-Mart is not breaking the rules. I just don't like the business model that trades American jobs for cheap foreign labor. And I don't like the business model that pushes wages down here in the United States.

I think that those corporations who push the outsourcing of production in order to discount-price their products back in our marketplace are shortsighted. They forget the Henry Ford model of wanting to pay his workers sufficient wages to allow them to purchase what they produced. And that mistake will likely be costly for our country in the long run.

Wal-Mart is America's largest corporation—the biggest in the world, as a matter of fact. So, it is not just any company. It is the one that perfected an entirely new business strategy—to get products created abroad with low-wage labor and sell the products in U.S. stores manned by poorly paid American workers.

This leads to low prices and lots of customers, but I believe it is a strategy that hurts our U.S. economy.

Wal-Mart workers take home an average of $250 a week, according to a PBS report, and about 70 percent of these workers leave in the first year (Wal-Mart disputes that figure, but did not provide a different one). One-third of the workers are part-time, so they are not eligible for benefits. The health insurance package requires a 35 percent contribution—more than twice the national co-pay average—so more than half of those Wal-Mart workers who are eligible can't afford it.

It clearly is a business plan that works to fatten profits, but I think, in the long run, it undermines much of the economy we have relied on to be a great, healthy country. I feel strongly that some important American values are being sacrificed in order to find the lowest-priced gallon of mustard or twelve-pack of underwear.

Wal-Mart has a right to pursue their business plan, but I also believe local governments have a right to make their zoning decisions based on whether they believe their next Wal-Mart superstore will help or hurt their local economy.

According to a 2003 *New York Times* report, Wal-Mart is the nation's largest grocer, toy seller, and furniture retailer. "More than 30 percent of the disposable diapers purchased in the country are sold in Wal-Mart stores, as are 30 percent of hair-care products, 26 percent of toothpaste and 20 percent of pet food. Wal-Mart has nearly 3,000 stores in the United States, and plans to add an additional 1,000 over the next five years. Increasingly, the company is taking its formula abroad; Wal-Mart is now the largest private employer in Mexico." (Wal-Mart has about 1.2 million American employees. And 1.5 million total when workers worldwide are included.)

That is an astonishing amount of economic power. Ask anyone who is trying to compete against Wal-Mart about what this power means. Ask the local lumberyard, the local grocery, hardware, or drugstore how they fare when Wal-Mart shows up. Ask the local community leaders if they notice a difference when the business community is dominated by one big-box retailer that runs all the small businesses out.

In WWII, soldiers venturing into newly occupied territory often found the words "Kilroy was here" scrawled onto a wall. The soldiers found it inspirational. What ought to be inscribed on the plywood covering boarded-up Main Street businesses is, "Wal-Mart was here," and that is hardly inspirational.

Wal-Mart CEO H. Lee Scott says, "We are at 8 percent of the nonautomotive, nonrestaurant sales in the U.S. I'm not sure why it couldn't be 24 percent. We've really done a great job for our customers, lowering prices, lowering the cost of living, raising the standard of living. Is it really unhealthy for us to be 32 percent? Could we be four times bigger right here? I don't know why not."

Well, I'll tell him why not. Good business is not just about low prices. It is also about good jobs. And the Wal-Mart business plan is antithetical to good jobs for Americans.

Progress is supposed to mean moving ahead. But in this case, "progress" in global trade has exported misery, turned a blind eye to child labor and slavery abroad while simultaneously eroding jobs and our manufacturing industry in America.

Wal-Mart has been a leader in constructing the new business model that I believe undercuts the middle class in our country. Yes, there are other companies that contribute to this exodus of good jobs. Target and Kmart come to mind. But, make no mistake, Wal-Mart is the leader of the parade and proud of it.

Through sheer buying power Wal-Mart can dictate the price they will pay, which forces companies to abandon any sense of loyalty to their workers. They must ramp up production and crank down costs. Inevitably, they must move production to China. Up goes the trade deficit. Wave good-bye to the American jobs. Then, Wal-Mart plants these stores on the edges of thriving communities where they become a death star, swallowing up all the small businesses that cannot compete with Wal-Mart's buying clout. Say good-bye to even more American jobs in these small towns. You can always put on a blue smock for less money and—likely no health-care plan. Because fewer businesses are paying taxes, local taxes rise and charities suffer because the mom-and-pop stores are cumulatively more generous than the Walton Gang.

The debate about the ravages of this model is growing in city councils around the United States. The inequities of global trade have come home to roost in small-town America as they debate about what a new Wal-Mart will do to their community. Some claim that those who work against a Wal-Mart store in their community are interfering with the free market system. "Compete or get the hell out of the way," they say, the notion being that businesses come and go, and if a local business can't compete—tough luck.

But the free market only works when you have *many* competitors. When one of the competitors becomes large enough to clog the arteries of the free market system, even on a local level, then the market is no longer free. Innovation is retarded, and in essence you have the same stagnation that exists when there is no competition.

On the local level, I believe wholeheartedly that towns have the right to determine through zoning what kind of community they want. Do they want to foster small businesses and a thriving Main Street? Or are they angling to play host to the largest big-box retailers that can sell the widest range of goods and services at the lowest prices even if it means drying up the rest of the town's local businesses?

Back in the 1950s we had some national companies like Woolworth's, Coast to Coast, Sears Roebuck, and Montgomery Ward that set up shop in towns across America, but these companies did not dwarf other businesses in the community. And they did not have the market power that a company like Wal-Mart now has.

With a one-two punch, Wal-Mart knocks businesses and their employees out. As these small businesses are put out of work, their employees are forced to get off the canvas and work for the source of their misery—Wal-Mart—and, according to a 2004 UC Berkeley study, Wal-Mart paid 31 percent less than surrounding employers.

Wal-Mart calls its employees "associates." Yeah, well there used to be a three-legged, one-eared blind dog with fleas in my hometown named Lucky. Being an associate sounds better than it is. The company scrimps on employee pay and is stingy with benefits. Lower operating costs for labor win out. And that forces other retailers wishing to compete with Wal-Mart to follow their lead, requiring suppliers to move their factories abroad and Main Street businesses to suppress the wages of their workers.

As grocery stores struggle to stay open when a Wal-Mart Supercenter comes to town, they are forced to cut wages. In 2003, seventy thousand union employees of Kroger, Safeway, and Albertsons went on strike in Southern California to protest wage cuts by the grocery chains that were in mortal fear of the forty new Supercenters opening in their territory. According to a PBS *Frontline* story, the average wage of the Wal-Mart employee, at $9.64, was about *$10 less* than the average hourly wage of a supermarket employee in that California job market.

Wal-Mart has nearly a *20 percent* market share of the grocery business and 16 percent market share of the pharmacy business. It is estimated that Wal-Mart will control *35 percent* of the grocery and pharmacy industry by *2007*. Wal-Mart has about three thousand total stores, including fourteen hundred Supercenters. For every Supercenter that opens, statistically, *two grocery stores close*.

This is what seems to escape every dissection of Wal-Mart. Not only does its immense muscle literally force major manufacturers to outsource, when Wal-Mart sets up shop in a community, it eliminates the competitors. It is economic cannibalism. Wal-Mart spokeswoman Sarah Clark says working families enjoy $2,300 in savings annually by shopping in Wal-Mart. That doesn't go very far if Wal-Mart costs you your job, health benefits, and/or forces your local taxes higher.

A 2004 economic impact study of the UIC Center for Urban Economic Development in Chicago concluded that a Wal-Mart on the west side, while bringing in 200 jobs, *would cost surrounding businesses 266 jobs!* That's less disposable income in a community, more workers on unemployment, and less tax revenue. Even though Wal-Mart would be paying more in taxes than the prior property owners, the severe decline in tax revenue from surrounding businesses creates a net loss.

Yet Wal-Mart, with its massive resources and polished pitch, pulls the wool over outgunned and overwhelmed city councils and zoning boards' eyes. If the company is ruthless in its efforts to set up shop, it is equally ruthless when the doors open. The *Capital Times* of Madison, Wisconsin, explained:

> By avoiding union contracts that spell out pay and benefits, it can keep a leg up on competitors. It's easier to keep prices low when the employees get less. Canadian workers are a bit more feisty, though, and those employed at the Jonquiere, Quebec, store voted last year to join the United Food and Commercial Workers Canada, becoming the first Wal-Mart store in North America to be unionized . . . The company's response to this brazen union move was swift and simple. Come May, the Jonquiere store will be closed and its 130 employees can just go someplace else to find work.

The company plays hardball the way Bob Gibson used to pitch. If you crowd the plate, you get a fastball under your chin.

Ironically, Wal-Mart wouldn't have to pay rock-bottom wages. *BusinessWeek,* in a 2004 story entitled "The Costco Way—Higher Wages Mean Higher Profits. But Try Telling Wall Street," said:

> Costco's high-wage approach actually beats Wal-Mart at its own game on many measures. *BusinessWeek* ran through the num-

bers from each company to compare Costco and Sam's Club, the Wal-Mart warehouse unit that competes directly with Costco. We found that by compensating employees generously to motivate and retain good workers, one-fifth of whom are unionized, Costco gets lower turnover and higher productivity. Combined with a smart business strategy that sells a mix of higher-margin products to more affluent customers, Costco actually keeps its labor costs lower than Wal-Mart's as a percentage of sales, and its 68,000 hourly workers in the United States sell more per square foot. Put another way, *the 102,000 Sam's employees in the United States generated some $35 billion in sales last year, while Costco did $34 billion with one-third fewer employees!!!!!!!!*

(The exclamation points are mine.)

Bottom line: *Costco pulled in $13,647 in U.S. operating profit per hourly employee last year, vs. $11,039 at Sam's.* Over the past five years, Costco's operating income grew at an average of 10.1% annually, slightly besting Sam's 9.8%. Most of Wall Street doesn't see the broader picture, though, and only focuses on the up-front savings Costco would gain if it paid workers less.

CORPORATE WELFARE FOR WAL-MART—YOUR HIDDEN BILL

Just in tax breaks and other sweetheart deals, local governments have subsidized Wal-Mart by at least $1 billion. There is no accurate tracking method to know exactly how much we are paying these guys to come to our towns.

But the costs of Wal-Mart run deeper, as Congressman George Miller's report shows:

Because Wal-Mart wages are in many cases not living wages, the company uses taxpayers to subsidize its labor costs. While the

California study showed how much taxpayers were subsidizing Wal-Mart on health care alone, the total costs to taxpayers for Wal-Mart's labor policies are much greater.

The Democratic Staff of the Committee on Education and the Workforce estimates that one 200-person Wal-Mart store may result in a cost to federal taxpayers of *$420,750 per year*—about $2,103 per employee. Specifically, the low wages result in the following additional public costs being passed along to taxpayers:

- $36,000 a year for free and reduced school lunches for just 50 qualifying Wal-Mart families.
- $42,000 a year for Section 8 housing assistance, assuming 3 percent of the store employees qualify for such assistance, at $6,700 per family.
- $125,000 a year for federal tax credits and deductions for low-income families, assuming 50 employees are heads of household with a child and 50 are married with two children.
- $100,000 a year for the additional Title 1 expenses, assuming 50 Wal-Mart families qualify with an average of 2 children.
- $108,000 a year for the additional federal health-care costs of moving into state children's health insurance programs (SCHIPs), assuming 30 employees with an average of two children qualify.
- $9,750 a year for the additional costs for low-income energy assistance.

But even if you don't want to take Congressman Miller's study as gospel, review the findings of the Institute of Southern Studies, which took a look at Wal-Mart's drain in their region:

- **Alabama:** The *Montgomery Advertiser* found in February 2005 that families of Wal-Mart workers are the top dependents on

Medicaid. Three thousand eight hundred sixty-four children of Wal-Mart employees depend on Medicaid for health insurance. The next highest company, McDonald's, has 1,615 employees' children on the program.

- **Florida:** In December 2004, the *Tallahassee Democrat* revealed that fifty thousand workers and their dependents rely on Medicaid for health insurance. McDonald's was the worst culprit in the Sunshine State, with 1,792 claims filed. Wal-Mart had 756.
- **Georgia:** Ten thousand two hundred sixty-one children of Wal-Mart workers rely on PeachCare for Kids, the state's program for low-income families, according to a February 2004 report in the *Atlanta Journal-Constitution.*
- **Tennessee:** Twenty-five percent of Wal-Mart workers in Tennessee are enrolled in TennCare, the state's health plan for the poor and uninsured, according to a January 2005 investigation by the *Memphis Commercial Appeal.* That's 9,617 employees.
- **West Virginia:** The *Charleston Sunday Gazette-Mail* revealed last December that 452 Wal-Mart workers in the state have children dependent on the State Children's Health Insurance Program, the most of any company.

Congressman Miller's California report concluded, "Among Wal-Mart employees, some single workers may be able to make ends meet. Others may be forced to take on two or three jobs. Others may have a spouse with a better job. And others simply cannot make ends meet. Because Wal-Mart fails to pay sufficient wages, U.S. taxpayers are forced to pick up the tab. In this sense, Wal-Mart's profits are not made only on the backs of its employees—but on the backs of every U.S. taxpayer."

Of course, that one won't show up on your receipt when you check out.

(Note: A November 2005 internal Wal-Mart memo that was leaked stated, "We also have a significant number of Associates and their children who receive health insurance through public assistance programs. . . . In total, 46% of Associates' children are either on Medicaid or uninsured.")

This isn't Wal-Mart bashing.

It is just a fact.

No single company in the world has benefited more from corporate welfare than Wal-Mart and no single company has cost this country more jobs than has Wal-Mart.

Examination of the connection between Wal-Mart, China, the trade deficit, and the economy it undermines can help us all understand how foolish and dangerous this headlong, unmanaged rush into globalism without rules has been. If Americans begin to understand how deep into their own lives these tentacles reach, they can begin to do something about it.

WAL-MART AND CHINA'S DOWNWARD CRUSH ON WAGES AND JOBS IN AMERICA

The ability and desire to hire low-wage workers in China has a dampening effect on wages in America. Even if you can't identify it, I would bet that most industries are competing with Chinese labor at some level. Workers fearful of losing their jobs in America may agree to forgo raises and even agree to wage cuts to defend their jobs.

Let me tell you, this country cannot move forward if the middle class is moving backward! A step backward now and then is fine if you are doing a cha-cha, but this is a lot like waltzing in front of a steamroller.

With its immense retail sales reach—*$258 billion* in sales for the fiscal year ending in January 2005—Wal-Mart has been able to force American companies to move factories to China so they can keep wholesale prices low. Wal-Mart has about thirty thousand suppliers, each under enormous pressure to squeeze every last bit of efficiency out of them.

So, as we have seen in the case of Huffy, Etch A Sketch, Fruit of the Loom, and countless others, Wal-Mart costs American manufacturing jobs. An unemployed workforce creates a drain on social programs, and that costs all of us money. And when companies like Huffy and Fruit of the Loom declare bankruptcy—you get the bill for that, too.

Try to put *$258 billion* in annual sales—*an 11 percent increase over 2004*—in perspective. That amounts to selling about $40 worth of merchandise annually to each of the 6.5 billion inhabitants of this planet. Wal-Mart CEO H. Lee Scott bragged in a 2005 speech that if his company were a country, economically it would be the twentieth largest in the world.

But things may be changing. Finally, Americans are taking notice and thinking before they shop. At the beginning of 2005, 69 percent of the population shopped at Wal-Mart at least once or twice a month. That was down to 51 percent in November.

A 2005 Zogby poll showed that 56 percent of Americans agreed with the statement, "Wal-Mart is bad for America. It may provide low prices, but these prices come with a high moral and economic cost."

And now let us connect this all to China, whose repressed labor force makes this all possible. Wal-Mart, as a company, is China's *eighth-largest trading partner*, ahead of entire countries like Russia, Australia, and Canada. In 2004, 80 percent of Wal-Mart's imports, some $18 billion worth, came from China.

According to U.S. government data, the United States imported $196 billion in goods from China in 2004 and was on track to hit $260 billion in 2005, while exports from the United States to China looked to rise from $35 to $44 billion. So China accounts for about *one-third* of our annual trade deficit, and Wal-Mart, as the leading importer, has led the charge in a race to the bottom line that no company can afford to abandon unless an international truce is called. Can we change it all overnight? No, but we most assuredly cannot continue in this direction.

Despite the fact that Wal-Mart has some forty stores in China and other companies have invested there, the potential for U.S. exports to China was vastly overestimated. That, coupled with the Chinese government's reluctance to allow more imports, has made wide-open trade with China a misstep of cosmic proportions. A few have come to recognize the danger, but with corporate lobbyists whispering in their ears, most Republicans in Congress and some Democrats as well have not heard our warning.

There is little reason for major corporations to do anything but advocate we stay the course. They are much more interested in their level of profits than the long-term economic health of the United States.

THE DANGER OF DEBT

A massive trade deficit, stagnant wages, plain old materialism, and recklessness have put us all in a tough spot. What has happened is that the American government and Americans have spent themselves into a deceptively deep hole—according to the Economic Policy Institute, that 660-billion-dollar 2004 trade deficit means that foreign lenders are gathering up our currency as they finance the gap created by our spending spree, a debt equivalent to $5,500 per household. *Per year.* Obviously, that sort of mounting debt cannot continue. But it did continue in 2005 and grew to over $700 billion.

As a measure of our individual financial vulnerability, consider that the average household credit card debt is over $7,000, and the savings rate is zero. Zero. You read that right. Meanwhile, Americans have an accumulated $8 trillion in mortgage debt, and 40 percent of that is interest. An accountant might tell the average American family that they are "exposed."

William E. Simon, former secretary of the treasury under presidents Nixon and Ford, wrote in his book *A Time for Action,* "*Deficit spending does not eliminate the costs of government. It only conceals them. Everything in life must be paid for.*"

A wise businessman always keeps debt manageable because it is impossible to predict disaster. This president and his willing cohorts have put this nation at great risk through inaction and inappropriate action. We have become the world's largest debtor nation. *The Washington Post* columnist David Broder wrote about the dangerous confluence of economic pressures we face:

> At a private dinner the other evening where many of the men and women who have steered economic and fiscal policy during the past two decades were expressing their alarm about this situation, one speaker summarized the feelings of the group. "I think it's 1925," he said, "and we're headed for 1929." I don't know whether that's true. I'm an optimist, not a pessimist. But, our current path should alarm even the most optimistic.

This president entered office with budget surpluses and a country on track to bury the national debt within a decade or so. Four years later his *8-trillion-dollar* national debt has left us exposed to the elements of the unknown.

Now, some economists will paint all sorts of rosy scenarios. It is wishful thinking. My palette runs much darker on this count, and if we do not find the political will to make a real change, we are headed for big trouble. The course we are on is unsustainable. We have been living on borrowed time and money. Interest rates have been kept artificially low in order to stimulate borrowing, investment, and homebuilding, auto purchases—you name it. That was the tonic for the recession in President Bush's first term. Inflation has been held back, which Wal-Mart likes to take credit for. But, if Wal-Mart gets credit for holding down prices, it must bear part of the responsibility for the increase in our trade deficit and job loss as well.

William Greider wrote in *The Nation* in 2004:

> I see the United States sinking into financial dependency—dangerously indebted to rival nations that are holding our debt paper, collecting the interest on Treasury bonds and private bank loans, or repatriating the profits from companies that used to be American-owned. A very wealthy nation can tolerate this nega-

tive toll for many years, but not forever. Unless the historic mean-
ing of debt has been repealed, no nation can borrow endlessly
from others without sooner or later forfeiting control of its destiny, and also losing the economic foundations of its general prosperity.

As Americans we have to understand that economic vulnerability is
as dangerous as military vulnerability; in fact, the former causes the latter. The fanatical terrorists who have us in their sights understand this
as well. When, as a nation, we carelessly allow ourselves to become as financially vulnerable as this president has, it is dangerous to our national
security.

It will be interesting to see what happens, in the way a car wreck is
interesting if you are not in it. China, as one of our major lenders, has a
stake in keeping the U.S. economy going. China needs our market. We
need their dollars to finance our indebtedness. Quite the conundrum
we have here, isn't it? So we have to lower the trade deficit methodically
without causing a major shock to either economy—it will, of course, be
a major shock to international corporations, and they will fight it tooth
and nail with their legions of lobbyists and barrels of political dona-
tions.

EMBRACING THE OPPORTUNITY—WITH EYES WIDE OPEN

Like it or not, we are in bed with the Chinese, and if they have cold
feet, we are just going to have to suffer. But if we have the vision, we
can negotiate a more equitable trade agreement, save our jobs, expand
the global economy, and improve conditions for the suffering Chinese
workers. There is incredible opportunity here.

To do that we have to be tough-minded at the negotiating table. Our
failure to negotiate from strength and enforce trade agreements—a
policy international corporations loved—has left us with less leverage
for the future.

Now let us look at China for a moment. Investment in their country can hold opportunity for American business. And I think it is fine to invest there with the purpose of fashioning products for their market-place, as long as we can begin to enforce a timetable for the improvement of labor and elimination of artificial subsidies. One of the great draws for companies like Wal-Mart is not just an easily exploitable and vast labor force, it is the fact that manufacturing is subsidized. Land is cheap, taxes artificially low, and fuel subsidized by the Chinese. All of that is a strategy by the Chinese government to lure manufacturing activity to their country. Low wages alone are very persuasive, but the communist government has the ability to sweeten the deal with deep subsidies.

This is not a new trick.

PROTECTING INDUSTRY IN THE NAME OF NATIONAL SECURITY

The nature of global trade has changed so swiftly, few people recognize that it is no longer just an economic issue but one of national security—and for an administration consumed with national security, it is amazing that the Bush administration has remained so blind to the wholesale dissolution of crucial industries.

On this point, we haven't a moment to waste. We must carefully inventory the infrastructure of this country's manufacturing might and identify what is essential to national security. Certainly our steel production and related industries are among those most crucial. Food and energy must also make the list.

Here's where the sanctimonious caterwauling comes in from those who don't want our country to have any type of industrial plan. But I think we should consider subsidies if necessary as a stopgap measure to protect essential businesses in the interest of national security. The fact is the IRS tax code is filled with subsidies and handouts to all sorts of companies that have no bearing on national security. Why not use them to invest in things that are essential to our national security?

PICKING OUR BRAINS AND OUR POCKETS

As we examine our approach to international trade, we have to answer questions about intellectual property. The Chinese have been famous (infamous, actually) for eliminating the need for research and development by copying American ingenuity and dumping copies on our doorstep to destroy our businesses. It is called piracy and counterfeiting. They copy books, CDs, DVDs, microchips, and more. Consumers love it, but it is literally stealing.

A recent story out of China makes it clear that the problem of piracy and counterfeiting is something the Chinese government can do something about if they really want to. According to press reports, some Chinese merchants were using the official logo for the upcoming Chinese Olympics without authorization. The Chinese government clamped down and stopped it immediately. So they've demonstrated that if they want to stop the cheating, they can. It is quite clear, however, that it has been in their economic interest to turn a blind eye to this wholesale cheating.

If we are successful in getting the Chinese to engage in fair trade practices, we could benefit in the long run from the much vaunted potential of a consumer base in China that will benefit our producers. But don't bet on it.

We were promised the same thing with Japan and yet, after several decades, we still have a staggering trade deficit with Japan of about $75 billion a year.

THE LONG-TERM POTENTIAL OF CHINA'S MARKETPLACE IS ENORMOUS

Slowly and surely, as we make global trade a more equitable process for countries, corporations, and workers there is opportunity—but we can't bankrupt the system on the way to the party.

In China, there are 320 million potential employees and buyers under the age of fourteen. As they are exposed to all the things technology has to offer, we cannot expect they will be satisfied in the long term to accept ten-cent-an-hour jobs. The Chinese government knows that, too. They have to raise wages and the standard of living, or face a revolution. Believe me, they are scared to death, which explains the recent attempts to censor Internet use. The communist government does not want its people to learn too much about democracy.

The Chinese leadership has immense challenges. A rural population equivalent to the entire U.S. population is expected to migrate to cities for employment, yet the electric grid is tapped out and housing must be built. We are seeing just a shadow of the Goliath China will become.

General Motors believes the Chinese auto market will be bigger than the American market within twenty years. According to Ted C. Fishman's book *China, Inc.*, China bought 3 million cars in 2003 while the stable U.S. industry sells about 17 million units annually.

It is estimated that there are now about 20 million cars in China. Some predict that it will grow to 120 million in the next fifteen years. That is a huge market, but don't hold your breath expecting American car makers to get a fair deal to compete for those sales.

U.S. negotiators, in the most recent trade deal with China, stuck it to the American workers and arranged a sweetheart deal for China. Believe it or not, our side agreed that the Chinese could charge a 25 percent tariff on U.S. cars sent to China, while we would impose only a $2^1/2$ percent tariff on Chinese cars sold in the United States. That is an outrage. One more stake in the heart of "fair trade."

Just as we have seen cars from Japan and Korea gain a foothold in our own domestic market, we will see Chinese cars on our highways in just a few years. Chinese auto manufacturing is intending to be on pace to pass the number two manufacturer of vehicles, Japan, by 2015 and nipping at the heels of the U.S. industry. Fishman reports that Wangfeng, one of the more than 120 Chinese automakers, sells luxury Jeep knockoffs in the Middle East for $8,000 to $10,000. As we contemplate China's future, we would do well to look back at our own industrial growth to understand where China is headed. While our economic evolution set a breakneck pace in a hundred years that took us from Model Ts to space shuttles, with the incalculable growth of technology, we can expect China's transformation to be swift.

I don't suggest that we ignore it. It is time to begin demanding that China meet the expectations of fair trade. It is time we stop treating these economic juggernauts as if they were the equivalent of ninety-eight-pound weaklings at the beach. We're the ones getting sand kicked in our faces.

I have focused on China and Wal-Mart in this chapter, because they are the seven-hundred-pound gorillas in the job loss and trade deficit area. But it is not China alone that has discovered the economic leverage of offering its employees for pennies an hour to the multinational corporations with sharp math skills and deficient consciences. Indonesia, Sri Lanka, India, Vietnam, and more are involved in exactly the same enterprise that has made China a formidable economic force. But the China and Wal-Mart connection is the most obvious example of what has gone terribly amiss on the way to a healthy and truly free market.

EIGHT

SOFTHEADED FOREIGN POLICY

THEY CALL IT *FOGGY BOTTOM*—THE NEIGHBORHOOD in Washington, D.C., where the State Department is located. It is where the deep thinkers about foreign policy hang out. We are told they spend their days evaluating the geopolitical relationships between countries and how all of it affects our country's vital interests.

But, in fact, they do more than that. Few people know it, but the State Department is the place where they make most of our decisions about trade policy. If you have ever wondered why we don't seem to have the backbone to take action against countries that engage in unfair trade practices against us, in most cases it is because of the State Department. They worry about offending or embarrassing another country. They look at trade issues as foreign policy equations, and they aren't very interested in the economic consequences for Americans.

So, unlike most of our trading partners, who treat trade policy as hard-nosed economic competition, the United States for the most part runs its trade policy through the fuzzy lens of foreign policy at the State Department. In short, foreign policy is masquerading as trade policy.

Here is a simple example.

The next time you pull up at a stoplight and find yourself next to a car from Korea, remember this. In 2004, according to the U.S. Automotive Trade Council, nearly seven hundred thousand Korean cars were shipped to the United States. At the same time, thirty-nine hundred U.S. cars were shipped to Korea.

Why the glaring disparity?

It's because Korea doesn't want U.S. automobiles sold in Korea.

Oh, the Korean government doesn't come right out and say that it is preventing U.S. cars from being sold there. It just erects all types of barriers that they know will prevent U.S. vehicles from making an inroad in their marketplace.

So this is a trade problem. What do we do about it? Not a damn thing. Why? Because Korea is an ally, and our State Department worries that if we were to take action against them for unfair trade practices, we might make the Koreans look bad or offend them. Bottom line, we don't want to hurt their feelings, and so a market for American automobiles remains largely closed to the cars our workers produce.

Nobody in the administration worries much about offending laid-off American workers. But until the Koreans get to vote in our elections, they ought to.

SOFTHEADED TRADE POLICY

Letting the State Department manage trade is a little like having the cheerleaders call the plays at the Super Bowl. For the State Department, it is not about demanding fair trade. They aren't interested in the issue of American jobs. They are interested in maintaining our relationship with other countries on a wide range of foreign policy issues. That's a legitimate thing to do. It just shouldn't be substituted for trade policy.

When it is substituted for trade policy, I call it softheaded foreign policy.

International trade is a competition—an economic Olympics. Countries and companies compete for the consumer dollar with prices and products. Each country regulates conditions of competition within its own marketplace. The trade agreements are supposed to make sure that these conditions result in a fair shake for everyone. But it is not the case. Most of these trade agreements have given other countries built-in advantages when trading with the United States.

Much of that is a hangover from the twenty-five years after World War II when we used concessionary trade policy to try to help other countries ravaged by the war to get back on their feet. We could do that back then. We were the biggest, the strongest, and we could compete with anybody in the world with one hand tied behind our back. Of course, times have changed. Those countries we deigned to help in the postwar period have grown up to become tough, shrewd international competitors. But our trade policies haven't changed much. We still end up giving others advantages when it comes to bilateral trade.

If this were the Olympics, would we agree to a set of rules that would give runners from other countries a ten-meter head start in the hundred-meter dash? Yet that is exactly what we have done in most of our trade agreements.

From time to time, I have threatened to require our trade negotiators to wear the type of jerseys that our Olympic athletes wear. You know, the ones that have a big USA on the front. That way, our negotiators could look down from time to time just to remember whose side they're on.

Nearly all of the other countries with whom we trade have a type of managed trade policy. They set goals for their country in the international trade competition, then they manage their trade to meet their goals. Our country, by contrast, has no such objectives. We stand lost in oblivion, allowing our pockets to be picked.

Even when our country does decide to take some action against the unfair trade practices we face from other countries, it is often half-hearted and pathetic.

In our dispute with Europe over American beef a few years ago, we finally took action. We slapped them with tariffs on their *truffles,*

Roquefort cheese, and goose liver. That'll teach them! That's bold action? I guess that's why others think we don't have the backbone to take tough action to defend ourselves in trade disputes.

We just have this notion that if we provide leadership by opening our markets, other countries will do the same. And if they don't, well, we can take some action to persuade them. But we will have to get permission from the State Department first, and that permission almost never comes.

As long as we're heavy into the sports analogies, it is akin to Tiger Woods spotting the field two strokes in every match. As good as he is, the competition is so fierce, he would sink to the middle of the pack.

So we lose. We lose good American jobs, and we sink deeper and deeper in trade debt (money we owe to foreign countries).

THE CUBA EXCEPTION

It's hard to know where to start describing the bizarre approach our country takes in its trade policies. Cuba seems like a good first stop. The island of Cuba is only ninety miles off the coast of Florida.

It's no secret that Cuba is a communist country run by Fidel Castro, a despot who has been sticking his finger in our eye for decades. In fact, he has now lived through ten U.S. presidencies.

The United States slapped a trade embargo on Cuba beginning with the Kennedy administration. (See, we can enforce a trade policy, even a dumb one, if we set our minds to it!) But a great deal has changed since 1961. The Berlin Wall has fallen, and the communist bloc splintered. Capitalism won. Yes, Cuba still has a communist leader, but our trade embargo has served to keep him in office.

With this embargo, over four decades later we continue to prevent the U.S. producers, including farmers and ranchers, from unimpeded selling of their products to Cuba. And even more, we still prevent U.S. citizens from traveling to Cuba.

The embargo never made sense. After all, our State Department constantly makes the point that travel and trade . . . *engagement* . . .

represents the best approach to deal with a communist country. It is the surest way for the United States to move communist countries like China and Vietnam toward greater human rights and democratic reforms, they say.

But according to four decades of government policy, that same logic doesn't apply to Cuba. We continue to view this poor island nation as a threat. A Mexican diplomat explained to the Kennedy administration its reluctance to join a boycott of Cuba because, "If we publicly declare Cuba is a threat to our security, 40 million Mexicans will die laughing." Today, the embargo is even harder to justify.

In order to slap around Fidel Castro, our government policy hurts our farmers and restricts our citizens from traveling. Punishing American citizens by restricting their right to sell farm products and their right to travel makes no sense. It is like shooting yourself in the foot. That's silly. But taking aim before shooting yourself in the foot . . . that's stupid!

Fidel Castro won't be around forever, so making overtures to Cuba is a sound strategy. Besides, I'll be willing to bet that Castro has never missed a meal because we had an embargo on food being sold to Cuba. The embargo hurt our farmers and it hurt poor, sick, and hungry people in Cuba. But not Castro.

Furthermore, I think using food as a weapon in foreign policy is immoral in every case.

America is better than that.

I've fought to open the doors to trade for the good of the Cuban people and for the good of American farmers. In the process I've joined forces with some unlikely allies. When John Ashcroft was a senator, he and I passed legislation over the president's objections to open the Cuban market just a bit to allow our farmers to sell some farm products there. The goods have to be paid for with cash, and the transaction has to be run through a non-U.S. bank. But even with the restrictions, we have now sold over $1.4 billion in agricultural commodities to Cuba since the Dorgan/Ashcroft amendment was passed.

In the fall of 2002, twenty-two train carloads of dried peas left

North Dakota bound for ships to Cuba. It was the first shipment of food from our farmers to the Cuban market in Cuba in forty-two years. We have continued to sell them more food in the intervening years despite the rising barriers erected by the Bush administration in an overt attempt to stop these sales.

Recently, President Bush has tried a new tactic in trying to shut down the sale of food from our farmers to the Cuban people. (Instead of requiring payment when the goods are delivered, he requires payment even before the goods are shipped.) In short, he is trying once again to shut off the sale of food to Cuba.

Why? Because the president's political agenda of satisfying the powerful anti-Castro Cuban-American community trumps the common sense of allowing our farmers to sell their food to Cuba just as the Canadians, the Europeans, and others do. Once again, this has nothing to do with thoughtful trade policy. Instead it is thoughtless foreign policy.

Let's face it. It's an election strategy. Florida, where the majority of expatriate Cubans live (and vote), was the key state in 2000, 2004, and will be in 2008. So despite all of the preaching about the virtues of free trade, the administration doesn't believe it applies to Cuba. And while this hard line pleases some in the Cuban-American community, it also disenfranchises many Cuban families who are barred from visiting loved ones.

Further compounding the problem, our U.S. embargo has become Castro's biggest excuse when explaining why the Cuban economy is such a wreck. He simply tells the Cuban people that of course the Cuban economy is in tatters. He says that's the case because the five-hundred-pound gorilla called the United States has had its fist around the Cuban neck for forty years with the embargo. He points the finger at us, then stokes up the sense of nationalism that exists in Cuba even among those who are not Castro fans. That kind of nationalism finds sympathetic ears in Cuba. Ironically, I think our trade policy has helped Castro to hang on to power in Cuba.

The Bush administration's obsession with Cuba has led it to take even more bizarre missteps in public policy. For example, it has turned the small agency in the U.S. Treasury Department called OFAC (which means the Office of Foreign Assets Control) from a group that is supposed to track the financing of terrorist networks into an agency spying on Americans suspected of taking a vacation in Cuba.

The Bush administration has diverted resources that were supposed to be shutting off the funding for Osama bin Laden and al Qaeda and used them to track American tourists under suspicion of vacationing in Cuba. That's right—taking a vacation in Cuba is against the law. We restrict our freedom to travel in order to punish Fidel. Here are some of the "bad people" the administration has nabbed:

Joan Scott is a young American woman who decided to go to Cuba to pass out free Bibles on the streets of Havana. Joan is simply a missionary who wants to spread the word of God. But that didn't mitigate the sins of her travel. OFAC tracked her down when she returned from Cuba and told her they were intending to fine her $10,000 for unauthorized travel to Cuba.

Then there is the case of Joan Slote, a seventy-five-year-old bicyclist who joined a Canadian cycling tour of Cuba. She spent eight days cycling in Cuba. When she returned to the United States, she discovered that her government was tracking her down to slap her with a ten-thousand-dollar fine and threatening to withhold her Social Security payments if she didn't pay up.

Or there's the fellow from Washington State who promised his dying father that he would take his ashes to Cuba and spread them on the church grounds where his father used to minister. For that the U.S. government tracked him down to fine him.

But the ultimate shame of this policy has to do with a young U.S. Army sergeant named Carlos Lazo, a Cuban-American who went to Iraq as an Army National Guard medic. While there he won a Bronze Star for bravery.

When this decorated soldier came back to the United States from Iraq, he learned that one of his teenage sons, who were living in Cuba with the boy's mother, was very ill. Yet Sergeant Lazo was denied approval to travel to Cuba to see his sick son by the U.S. State Department. When I visited with Sergeant Lazo, he was deeply saddened and dismayed that he had fought for freedom in Iraq only to discover the country he fought for was denying him the freedom to travel to see his sick child.

I was so incensed by this injustice that I forced a vote in the U.S. Senate to give Sergeant Lazo the right to visit his sick child. Because of the parliamentary situation in the Senate, I needed sixty-seven votes to win that vote. I got only sixty-two votes. That's right. Thirty-eight senators agreed with President Bush that this soldier shouldn't be free to go to Cuba to see his sick son. Unbelievable.

THE CHINA SYNDROME

There is probably no clearer example of the U.S. government substituting foreign policy for trade policy than with China and agricultural trade.

For instance, on March 17, 2003, Bruce Quinn, the director for China Trade Policy at the Office of the U.S. Trade Representative (USTR), in a moment of unusual candor, told a wheat industry meeting that he felt that the United States should file an action against China because of China's unfair trade practices on agricultural trade.

Despite all of the assurances by China, our American farmers felt they were being shut out of the markets China promised would be open to them. Quinn said the Trade Policy Review group in the Bush administration had already given permission to USTR to take action against China. But he said that many in the Bush administration "feel it is an in-your-face thing to do to China" so soon after it became a member of the World Trade Organization.

So, while American farmers are faced with unfair trade practices by China, instead of having our country stand up for our farmers' economic interests, the thinkers in Foggy Bottom are worried about the Chinese being insulted if we complained.

Quinn said, "It would be hard for American farm exporters to realize the commitments for expanded sales to China that the Chinese made when they joined the WTO ... because of rampant corruption, China's desire to be self-sufficient in its food supply, and new leadership that will want to protect its farm sector."

So what does the United States do about that? Nothing! They assume the position of a potted plant.

Of course, China wants to protect its farm sector! It is crucial to the national security of the country. In Washington, though, most have not figured out that it applies to us, too.

The State Department's fingerprints are on virtually every part of our China trade policy. The issue of counterfeiting and piracy of products in China is an epidemic. It is estimated that in 2003, 75 percent of the pirated and counterfeit goods seized at the U.S. borders came from China. *Newsweek* reported, "Counterfeiters in China are using computer programs (often pirated themselves) to produce increasingly exact replicas of everything from sneakers to sweaters."

You have seen in chapter 5 that I am not all that sympathetic to the behavior of the large pharmaceutical companies. But what they face in China is a good example of what all American companies are struggling against.

Consider the case of Viagra. Pfizer has to watch as the Chinese reverse-engineer to make an exact copy of the drug and produce it in China, paying nothing to the companies that hold the patents. The Chinese authorities denied patent protection for Pfizer and instead allowed Chinese companies to copy the drug and market Viagra in China. Where I come from, that is called stealing.

Now, I'm not suggesting we start a trade war with China over Viagra. But it doesn't matter what product we talk about. Handbags, movies, music, software, computers, shoe polish, golf clubs, and much more are all found copied, imitated, pirated, or counterfeited in China with impunity. And we open the doors and let them dump the counterfeits on the American market.

Another trade strategy used by China is to undervalue its currency in order to give it an advantage in our bilateral trade. It's complicated, but the gist of it is that unlike most other developed countries, China doesn't allow its currency to float—that means allowing the currency markets and global economic situation to set the value of its currency. Until recently China pegged its currency to the U.S dollar to maintain a specific advantage that led to the unprecedented U.S. debt held by China.

As a result, in the past few years the yuan (China's currency) has been undervalued. Had it been allowed to float, it would have naturally increased in value, making Chinese imports from the United States more attractive and Chinese exports to the United States more expensive.

The market would have compensated for the imbalance.

It has been estimated that the yuan is undervalued by 15 to 40 percent. It's an almost impossible hurdle for American exporters to overcome. If you don't have markets, you cannot produce. If you cannot produce, there is no need for workers. And that is why the American job market has not seen such turmoil since the Great Depression.

What have we done about this problem? Nothing really. We did a little jawboning, but without result. And once again, when Congress was about to take action against the Chinese for this currency manipulation, the White House—expressing the concern of the State Department—headed Congress off at the pass.

One lesson we should have learned from this economic debacle is that we should never negotiate a trade agreement with another country without providing for fluctuations in currency values.

A few years ago our negotiators made a big deal about the trade agreement they had negotiated with Mexico, which they said reduced tariffs that were applied to American goods being shipped to Mexico. But shortly after the agreement was done, Mexico devalued its currency by 50 percent, which meant that whatever progress was made in forcing Mexico to reduce their tariffs was canceled by the devaluation of the peso by the Mexican government.

No wonder we are called Uncle Sucker in some circles.

Why don't we do something about these issues? Simply, it is because our foreign policy "big picture" thinkers put the brakes on any effort to enforce trade agreements. They see these as foreign policy issues rather than trade matters. However, if our trading partners are viewing these trade issues through an economic lens, and our government is viewing them as foreign policy, we are at a very big disadvantage.

And that is why we are losing in international trade.

CANADA DUMPS ON THE AMERICAN FARMER

Here's another perfect example of why our family farmers feel their own government is cheating them. The unfair grain trade from Canada after the passage of the U.S.-Canada Free Trade Agreement hurt our family farmers badly, but our government wouldn't lift a finger to help.

Canada sells its wheat through the Canadian Wheat Board, a government-sponsored monopoly that would be illegal in the United States. When Trade Ambassador Clayton Yeutter negotiated the infamous trade agreement with Canada, he assured American farmers that they would not become victims of unfair trade from the Canadian Wheat Board, and he put those assurances in writing.

But it wasn't the truth. And he had to have known it.

Almost immediately following the approval of the U.S.-Canada Free Trade Agreement, massive quantities of unfairly subsidized Canadian durum and spring wheat began moving south across the border. It was taking money right out of the pockets of American farmers. And, of course, our country did nothing about it. I protested and railed about the unfairness of it all, but it fell on deaf ears.

One day, to prove my point about this one-sided deal, I went to the U.S.-Canadian border at Fortuna, North Dakota, with Earl Jensen, who was driving his twelve-year-old orange grain truck. We had about one hundred bushels of durum wheat on board, with the intention of taking that wheat into Canada.

All the way to the border we met eighteen-wheelers hauling Canadian durum wheat down into the American market. But when we tried to cross into Canada with some American durum, we were stopped at the border and told we couldn't bring the wheat into Canada.

I had alerted the television stations and the press that we were going to demonstrate the unfairness of the U.S.-Canada Free Trade Agreement, so they were all waiting at the border to record the action. It was the first time that people saw clearly that the trade agreement we had negotiated with Canada had double-crossed American farmers.

In fact, we would find out later that Trade Ambassador Yeutter had deceived both U.S. farmers and the Congress about the details of agriculture trade in that agreement. He had made a secret, undisclosed deal with the Canadians that would undermine our efforts to argue successfully that they were dumping their grain into our marketplace at below cost. He did that by secretly agreeing that the Canadian "cost of acquisition" would not include the farmers' final payment from the Wheat Board. In short, the agreement allowed the Canadians to sell at below their total costs into the United States and claim that they are not selling below cost. It was an agreement that the Canadians could use a sleight of hand when competing with our U.S. farmers.

I still get steamed just thinking about it.

But did our government stand up for our farmers and take action against the Canadians for their unfair trade? No, except for a brief moment of sanity exhibited by Trade Ambassador Mickey Kantor, who took some temporary action, our government worried about what it would do to our relationship with Canada if we stood up for our farmers. Kantor, for a brief period, imposed some import duties on Canadian grain exports to the United States after the Canadians told us to take a hike when we pushed them to open the records of their grain monopoly, the Canadian Wheat Board.

But that lasted for a very brief period. In the main this issue has once again been a case of foreign policy trumping trade policy. Apparently, some think there aren't enough farmers to be a political threat, so they are easy to trample in trade agreements. But those farmers are crucial to the strength of this country. They deserve better.

WHERE'S THE BEEF (COMING FROM)?

I come from cattle country, so I know a few things about the cattle industry. I know a good cut of meat and I also know a raw deal when I see one. Consider the issue of meat from Mexico.

"How would you like your steak?" Well, for starters, don't cut a slice off the carcasses that our meat inspectors found hanging in the Mexican meat-processing plant.

Although inspectors rarely visit a Mexican meat-processing plant, in May of 1999 one American inspector paid a surprise visit to a meat-packing plant in Hermosillo, Mexico.

Here is what he said he found: "Shanks and briskets were contaminated with feces . . . diseased-condemned carcass was observed ready for boning and distribution in commerce."

That plant was decertified and barred from sending meat into the United States. But then the Mexican officials went to work to restore the plant's ability to sell meat into the United States. It switched owners, changed its name, and regained an export license. Now this very plant sells meat into the U.S. market. And no USDA inspector has ever returned to inspect it. *So, how do I like my steak?* Without feces, please. And please, not from that plant in Hermosillo.

This is part of a bigger story about big business, safe food, and foreign policy. Naturally, as a consumer concerned with your family's health, you would want to avoid potentially hazardous meat. Good luck.

In January 2004, I held up a two-pound piece of raw beefsteak on the floor of the U.S. Senate and asked if anyone there could tell me where that meat came from. I recounted the story about the Mexican beef-processing plant and asked if anyone could be sure that this piece of meat hadn't come from that plant.

So I, and others in Congress, passed a law in 2002 that requires that meat be labeled. It is called "Country of Origin Labeling"—COOL for short. The basic premise is that if you want to buy American and get the protections of the inspections of our meat-processing plants, you get to make that choice. It is the law of the land. But you can search all day and will find that meat is still not labeled as to country of origin.

This is a prime—excuse the pun—example of the arrogance and disdain this administration has for any rule they don't like. It is a typical story about the clout of the big economic interests and their friends who do their bidding in the Congress. These people drag their feet so much I'm surprised you don't see smoke coming from their shoes.

First the USDA stalled in implementing the COOL law. Then the U.S. House has twice stuck amendments in big appropriation bills to delay the implementation of the meat-labeling law. The Republican leadership in the U.S House of Representatives dances to the tune of big business. So when the big meatpacking houses and the big grocery chains weigh in with the GOP, they get what they want.

The Republicans who are working to prevent this law from being implemented parrot the line of the big business foes. "It is too complicated," they say. Right. We can drive vehicles on the surface of Mars, but we can't figure out how to label meat? I know where my underwear is made, but I can't figure out if I'm supporting American ranchers when I buy that steak? We do require labels on shirts, shoes, neckties, canned food, packaged food, and most everything else we buy. But not meat!

Our cattle ranchers are getting the short shrift, and consumers' rights are being ignored.

Food safety should not be a Democrat or Republican issue, but it is. At the end of the day, it appears that as long as President Bush is in the White House and his party controls the Congress, the consumers won't have the opportunity to see a label on the meat they buy in order to know where it came from.

Oh, by the way, nearly twenty years after we reached a "beef agreement" with Japan, there remained a 50 percent tariff on every pound of American beef sold in Japan. How could that be? Once again, incompetent trade agreements that shortchanged American producers (in this case ranchers) over and over again.

AUTO TRADE STUCK IN REVERSE

Earlier in this chapter, I described the imbalance in our automobile trade with Korea. They ship over seven hundred thousand Korean automobiles to the United States each year while we ship about four thousand U.S. cars to Korea to be sold in their market. It is hardly balanced trade.

Is this imbalance some sort of curious accident? No. Here is a sample of how the Koreans get by with it.

In February 2003, DaimlerChrysler started to sell the Dodge Dakota pickup truck (made in Detroit) in Korea. Korea does not manufacture pickup trucks like the Dakota, so DaimlerChrysler thought there was some potential in the Korean market. They started to market it to small business owners in Korea. They thought it was going to be successful after they sold sixty pickups in February and another sixty in March.

But in March 2003 an official with the Ministry of Construction and Transportation decided that the pickups posed a hazard. He said that some people were putting optional cargo covers on the vehicle, and that it might be dangerous if passengers rode in the back. So he announced that cargo covers on Dodge Dakota pickups were illegal and that drivers would be fined if they did not comply.

The Korean newspapers had big headlines "Government Ministry Finds Dodge Dakota Covers Illegal." The result? The Koreans got the message. Fifty-five out of the sixty orders that had been placed for March were canceled. So much for Dodge Dakotas in Korea!

In November 2003, the Korean government quietly reversed its rule and allowed Dodge Dakota pickups to be sold with the cargo covers. But by then the less-than-subliminal message had already been received by the Korean public. Don't buy U.S. automobiles. Even two years later, in 2005, DaimlerChrysler was only selling about fifteen Dodge Dakota pickup trucks a month in Korea. I'd be willing to bet that an American dealership could sell that many on a good day.

This wasn't an accident. It was the Korean government, supported by the press, sending a message to the Korean people: *We don't want you buying the Dodge Dakota pickup.* It's the way they do things in Korea to keep American products out even as they take advantage of a wide-open American marketplace.

Now, 99 percent of the cars on the road in Korea are Korean-made. That's the way they want it. And they erect many sophisticated barriers that prevent access to their markets by foreign car companies. The Korean car market is certainly mature enough to compete fairly. There is no excuse for them to access our market while restricting theirs. (And by the way, 95 percent of the cars on the road in Japan are Japanese-made—same deal.)

These are representative of literally hundreds of similar barriers U.S. corporations must overcome to compete globally. The U.S. government *should* intervene on their behalf, but the State Department would consider that an impolite thing to do. Once again, that is because the question of whether to do that runs through the State Department, and there the analysis is not largely about economic considerations. Rather, it is about foreign policy relationships.

I have described just a small sample of the problems that exist with a trade policy that is run through the eye of the needle of foreign policy. It means, in the end, our country does not have the backbone or the will to demand fair treatment from our trading partners. And as a result, we continue to lose both opportunity and jobs.

While most of our trading partners are making their decisions based on hard-nosed economic choices, the United States is still running its trade agenda through the softheaded foreign policy apparatus of the State Department.

If I were going to use one more sporting analogy, it means our competitors are playing tackle football and we are playing touch. So we suffer the injuries. And no wonder we are running the largest trade deficits in the history of civilization and shipping jobs abroad at the same time.

NINE

THE TOXIC WASTE OF
WORLD TRADE

F OR RESIDENTS OF MANILA IN THE PHILIPPINES, THE good news in the summer of 2005 was that malaria would not be a problem. The bad news? It was because malaria-bearing mosquitoes couldn't survive the air pollution in Manila, a disease expert reported.

How bad does the air have to be that it cannot support insects, I wondered when I read that news story. As I thought about that, I considered the fact that as jet streams and trade winds move air around the globe, at some point I, too, would be breathing in some of that poisoned air.

In 2002, the *Los Angeles Times* reported:

In one severe dust storm in spring 1998, particle pollution levels in Oregon, Washington and British Columbia soared. In Seattle, air quality officials could not identify a local source of the pollution, but measurements showed that 75 percent of it came from China, researchers at the University of Washington found. "A larger fraction of the haze we see is Asian, far more than we ever dreamed," said Tom Cahill, professor of atmospheric science and physics at UC Davis. "We're a small world."

That news item reminded me of an almost forgotten incident from my childhood when I won a goldfish at a carnival. I remember the joy of bringing it home in a plastic bag and putting it in a glass bowl. I called my new friend Popeye, and I visited with him every day as I watched him swim in that bowl.

But I was irresponsible.

"That goldfish is going to die if you don't clean the bowl!" Mom warned. "How would you like it if you had to live in a dirty glass bowl?" It was a rhetorical question, and I was not given to pondering such things. In my defense, I was only six years old.

Predictably, one morning Popeye wasn't swimming anymore. The goldfish looked like he was napping while floating on his back. Mom took a look and pronounced him dead. Saddened, I gave the poor thing a funeral with interment between the carrots and the cabbage.

Mothers are wise when it comes to such matters. I should have cleaned the bowl. That simple lesson is worth remembering as we consider how the new global economy affects the glass bowl in which we live.

This earth of ours is a planet with finite resources very much like a glass bowl. What happens in one part of the world affects us all. Air pollution drifts across international borders. Mercury poisons everyone's fish. We all breathe the poisons and ingest the toxins.

If the economy is global, so too is pollution. And when corporations move jobs away from America to avoid the regulations that prevent them from dumping chemicals into the air and water, we lose twice. We lose the jobs, and we still suffer the consequences of the pollution these corporations create in the other parts of our planet.

According to the previously mentioned *Los Angeles Times* story, the so-called Made in China Haze has been "spotted at ski resorts from Lake Tahoe to Aspen, Colorado, and above Los Angeles and Vancouver, Canada. At its worst, it can cast a faint, yellow hue across a twelve-hundred-mile front from Arizona to Calgary, Canada, and beyond before it peters out somewhere over Greenland, studies show."

Yet some corporations have been licking their chops as they think about how much money they will save by outsourcing manufacturing to areas of the world where they don't have to pay the cost of cleanup. The fewer rules, the better, they figure.

Some call it environmental imperialism.

And you don't have to look far to find examples.

OUTSOURCING JOBS AND POLLUTION

American energy companies are increasingly looking south to Mexico to build new power plants to feed our voracious energy appetite. Unfortunately, the pollution they launch into the skies will not stop at the border.

In 2003, when InterGen (a partnership between Shell and Bechtel) cranked up a thousand-megawatt power plant just across the California border in Mexicali, Mexico, Reuters cautioned that "pollution is likely to worsen because the companies are skirting U.S. laws by building in Mexico, where they are not required to offset particulate matter emissions—or air pollution—with community projects that reduce regional air contamination."

About half the power the InterGen plant produces was earmarked for California, whose emissions standards the plant admittedly could not meet, according to *The New York Times*. Of course, the big picture is that California has an energy crisis, but if every country abided by the same environmental and regulatory standards, the jobs might have stayed in America.

The plant went south.

The jobs went south.

The pollution still floats to the north.

California gets the electricity, but in the long run, it is a bad deal.

It was a simple case of a power company dodging U.S. regulations. But they had help in high places. President Bush and the U.S. Department of Energy issued special presidential permits for the InterGen plant and another owned by Sempra Energy to allow them to send the power from the polluting plants north.

U.S. District Judge Irma Gonzalez later ruled the permits illegal because they failed to include an environmental study on the effect on air and water in California's Imperial Valley, which already has the highest incidence of childhood asthma in the state.

According to the U.S. Department of Health and Human Services, "Residents living along the U.S.-Mexico border experience greater rates of communicable illnesses such as tuberculosis." The Health Resources and Services Administration (HRSA) also reports a higher incidence of intestinal infections and hepatitis, due to a shortage of clean water.

"Most of the pollution may be coming from Mexico, but in many cases it is driven by capital from the U.S., Japan and Korea," observed Erik Lee, assistant director for U.S.-Mexican Studies at the University of California in an article in *Environmental Science and Technology.* "We've outsourced our jobs and pollution."

In Mexico, officials say that one-third of the country's diseases are caused by environmental factors—mostly air pollution. The fact is, citizens of Mexico and many of the countries in which the United States has corporate interests have far fewer rights than do Americans. Citizens are likely to remain unaware of toxins released into the air and water by these companies—until people get sick and start dying. Global corporations are quick to exploit the unprotected people in third-world countries.

The choice is obvious.

Lower our standards or raise those of our trading partners. The enlightened option is the latter. In the meantime, corporations are setting up shop in Mexico because officials are likely to look the other way.

Ernesto Ruffo, Mexican government border commissioner, says matter-of-factly, "Building anything on the Mexican side of the border is much cheaper, mostly because of the regulatory system." Ironically, if our trade agreement had been honored, the issue would never have arisen. A key provision of NAFTA mandated that Mexico raise environmental standards to meet those in the United States. But they have not.

The InterGen power plant sends an estimated thirty-eight hundred tons of pollutants into the air each year, says Steve Birdsall, director of the Imperial County Air Pollution Control District. That's about ten times the pollution the smaller Sempra plant produces. Birdsall called InterGen "the epitome of corporate arrogance."

The controversy over the pollution-belching power plant did lead to one victory. InterGen agreed to install nitrous oxide controls by early 2006, after Senator Dianne Feinstein, D-CA, introduced a bill requiring plants within fifty miles of the border to meet regional American standards or forfeit rights to buy natural gas from the United States.

Sempra Energy made no bones about the fact that the wheels of commerce move more quickly in Mexico, which made building there more attractive. Sempra was able to get a Mexican permit in five months. In the United States, stringent environmental studies and a more detailed process take twenty-two months to license one of these natural gas power plants.

Sempra Energy says they built their six-hundred-megawatt plant, which is located three miles from the border, to meet California standards. Still, the impact the plant has on the already heavily polluted border environment is not inconsequential. According to Greenpeace, this new plant emits approximately 378 tons of nitrogen oxides, 376 tons of carbon monoxide, and nearly four megatons of carbon dioxide annually.

In addition, the plant is cooled by river water. About 3 million gallons of water from the New River, which flows into California's Imperial County, is evaporated or lost daily, Greenpeace says. And about 750,000 gallons of highly saline wastewater is dumped back into the riverbed daily. Mexican environmentalist Fernando Medina told Reuters that he worries about the consumption of such a valuable resource. "Mexico and the United States are fighting over water from one end of the border to another," he said. "How much sense does it make to allow big consumers of water to locate here?"

While America is desperate for energy, so too is Mexico. *The New York Times* observes, "The irony of exporting power from these plants when Mexicans need more—and when their electricity bills are doubling—is not lost on the populace. But support for the new plants among politicians is near total. Public opposition to the plants was muted by the fact that they were a done deal before the public knew anything about them."

Environmental imperialism? Exploitation? One could make the case.

At any rate, the cover of Pandora's box has been flung wide open. Sempra has plans for a vast network of pipelines to send natural gas south to power as many as twenty-two Mexican power plants, adding even more pollutants to the skies. J. P. Ross, who wrote a scathing report for Greenpeace about the San Diego–based Sempra's plans, said the North Baja pipeline will run 135 miles ending just south of the California border, allowing Sempra to "once again dodge the regulations of its home state."

Of course, we need energy production—an industrialized nation cannot survive without it. But we need *responsible* energy production.

LEAVE THE DIRTY WORK FOR OTHER COUNTRIES

Now, let us look past our immediate borders and see the impact corporations and a wide-open global market can have on countries with loose environmental protections.

China has emerged as a world economic power, but the internal cost has been high. The ecological impact is widespread. Cyclists in Beijing have been spotted wearing masks to filter out smog. Fish farmers on the Huai River basin have been economically devastated by industrial pollution spills.

In China today, water pollution is so severe that officials say more than 100 of China's 660 largest cities face extreme water shortages. The country supports one-fifth of the world's population—1.3 billion— with just 7 percent of the water supply. That is just asking for trouble, and trouble is already brewing. A serious rural insurrection could become reality as pollutants seep into the ground, ruining watersheds in agricultural communities.

In April 2005, police and villagers clashed in Zhejiang Province as citizens occupied an industrial complex blamed for crops ruined by polluted water supplies. In the village of Huaxi, toxins from manufacturers were blamed for a withered cabbage crop. "It is rotten from the inside. It doesn't grow," Li Xian, a local farmer, said.

In Xinchang, a village 180 miles south of Shanghai, according to a July 2005 *New York Times* report, "As many as 15,000 people massed and waged a pitched battle with the authorities, overturning police cars and throwing stones for hours, undeterred by thick clouds of tear gas." The issue stemmed from a severe degradation of the local environment by the ten-year-old Jingxin Pharmaceutical Company. An explosion in the plant touched off the riot.

Many of you will remember Pearl S. Buck's poignant novel *The Good Earth,* which so beautifully captured the simple yet difficult life of a Chinese peasant couple. It lends insight into the anguish these gentle farmers feel over the changes in their lives and the degradation of the Good Earth.

"Our fields won't produce grain anymore," said a woman who lives near the pharmaceutical plant. "We don't dare to eat food grown from anywhere near here." Her husband added, "They are making poisonous chemicals for foreigners that the foreigners don't dare produce in their own countries."

Exactly. Corporations, either directly or indirectly, have outsourced their dirty work. As long as we consume without asking questions about the origin of these low-priced goods, nothing will change. Though prices at the counter may seem cheap, the long-term costs to Mother Earth are steep.

C. L. Cook, in a commentary for *Peace, Earth & Justice News,* had these dire observations: *"Occurring throughout China's 'miracle economy' are masses of dispossessed peasants, driven from the land to a Dickensian industrial nightmare, destined to toil endlessly for survival in conditions promising less. Staying in the country often means victimization at the hands of local crony pols, the remnants of China's communist legacy now comprising a network of 21st century company towns."*

Have we returned to the exploitation of the early days of the Industrial Revolution? It appears so, but today, the potential for ecological damage is far greater.

The *Taiwan News* reports, "Across China, entire rivers run foul or have dried up altogether. Nearly a third of cities don't treat their sewage, flushing it into waterways. Some 300 million of China's 1.3 billion people drink water that is too contaminated to be consumed safely. In rural China, sooty air depresses crop yields, and desert quickly encroaches on grasslands to the west."

An old farmer, who rioted to protest pollution from chemical plants in one coastal village, told the *Taiwan News*, "We had to do it. We can't grow our vegetables here anymore. Young women are giving birth to stillborn babies."

The New York Times observed, "The riots in Xinchang are a part of a rising tide of discontent in China, with the number of mass protests like these skyrocketing to 74,000 incidents last year [2004] from about 10,000 a decade earlier, according to government figures." While outsourcing and global trade have shaken China's environment and its people, they are not suffering alone.

INDONESIAN CHAIN SAW MASSACRE

In Indonesia in 2004, police suspended operations at the American-owned Newmont Minahasa Raya gold mine for dumping deadly heavy metal mine waste laden with mercury and arsenic into Buyat Bay—two thousand tons daily. Locals reported health issues including nervous system disorders, lumps forming under the skin, and other skin ailments.

The fish have fared far worse. The sea was filled with bloated corpses of fish near the pipe that discharged cyanide, among other waste, into the ocean. According to the *National Newspaper*, the fish had "hemorrhaging in the liver, diaphragms broken, and eyeballs bulging from the socket."

Meanwhile, Indonesia's endangered rain forests continue to be exploited by global corporations including BlueLinx Holdings, Inc., the largest wood distributor in America. An agency of Homeland Security documented that BlueLinx, a former subsidiary of Georgia-Pacific, purchases wood from mills with a history of trafficking in illegal timber. The American Forest & Paper Association estimates that 55 percent of the plywood exports from Indonesia are illegal.

A *BusinessWeek* editorial described the unprecedented deforestation as "Indonesia's Chainsaw Massacre." Timber companies are wiping out forests at the rate of three hundred soccer fields *every hour*. Seventy percent of the old growth has vanished. Within fifteen years it will be gone, devastating the 40–50 million indigenous people who depend on the ecosystem for their sustenance. Imagine, if you can, 40–50 *million* displaced people.

THE REAL THING

In India, American icon Coca-Cola's largest bottling plant stands accused of sucking up well water supplies and poisoning the land around the community of Plachimada with sludge the company calls fertilizer. The British newspaper *The Guardian* reports that the sludge contained cadmium and lead—both deadly. That sort of "fertilizer" leaches into the food chain when plants are grown or slaughtered animals that eat the plants are consumed. And that is just what happened. Locals claim the land around the bottling plant has been devastated.

A 2003 report to the World Trade Organization says Plachimada was a thriving farm community employing thousands, before the opening of the Coke plant in 1998. Critics say the once-vibrant agricultural community and those thousands of jobs have been laid waste in exchange for a bottling plant that employs a mere 140 with another 250 described as casual laborers.

Indian environmentalists say that most communities near the bottling plants are experiencing severe water shortages as a result of

Coca-Cola's massive extraction from aquifers. According to the *Hindu* newspaper, a "hydro-geologist, who preferred anonymity, pointed out that the shallow aquifers in the Kaladera region had already dried up, as indicated by the depth of water level in the wells and hand pumps, and the deeper aquifers were now threatened by the Coca-Cola plant's activities. The water table in the region has fallen to an alarming 125 feet over the past decade."

Suffering at the hands of foreign interests is nothing new for Indians. In 1984, Union Carbide's Bhopal disaster killed 8,000 by pesticide poisoning in three days and sickened another 120,000.

Pollution from the Kazipally industrial area has been destructive to the surrounding countryside. Wells are polluted with green water. Streams run with purple sludge. A lake has turned the color of wine, but it is no biblical miracle. Livestock have died and villagers have had strange skin rashes.

Ironically, some of the biggest polluters are pharmaceutical makers who supply India's billion people with medicine. And Indian drug exports to the West continue to rise and are expected to reach the 6-billion-dollar mark by 2010. Increased demand ensures the continued growth of the pharmaceutical industry. However, the pollution that accompanies that growth has one local activist, Dr. Allani Kishan Rao, calling it "another Bhopal—but in slow motion."

THE THREAT OF GLOBAL WARMING

In recent years, as globalization has galloped forward, a new environmental threat has emerged. It's called global warming. The temperature of the earth is rising, we are told, and it is now a consensus of the overwhelming majority of scientists that something is happening that could have dire consequences for our future. Oh, there are still some doubters who claim that this isn't settled science and these days President Bush, for one, says he is not sure there *is* such a thing as global warming. Certainly, more solid, objective scientific studies are needed—we need to better understand what is happening.

But the heavy weight of evidence points to a real problem with global warming. The question isn't *whether* we address it, but rather *how*!

The evening weather has become a freak show of strange, violent storms of unprecedented velocity. In fact, Massachusetts Institute of Technology climatologist Kerry Emanuel told *USA Today* in an August 1, 2005, story that "storms are lasting longer at high intensity than they were 30 years ago." Peak storm speeds have increased on average 50 percent since the 1970s.

When former president Clinton traveled to South Africa in 2005, he discussed the perils of global warming. "Not very far from you in the South Pole in the last 10 years, twelve chunks of ice the size of Rhode Island have broken off," he said. "If this continues for another couple of decades, part of South Africa will be under water [*sic*], and we will lose 50 feet of Manhattan Island in New York." Your children and grandchildren may someday look at a globe that has been drastically altered from the one you know today.

While our current President Bush scratches his head and mulls it over, melting ice and rising water are changing the very face of the globe. Mark Serreze, a polar scientist at the University of Colorado, says 6 percent of the arctic ice has melted since 1978. Whole Alaskan villages are being swallowed up. By the year 2100, a UN panel on climate change predicts, worldwide temperatures will have risen by two to ten degrees.

The science suggests that carbon dioxide and other "greenhouse gases" trap the sun's heat in the atmosphere, causing global warming and melting of the ice caps. As the ice melts, less sunlight is reflected, more heat is retained in the earth's atmosphere, and the process is accelerated.

In addition, power plants, automobiles, and other fossil-fuel-burning industries all increase the natural carbon dioxide level in the earth's atmosphere.

The U.S. Congress is funding Clean Coal Technology programs to try to develop a zero-emission coal-fired electric-generating plant in the future, an approach necessary in order to be able to use our domestic abundance of coal in the future. And I think it is possible we will, through science and technology, be able to build zero-emission coal-fired electrical-generating plants.

Those technologies, when perfected, will allow us to produce clean energy while using our most abundant source of energy. But, just as important, that new technology will need to be used in the so-called "developing countries" as well if we are to reduce the emissions worldwide.

This planet cannot address climate change issues by imposing emission standards on U.S. producers that foreign countries can ignore for their producers. That is not a way to address global warming. It is a way to tip the scales and send more and more U.S. jobs overseas. I favor thoughtful approaches to address global warming and strategies to keep jobs here at home. We can do both if we are smart about it.

The Union of Concerned Scientists estimates that just 122 corporations account for more than 80 percent of all global emissions. They say just five companies—ExxonMobil, BP Amoco, Shell, Chevron, and Texaco—produce 10 percent of the world's carbon emissions.

Rush Limbaugh and other "experts on everything" still contend nothing is happening. And some think tanks funded by the very same energy corporations who are the largest producers of greenhouse gases question the credibility of various scientific studies. But something is clearly going on, and we need to respond to it.

Certainly, climate change has occurred in the past centuries without the contributions of man. But this time it seems to me that our planet has significant contributions from man that affect our climate.

Why does this administration continue to deny the problem? Because they are oil/energy men and talk about global warming hurts the "oil bidness."

In 2005, Philip Cooney, the former chief of staff to President Bush's Council on Environmental Quality, quit two days after it was learned he had altered global warming reports from government scientists to soften the concerns about global warming.

In the wake of the scandal, ExxonMobil hired him. They ought to get along well. Exxon's company line is that there is no global warming.

If one digs deeper into company policy, you might find they also adhere to the notions that the planet is flat, the sun revolves around the earth, and Elvis is on tour.

Before his administration post, Cooney worked for the American Petroleum Institute, not exactly an indication of objectivity. Of course, I would be shocked to learn that the petroleum industry has been driving public policy.

Environmentalist Robert F. Kennedy Jr. hit the nail on the head when he observed in a recent interview, "Polluters have been put in charge of agencies that are supposed to protect Americans from pollution. These individuals have not entered government service for the public interest, but rather to subvert the very laws they're now charged with enforcing."

At the root of most of these ills are the tentacles of corporate influence over government. It is nothing new, but never has it been more pervasive. It is astonishing in its breadth. Corporations fund campaigns, sponsor deceptive advertising, and sometimes write their own legislation.

President Eisenhower saw it coming, and it is here. Patriotism no longer exists among many of these corporations. Some companies have more economic clout than entire *countries*. They can make or break a politician.

Senators John McCain, R-AZ, and Russ Feingold, D-WI, were right in their campaign reform efforts to lessen the monetary influence of multinational corporations. The U.S. government should serve U.S. citizens, not corporations that demand tax breaks for the privilege of outsourcing American jobs and trashing the environment.

Observers from another planet would view us as suicidal. The willful destruction of the environment and the middle class that is the economic engine that keeps Corporate America running might seem puzzling until you understand that corporations (with some exceptions) are entities designed to make the selfish decision that will enhance profits. The bigger they get, the less humanity they exhibit. There is but one goal: *profit*. Corporations can live in perpetuity, but their vision rarely extends beyond the next quarter. The flag they salute is currency. The euro, yuan, franc, or peso—it doesn't matter. *People* don't matter. They are disposable. Workers may be used, discarded, and replaced. If American workers won't work cheap enough, they'll find third-world workers—including children—who will. And the environment doesn't matter. As long as short-term profits are strong, the long-term effects don't matter.

As I said earlier, there are some courageous exceptions to this rule. But far too few.

WHERE IS THE LEADERSHIP?

As the world's only true superpower, the United States is in a unique position of influence. We have a rare opportunity to lead the fight against pollution, global warming, and the global exploitation of workers. But the present one-party, pro-business regime has shown only a willingness to continue the relentless drain of the earth's resources.

Russell E. Train, who headed the EPA from September 1973 to January 1977 under Presidents Nixon and Ford, said before the 2004 election, "It's almost as if the motto of the administration in power today in Washington is not environmental protection, but *polluter* protection."

Every generation is called upon to sacrifice. This generation seems content to pass its troubles to our children. But are we really willing to leave our children an overheated planet and a national debt so monstrous that taxes must be raised and vital social programs cut? Are we prepared to sacrifice their very health?

According to the Environmental Protection Agency, almost 20 million Americans, including 6.3 million children, have asthma. The biggest growth in asthma cases is in children *under five*. Does that suggest we can safely ignore the air quality in the United States? I don't think so!

Over the years, Republicans in Congress have been faithfully pushing something called "regulatory reform." Regulations that prohibit companies from polluting cost these companies money, and they don't like it. So they trumpet a plan that sounds almost downright patriotic. "Regulatory Reform!" they chant in the same manner Texans once rallied behind a cry of "Remember the Alamo!" For the most part, common sense has prevailed because enough senators and congressmen have grave concerns about the environment.

So, it's reasonable for you to ask, if global warming and pollution is a serious matter, how is it that the U.S. Senate voted ninety-five to zero against ratifying the Kyoto Treaty? Simple. Everyone in the Senate understood that if we sign up to a treaty that imposes burdens on the United States but delays implementation in countries like India and China from the same requirements, in the new global economy jobs will move even more quickly away from the United States.

It was a recipe for economic *and* ecological disaster.

We've seen how unmanaged trade and this unconscionable corporate race to the bottom line has led to rampant outsourcing and a flood of American jobs going overseas. If we had further raised the cost of doing business in America because of environmental regulations while exempting other, low-wage countries from the same requirements, the exodus of our jobs would have increased in scale from devastating to catastrophic, and the pollution abroad would continue.

It is already easy for American companies to pack up and move overseas where unions are not allowed, working conditions are abysmal, and environmental regulation is not an issue. To accomplish fair trade and an improved environment, all countries must play by the same rules from the start.

A much better approach would be to allow only the importation of goods manufactured in an environmentally sound manner. Public pressure and effective laws have forced American companies into cleaning up their pollution. The job isn't completely done, but we've made a lot of progress here at home. What if we used trade policy to do the same for companies that move to produce abroad?

We are still the world's most attractive marketplace. If we use that clout in a responsible manner, we can simultaneously improve environmental conditions around the world, better working conditions, and raise wages in other countries while protecting our own. We should seriously consider a worldwide emissions standard and a strategy for minimum wages in other countries as an admission price to our U.S. markets. It might well be one of our finest successes.

Under this scenario, there will still be abundant trade. There will still be economic growth. By more carefully managing it and insisting upon some basic fairness, we can lead other nations toward a cleaner planet. Loosely managed trade, which encourages corporations to place short-term profit above ecology, has accelerated the problem, and now we find ourselves literally swimming in our own sewage, breathing our own filth.

Think about it. We all breathe from the same giant air tank. Allergies have become commonplace as our bodies recoil from the daily contact with pollutants. Cancer is pandemic. Yet we all wear blinders, believing that we are all safe in our neat little boxes, when in fact we are all in this together. That means we all have to abide by the same standards. And those standards need to be tougher. What is unsafe in America is unsafe in third-world countries.

Remember the movie *My Big Fat Greek Wedding*? The colorful father who believed Windex was a cure-all reminded me of my father. My dad was like that with a chemical called 2-4-D. He killed everything in our yard and surrounding yards with his sprayer filled with 2-4-D. No weed was safe from his chemical wrath. Canada thistle, creeping Jenny, and dandelions all succumbed to his chemical assault.

It was much later that we found out that 2-4-D had to be banned because it was also dangerous to human health. But we now find that we are importing the residue of this deadly chemical because it is used in other parts of the world and finds its way to the United States in the pollution that we inherit from other areas of the world.

CHEMICAL BABIES

When the dust blows off farmland in China and travels six thousand miles to American skies, pesticides like DDT, 2-4-D, toxaphene, and dieldrin, long deemed too dangerous to use in our country, are sucked into American lungs.

A report released in July 2005 by the Environmental Working Group found an average of over two hundred industrial compounds, pollutants, and other chemicals in the umbilical cord blood of newborns, including seven dangerous pesticides—some banned in the United States more than thirty years ago. Scientists point out that the presence of pesticides in the blood of babies is because it takes many decades for some of the compounds to break down and also some of them are still used in foreign countries which export produce to the United States.

In general, there are some very real concerns about the dangers our disposable society has created for the unborn. A *USA Today* report on August 3, 2005, cited the concerns of epidemiologist Shanna Swan at the University of Rochester in New York, whose research found that higher phthalate levels (from plastics) in pregnant women were associated with changes in the genitals of baby boys; specifically, they had lower concentrations of male hormones. The Centers for Disease Control's Jim Pirkle says, "The big concern of the phthalates is that they have anti-androgen activity. They get rid of things that are in the testosterone line, the things that make a man a man."

Cleaning up our environment and protecting it from further damage seems to me to be the preeminent security issue of our species. Consider the Green Cross mission statement, *"We desperately need to recognize that we are the guests not the masters of nature and adopt a new paradigm for development, based on the costs and benefits to all people, and bound by the limits of nature herself rather than the limits of technology and consumerism."*

In the summer of 2005, as the space shuttle *Discovery* circled high above the earth, the scars of this delicate planet were evident to shuttle commander Eileen Collins. "Sometimes you can see how there is erosion and you can see how there is deforestation. It's very widespread in some parts of the world," Collins told Japanese officials in Tokyo, including Prime Minister Junichiro Koizumi, in a conversation from space. "The atmosphere almost looks like an eggshell on an egg, it's so very thin," she said, on this, her fourth journey to space. "We know that we don't have much air, we need to protect what we have."

It is time for America to take a hard look in the mirror and face the reality that through our individual overconsumption and lackadaisical attention to the environment, we have dug ourselves a very deep hole.

We must outline a long-term vision for this nation that transcends four-year presidential terms. It should include the long-overdue goal of complete energy independence. In the meantime, in light of national security and the economy, we must make pragmatic decisions. We are going to continue to need fossil fuels, but we can also begin a swift transition to cleaner energy. We can aggressively support alternative energy, and we must. And we can use our technology to allow us to use our abundant coal resources without contributing to the degradation of our environment. All of this is possible if we have the will.

Each day, in some manner, we are writing our last will and testament and outlining an inheritance for the next generation. Can we, in good conscience, leave such a legacy of hardship to our children? Our predecessors—the Greatest Generation—sacrificed mightily and created for us the framework of a great nation. Can it be that the next generation will squander all they have left us? Let us be mindful of the question: What will history say? Will our epitaphs indict us as greedy, shortsighted destroyers of our planet? That is the path we are on and will remain upon until we have the will to put the power back in the hands of the people.

It's time now to clean the fishbowl.

TEN

THE GOATS OF TRADE—GREASING THE SKIDS

No GOOD STORY IS COMPLETE WITHOUT HEROES AND villains. And lurking in the shadows of our trade failure are plenty of bad characters. Maybe the term *villain* is too strong. After all, we're not talking about evil. In some cases it's just bad judgment, with others it is incompetence, or maybe ignorance on the part of certain policy makers. But sadly, greed and underhanded behavior explain a lot of what has happened.

But for the sake of simplicity, I'll still just refer to the entire herd as "goats." It may not be an elegant way to label those who have been driving the getaway car, but I think it is fair. And you can easily distinguish these goats from the "heroes" list you'll find in the very next chapter.

My list of goats will include some of the people who were supposed to work for us negotiating good trade agreements, but who, when finished with their government service, went to work for *them*—the "them" being those on the other side of the negotiating table from "our guys."

Much of the bad behavior exhibited by trade negotiators and other government officials isn't illegal—it's just wrong. Until ethics and legality become close neighbors, the abuse of power and position will continue with these characters. Let's make them blush, at least.

Be aware that my list is not exhaustive. I just picked a small sample of the smarmy lot that has gotten us into this mess.

SEÑOR BROCK-'OLE!

Take the case of Bill Brock, a former four-term congressman from Tennessee and Republican U.S. senator from 1971 to 1977. In the early 1990s, according to published reports, Brock, who was the U.S. Trade Representative from 1981 to 1985, with his company, reportedly earned nearly $1 million assisting the Mexican government in the passage of the now-infamous North American Free Trade Agreement (NAFTA). Brock also represented Mexico during the U.S. debate over fast-track authority.

Do you wonder why a former U.S. Trade Ambassador would represent a foreign country? That's easy. Money! Lots of money! A plethora of pesos!

Fast-track authority is an unusual procedure, with Congress ceding much of its original constitutional trade oversight to the president under a procedure with mandatory deadlines, no amendments allowed, and limited debate. It's proved to be a horrible idea. The slow, deliberate pace and consideration of democratic trade agreements of old is a much better alternative to the wham, bam, thank you, ma'am trade agreements since NAFTA that have gutted manufacturing jobs and have us up to our nostrils drowning in trade deficits and historic national debt.

Bill Brock testified before Congress about what a great deal both fast track and NAFTA were going to be for America. I don't think he mentioned that he was being paid handsomely at the time to represent Mexico. That's a little like getting a job reference from your mother.

People like Brock said NAFTA would create a lot of good American jobs while I was warning that NAFTA would cost half a million jobs.

Turns out I was wrong.

It was much worse.

The combined effect of changes in imports and exports as a result of NAFTA was a net loss of *879,280 U.S. jobs.*

According to the Economic Policy Institute, between 1993 and 2003, NAFTA resulted in an increase in exports that created 794,194 jobs, but it displaced production that would have supported 1,673,454 jobs. That's called going backward.

Yet Brock, who, after serving as the Trade Ambassador, was secretary of labor under Ronald Reagan, led the charge on NAFTA. I've always thought that the secretary of labor ought to have some working knowledge of the labor market. Just like, say, a FEMA director ought to know how to manage disasters—not *be* one. Maybe I'm old-school that way.

Brock should have known better. American workers paid for his mistakes. By contrast, he ended up doing real well.

THE WASHINGTON POST

I know it's hard to call an entire newspaper a "goat." After all, it's one of America's premier newspapers. . . . and the sports section of *The Washington Post* is outstanding. But the *Post* has done this country no favors in its role as head cheerleader for our failed free trade strategy.

Over the years it has been disappointing to me that *The Washington Post* and some other major newspapers were systematically unfair in their treatment of trade issues. Both the reporters and the editorial writers were notorious for going to the same tired, discredited old sources to preach the next sermon on free trade.

It didn't matter much what the trade news was. Their long-ago discredited sources would spin it like a top. And each new article telling us about how the trade deficit was ballooning would be explained away by the reporter, an editorial, or more likely accompanied by a predictable quote from one of the missionaries that shared the *Post*'s obsession with the virtues of our trade strategy.

For example, on March 27, 2000, *The Washington Post* noted that the

January trade deficit of that year had grown to $28 billion (a new record high). They editorialized that "this is understandable. . . . the deficit is more a symptom of strength. America's economy is growing faster than those of Europe and Japan, so naturally it sucks in lots of imports."

Five years later, on December 16, 2005, a *Washington Post* story announced another record-high trade deficit of $66 billion in October. That was explained away in part by reporter Paul Bluestein who wrote: "The continued robust growth of the U.S. economy, which draws imports at a much more rapid rate than the more anemic economies of Europe and Japan—a point the Bush administration has made repeatedly."

So, these giant trade deficits are a sign of strength? Well, then, why worry? Just keep reporting with those rose-tinted glasses.

Another monthly record trade deficit! Trot out the apologists to explain it away and maybe even suggest it was good for us. Well, maybe the Asian countries weren't growing fast enough. Or maybe it was a sign of how strong our economy was. Or the dollar was too expensive. Or, or, or, or. We got the same tired excuses from the same brain-dead commentators and analysts who wanted to spin failure into success.

Yawn.

I do credit the *Post* for doing the occasional well-researched story about sweatshop labor in foreign countries (see the Li Chunmei story that I cited in chapter 3).

But those of us who tried to get our op-ed pieces published by the *Post* to offer another (enlightened) perspective on the trade mess were usually turned down. Once in a while they would print a lonely dissent. But by my count, *The Washington Post* prints far more column inches in opinion pieces that are pro–free trade than it does those that question the giant trade deficits and blatant unfairness of recent trade agreements.

In fact, I did an analysis of the amount of space that *The Washington Post* devoted to the trade issue on their op-ed page. It turns out that 69 percent of their space was devoted to the pro–free trade side while only 31 percent was devoted to those who are demanding "fair trade" agreements. Now, according to Rush Limbaugh and Fox News, the media is supposed to be on my side—Democrats have a stranglehold on the media, remember? Apparently no one at the *Post* got the memo. They could learn a few things about Fair and Balanced.

It's probably safe to say that none of the editors or the columnists in the *Post* has ever lost a job to outsourcing. The same can be said for the blue-suit, cigar-and-suspender crowd that gets their op-ed pieces printed by the *Post*.

Take some of my complaints about the *Post* with a grain of salt. I've been so sore that they treat my side of the debate so unfairly I have taken to insulting them from time to time. I haven't learned not to argue with those who buy ink by the barrel, and finally I have a small ration of ink and paper to take a stand on that front.

In an intemperate moment during a trade speech, I once told an audience that I had a very specific routine when I campaign for office. I get up early in the morning and drink a big glass of water, then read *The Washington Post*. That way when I hit the campaign trail I have *nothing in my stomach and nothing on my mind.* Okay, so I was upset. It really is a great newspaper except for their position on trade and their habit of not allowing fair coverage of the issue.

Some years ago, after they had declined to publish an op-ed piece of mine on trade, I wrote them a letter telling them that they reminded me of something Clement Freud (Sigmund's grandson) once said: "When you hit someone over the head with a book, and get a hollow sound, it doesn't mean the book is empty."

So now I think I'm off their Christmas card list. But they made my list of goats and that's something.

TEN PERCENT BOB

And then there is Robert Bostick, a real piece of work. He was the associate deputy undersecretary for international labor affairs at the Department of Labor during the negotiation of NAFTA and a member of the U.S. negotiating team.

As it turned out, Bob was doing a pretty good job of negotiating, for himself. As part of his responsibilities, Bostick was involved in an effort to promote low-income housing subsidized by the Mexican government for low-paid Mexican workers living along sections of the U.S. border. It was a 120-million-dollar project.

According to published reports, in 1992, Bostick accepted an offer of 10 percent of the net profits generated by the project involving construction of six thousand condominiums.

While he was supposed to be representing Uncle Sam, Bostick was apparently doing a little business for himself on the side. He pled guilty to accepting the illegal cash and to a count of conspiracy. He was sentenced to probation for five years. The pair who offered the bribe, Leonard Malcolm and Terence Nolan, got three years probation.

Probation. That'll teach 'em.

CARLA HILLS AND VALLEYS

When it comes to working both sides of the street, Carla Hills is a tough act to follow. She was the U.S. secretary of Housing and Urban Development in the Gerald Ford administration. She went on to represent the Korean conglomerate Daewoo, which makes everything from electronics to cars. She also provided legal advice to the Matsushita Corporation of Japan.

But Hills really made her mark as a U.S. Trade Representative from 1989 to 1993 under President George Herbert Walker Bush, when she was the primary U.S. negotiator of NAFTA. A lawyer by trade, Hills drafted a controversial provision in the treaty called Chapter 11, which allowed lawsuits against the three governments involved in the treaty— Canada, Mexico, and the United States—for (get this) passing environmental, health, and land use regulations. In short, it allows companies, under NAFTA, to bring actions against a country because of environmental laws they may pass that disadvantage the companies' ability to sell products across borders.

Essentially, this provision circumvents our laws. It allows multinational corporations to do an end run around democracy and intimidate American governments at all levels. Often, just the threat of a billion-dollar lawsuit can cause opposition to crumble.

Public Citizen, a nonprofit public-interest organization, reported in February 2005:

> With only 11 of 42 cases finalized, some $35 million in tax-payer funds have been granted to five corporations that succeeded with their claims. An additional $28 billion is known to have been claimed by companies against all three NAFTA nations. The U.S. government's legal costs for the defense of just one re-cent case topped $3 million; 11 other cases have reached arbitra-tion.

When she crafted this provision, Carla Hills in effect traded away democracy. Washington lawyer Daniel Price, who was the lead U.S. ne-gotiator on Chapter 11 a decade ago, doesn't feel too bad about it. He told columnist William Greider that anyone troubled by the intrusions on U.S. sovereignty should "get over it."

Get this: In 1999, California governor Gray Davis ordered that MTBE be phased out of all gasoline sold in the state. The dangerous pollutant leaches into soil and taints water supplies and threatens hu-man health. Curiously, methyltertbutyl ether is also used medically to dissolve gallstones.

So Governor Davis did the right thing. He banned the stuff. But Methanex, the Canadian company that is the world's largest producer of MTBE, sued California (but ultimately lost) for loss of profits under the Chapter 11 provision of NAFTA.

But it is not just Canadian polluters who sue to pollute. The Ethyl Corporation, the American manufacturer of the chemical MMT, methylcyclopentadienyl manganese tricarbonyl, decided to sue under NAFTA's Chapter 11 because Canadian health officials thought the neurotoxin was a health hazard. The manganese in MMT has been linked to Parkinson's-like symptoms. Studies show that miners exposed to excess levels of manganese have a high rate of psychosis, severe neurological disease, and premature death.

Besides, it does nothing for gallstones.

But the lawsuit forced Canada to lift the ban and pay the Ethyl Corporation $13 million for the time lost polluting Canada. Ironically, MMT is banned from use in most gasoline sold in the United States.

We can thank Carla Hills for this subversion of democracy. She runs her own trade-consulting firm, and now freely wields the power of the Chapter 11 cudgel she created. William Greider, national affairs correspondent for *The Nation,* said in a Bill Moyers PBS exposé called "Trading Democracy":

> Carla Hills . . . supervised and led the negotiation of NAFTA, then left government and started her own international consulting firm, and sent her chief negotiator [Julius Katz] to tell the Canadian government that if they went ahead with a regulation on cigarette packaging, which they were considering, her clients, big tobacco, would file a huge claim against them. Canada backed off, and the reason they backed off is because they could read the terms and see that, my God, they're right, if we do this—which they regarded as a health regulation—we're gonna get stuck with a big bill for it.

CLAYTON "SERVICED" OUR FARMERS

Clayton Yeutter now works for Hogan & Hartson, but he was the U.S. Trade Representative from 1985 to 1989 under Ronald Reagan. I never saw a man who smiled as much as he did. You kind of got the feeling that he was just a good old boy . . . wearing Ferragamo shoes.

But if you watched him closely for a while, he would remind you of the guy in the old Western movies who went from town to town in his covered wagon peddling a bottle of medicine that he claimed would cure all of your ills from gout to the hiccups. You remember that guy.

He wore striped pants, silk shirt, bowler hat, and had a fast tongue that convinced you to buy several bottles of what he was selling.

I watched up close as Clayton Yeutter negotiated a free trade agreement between the United States and Canada. He smiled and cajoled and assured everybody that things were going to be just fine. The problem was that behind closed doors he literally gave away the farm. He signed up to a deal with Canada that undermined American farmers and left them helpless to do anything about it.

I was serving in the U.S. House of Representatives at the time and was on the Ways and Means Committee, where his trade agreement had to be approved with implementing language. At the hearings I pointed out that I felt he had set up American farmers for failure. He allowed the Canadian Wheat Board monopoly to ship unlimited quantities of grain into the United States at secret prices (described in chapter 8) and undermine our farmers.

When the dust settled, the Ways and Means Committee approved his free trade agreement with Canada by a vote of thirty-four to one. You can probably guess who the one was. Yup . . . that would be me. Congressman—now Senator—Quixote. I refused to budge because I felt Clayton Yeutter had negotiated an agreement that sold out our farmers. It didn't take long to prove that was the case. Very quickly an avalanche of unfairly traded Canadian grain headed south to undermine our family farmers.

It was a schizophrenic time for trade. Reagan declared he was a free trader even as he slapped a 100 percent tariff on some Japanese electronics in 1987. And, as the Cato Institute noted,

Two days before the November 1987 trade statistics were due to come out in January 1988, Reagan said the trade deficit was a sign of strength and noted that the United States had incurred trade deficits during its great period of growth in the nineteenth century. But when those numbers actually showed a 25 percent drop in the deficit from the month before, Reagan declared this an improvement in the trade picture. If the deficit was a sign of strength, how could a reduction in the deficit be an improvement?

But no one ever accused the champions of free trade of being consistent. The convoluted rhetoric has not varied much from that administration to the present one. The playbook is the same.

If Clayton Yeutter did not care a fig about farmers in my part of the country, by no means did he abandon agriculture altogether. He was smokin' when it came to protecting the tobacco growers. See, trade is crucial to tobacco, because Americans are wising up and smoking less. According to *USA Today,* while cigarette sales fell by 4.5 percent in North America between 1990 and 1995, they had increased by 5.6 percent in Eastern Europe and 8 percent during the same period in the Asia-Pacific region.

According to 1997 figures cited by the *San Francisco Chronicle,* approximately 1.1 billion people fifteen and older were smokers. Seventy-two percent of those smokers live in developing countries, a rate expected to rise to 85 percent by the year 2025.

If you want to keep people puffing away, you gotta go where the action is. So Yeutter bullied countries like Japan, Korea, and Taiwan, under a provision of U.S. trade law (Section 301), into opening their markets to tobacco. Meanwhile, the same administration, led by Surgeon General C. Everett Koop, was launching a campaign against domestic tobacco use.

While Yeutter was aggressive on behalf of tobacco trade, you didn't see him take action against the Canadians for the unfair trade targeted at American farmers. No time? I think it was a case of no interest.

Clayton Yeutter never admitted to doing tobacco companies any special favors, but the record speaks for itself. After he completed his term as a trade representative, he joined the board of British American Tobacco, the British tobacco conglomerate. I rest my case.

In 1986, Ronald Reagan said, "Our trade policy rests firmly on the foundation of free and open markets. I recognize . . . the inescapable conclusion that all of history has taught: The freer the flow of world trade, the stronger the tides of human progress and peace among nations."

That's true if the free and open markets are the product of rules that respect workers and the environment and protect intellectual property. Without those protections, the free markets are just profit opportunities for producers. Nothing more.

CAPITOL HILL GOATS

Maybe it is because the sting of the Central American Free Trade Agreement is still fresh, but I want to add to the list of goats some of those involved in the last-minute arm-twisting and pork barreling used to swing enough votes to pass this trade act in July 2005.

I had hopes the U.S. House of Representatives would not ratify the treaty—I thought some lessons had been learned from the devastating effects of NAFTA and those trade agreements with other countries like China. The trade deficit was at record highs and so was the national budget deficit. Job loss to other countries continued at a record pace. In fact, CAFTA was on its way to defeat—which would have given the country time to reassess our trade policies and the harm they have done to the working people of America. Like NAFTA, CAFTA is good for megacorporations and bad for working people.

CAFTA passed the U.S. House by the slimmest of margins—217 to 215. And it took President Bush and Vice President Cheney's visit to the Capitol the morning of the vote to lobby some Republicans who were in danger of doing the right thing.

Then the House Republicans limited the debate on CAFTA to two hours. They did this because during debate common sense starts to win out, and that would have sounded the death knell for this trade agreement. When the "debate" ended CAFTA opponents still held a majority. When the fifteen-minute roll call expired, the nays were ahead by five votes.

That should have been the end of it. But when the Republican crowd in the U.S. House loses, they don't slink away with their heads in their shoes. No, they just change the rules and declare themselves the winners.

At the end of the allotted time during the House vote, then House Majority Leader Tom DeLay—the one who had a standing appointment with the Ethics Committee—kept the roll call open as the arm-twisting and political favors were doled out. Administration officials, U.S. Trade Representative Rob Portman, and Republican leaders did their rounds and negotiated pork-barrel deals for the holdouts.

It took them over one hour to twist enough arms and turn defeat to victory. When they finally had the swing vote from North Carolina representative Robin Hayes, the gavel went down and CAFTA was approved. Were they embarrassed or ashamed by breaking the rules of the U.S. House of Representatives to achieve their victory? No. This crowd doesn't embarrass easily.

It was reported that an estimated $47 billion in pork-barrel money (*your* tax dollars) was used during the CAFTA vote by Tom "The Hammer" DeLay and Speaker Hastert to purchase those final votes.

The Washington Post said the next morning:

> The last-minute negotiations for Republican votes resembled the wheeling and dealing on a car lot. Republicans who were opposed or undecided were courted during hurried meetings in Capitol hallways, on the House floor and at the White House. GOP leaders told their rank and file that if they wanted anything, now was the time to ask, lawmakers said, and members took advantage of the opportunity. . . .
>
> Lawmakers also said many of the favors bestowed in exchange for votes will be tucked away into the huge energy and highway bills that Congress is scheduled to pass this week before leaving for the August recess.

So President Bush and his pals won! CAFTA is now law. Our U.S. trade deficit is increasing, jobs are leaving, and the president and the Republican Congress have some of the lowest approval ratings ever recorded. A coincidence? I don't think so.

But already the president is looking beyond CAFTA. Now he is trying to land a free trade agreement with South Korea and another trade deal called the Free Trade Agreement of the Americas. In November of

2005, the president attended the Summit of the Americas in Argentina, where there were massive public protests and street demonstrations in opposition to his plans.

The president says that all nations involved in his trade plans will benefit economically. But the fact is, labor in America and labor in other countries are against the plan—because they know it will be one more trade agreement that benefits the giant corporations and tramples workers' rights and opportunities.

People from the United States and other countries have seen enough. They know this is not about opportunity. It is about exploitation. The president and those who work with him can't convene a meeting on trade anywhere in the world these days without inciting protests among the workers who have been exploited by the agreements.

How times have changed. There was a time when our country's political leaders understood the value of labor and the need to support the labor movement. The United States supported the Solidarity labor movement in Poland as long as it was demonstrating for the dignity of workers and the rights of working people in foreign countries.

These days President Bush and his supporters do their best to ignore the call of our workers for a fair deal. The presidential motorcade is usually given a travel route that allows them to avoid seeing the citizens who take to the streets to protest these trade deals. It's a shame.

President Bush is restricted to doing "drive-by" trade deals.

YOU, TOO, CAN BE AN ECONOMIST

While CAFTA is still fresh in our minds, as well as those rosy proclamations of all the good it will do, it might be interesting to see what was being said before CAFTA's big brother, NAFTA, was being debated.

This 1993 excerpt comes from the ultraconservative think tank the Heritage Foundation:

> According to Gary Hufbauer and Jeffrey Schott, authors
> of the Institute for International Economics book *NAFTA: An*

Assessment, "If the NAFTA is rejected, the U.S. is likely to experience job losses" . . .

While Hufbauer's and Schott's estimate of job increases is slightly different from those predicted by the ITC or the Clinton Administration, they still calculate that under the NAFTA, a gross total of 316,000 U.S. jobs will be created, while a gross total of 145,000 U.S. jobs will be lost—leading to a net gain of 171,000 new jobs.

Okay. Reality check. The United States has lost nearly 880,000 jobs to NAFTA. Hufbauer and Schott's calculations were off by more than *a million jobs!*

They were not just wrong. They were boneheaded wrong. And let's be fair. Bill Clinton had it wrong, too. He did, however, get a lot more right on the economy than the present gang has. So what are Hufbauer and Schott doing today? Well, you know, the study of economics is a no-fault profession. Kinda like being a television weatherman. And I'm sure that these two economists are being paid handsomely for their opinions on the next trade proposal. (They predict sunshine with scattered goofiness.) Corporations that benefit from trading away American jobs will pay big money to economists who will give them the answers they want.

When it comes to consistent convoluted thinking, it is hard to beat the Heritage Foundation. Michael G. Wilson asserted in his 1993 article:

Since labor represents only between 10 percent to 20 percent of production costs for most businesses, Perot's argument about lower wage levels in Mexico luring U.S. plants south of the border is greatly exaggerated and in most cases wrong . . .

U.S. workers earn high wages because they are the most productive workers in the world. By contrast, Mexico's wages are low because the economy is poor. U.S. companies wishing to relocate to Mexico must deal with the consequences of what is essentially a Third World economy. For example, the operating costs for U.S.

firms doing business in Mexico are raised considerably by higher levels of worker absenteeism, lower educational standards, political instability, limited access to raw materials, and the problems associated with long distance [*sic*] management.

Consequently, few companies base plant locations on a simple calculation of wage differentials; for most U.S. manufacturers, the cost of labor is less important than such factors as access to technology, the skills of the local work force [*sic*], and the quality of the transportation network.

Oops! The three largest imports from Mexico are auto parts, automobiles, and electronics—all the product of high-skill labor. Where are you now, Michael Wilson? How do you answer to this?

Look, these folks could put out a paper that projects with confidence that they can make a pig fly, but most people with a lick of sense know better.

MISCELLANEOUS GOATS

There are many goats I haven't named. But they know who they are. When the roll is called for those who stepped forward to support American jobs, their names won't be on it. That list includes some politicians with whom I served in Congress (Newt Gingrich, for example), some business leaders who now think of themselves mainly as international citizens, and the pundits and columnists who, insulated by their jobs, foolishly support the export of good jobs.

Jack Welch, the former CEO of General Electric, makes the list. Sure he was an all-star executive. But the title of his recent book, *Winning*, didn't apply to those whose jobs were lost when Jack was busy outsourcing jobs overseas.

And while President Ronald Reagan and President George Bush set the stage for the new trade agreements that began eating away at the manufacturing base of our country, they passed the baton to President Clinton, who pursued the same strategy.

During the twenty-five years between 1980 and 2005, we have had seventeen years of Republican presidencies and eight years of a Democratic administration. But, with only a few differences (the Clinton administration did try to do something about labor and environmental standards in some of their negotiations, and that was a step forward), if you closed your eyes and just listened to the rhetoric on trade, there wasn't a dime's worth of difference in the strategy of the two political parties' trade policy.

And President George W. Bush, well, he's a chip off the old block on trade issues. Or maybe it's a block off the old chip. Under his watch the trade deficit has climbed to record heights, but he seems unaware or uninterested. His is an administration where big business is invited to help draft the rules and regulations, so he is hardly the one who is going to tell big business that this isn't working.

But still, there is a difference between the two political parties on trade today. Judging by the Democratic opposition to CAFTA, I think it is fair to say most Democrats (not all) have now learned a lesson or two about the pitfalls of unregulated, unfair global trade and have returned to their roots in defense of the working people. There are still some Democrats who fancy themselves "new" and who think that cuddling up to big business and shipping jobs overseas is good for the country. You can recognize them by their waxy complexions as they read the monthly bad news on trade deficit and their red faces as they try to explain to their constituents how this is all good for them.

As for the Republicans, they've almost completely caved in. There are just a few brave souls who recognize the damage being done to this country and its workers. The majority of them don't dare cross their corporate benefactors.

But I believe they are on the wrong side of history.

ELEVEN

SOME HEROES—BUCKING THE TIDE

OKAY, ENOUGH TIME ON THE GOATS OF TRADE. THEY'VE had their fifteen minutes.

There are also some heroes in this trade saga—people who are willing to put principle before profit.

We are constantly reminded that a corporate executive has the responsibility to do what is right for the shareholders. That usually means the search for maximum profits. But shouldn't there be other considerations? Is profit the only motive of corporate decisions? Or does the corporation have some responsibility to workers, too?

Regrettably, we read about many executives who think of employees as useful tools to be discarded when it looks advantageous to do so. And many of the economists and reporters who wallow in the world of trade have made their bed with the corporate interests on this matter. But there are some exceptions—including some executives with courage who abide by the principle of loyalty to their workers. I mentioned the example of Jake Marvin from Marvin Windows in chapter 2. But there are more.

And there are some academics, some politicians, and public-spirited citizens who have had the courage to speak out against what they see as failed policies that weaken our country. Here is a partial list of some of my heroes.

THE PRICE OF AARON FEUERSTEIN'S LOYALTY TO HIS WORKERS

I learned about Aaron Feuerstein from press reports. Months later, I met him. His company, Malden Mills, which was founded by his grandfather in 1906, invented a fleece they called Polartec. And that helped make the company a very successful one.

But on December 11, 1995, bad luck struck. A boiler exploded at the textile plant in Lawrence, Massachusetts, and the plant burned to the ground. It was a bitter cold night with 50 mph winds. Yet, in that viscous brew of fire and ice, two managers, Bill Perez and Alan Kraunlis, braved the blaze and salvaged the personnel files so that the families of the injured workers could be called. Twenty-two workers of a workforce of three thousand were hospitalized, but Aaron Feuerstein was relieved that no one was killed.

In all, the company lost 750,000 square feet in three of nine buildings. It was a pretty tough blow for Aaron and the workers in the twenty-third-poorest community in the United States. Some Christmas this was going to be!

The easy thing to do would have been to lay off the workers and maybe even rebuild overseas. But facing the crisis of a lifetime, Aaron Feuerstein did something astonishing. He gave each worker a 275-dollar Christmas bonus, three months' salary, and health insurance. And the company set up a crisis team to address the needs of his employees. They even collected Christmas presents for the children of the workers.

He ultimately paid out an estimated $20 million to his workers—a stunning act of loyalty in this day and age of disposable workers. Aaron explained, "I have a responsibility to the community. It would have been unconscionable to put 3,000 people on the streets and deliver a deathblow to the cities of Lawrence and Methuen. Maybe on paper our company is worthless to Wall Street, but I can tell you it's worth more."

Quitting would have been easy. But Aaron took the $300 million in insurance money and borrowed another $100 million to build a better, worker-friendly plant. In less than four months Aaron had most workers back on the job. Nine months after the fire, the plant was fully operational.

Aaron Feuerstein's ethics were widely applauded. He was invited to the White House by President Clinton and received twelve honorary degrees, yet he seemed almost embarrassed by the reaction. "I get a lot of publicity," he said, "and I don't think that speaks well for our times. At the time in America of the greatest prosperity, the God of Money has taken over to an extreme."

In spite of Aaron's best efforts, the company was financially vulnerable. Reeling from debt, cheap foreign imports flooding the market, and the financial effects of September 11, 2001, the company was forced into bankruptcy. Sales fell from $400 million in 1995 to $236 million in 2001.

The company emerged from bankruptcy in 2003, and I'd like to give you a happy ending to this good man's story—but I can't. After the failure of the business, Aaron found himself scorned in some business circles for caring more about his workers than his creditors. Marianne Jennings, a business columnist for *The Washington Post*, blasted Aaron for his business practices.

But it is hard for me to fathom that in the cutthroat arena of global business, loyalty to one's employees is deemed a mistake.

That's the mind-set. And it has to change. People are more important than money. We have completely lost track of the purpose of government—which plays a huge role in business by making the rules or, these days, ignoring them. The role of government is to help create a society beneficial to people. People are the priority. Not corporations. Certainly commerce plays a huge role in the betterment of any great society, but any society that forgets that *its primary purpose is to serve the people* cannot ever be great.

Aaron Feuerstein managed to hang on to a figurehead role in the company, but the new owners did what he was loath to—they outsourced the production of Polartec to China.

REMEMBERING THOSE WHO HELPED
GET YOU THERE

Another guy in a white hat is Robert Naegele, the former owner of RollerBlade. And if you can get past all the skinned knees and scraped elbows he's been responsible for over the years (wear pads!), Robert Naegele should be remembered for doing a good thing for his employees. When he sold the company to Nordica, it would have been easy just to walk away with a smile on his face and over $200 million in his pocket—admittedly a very large pocket.

But Robert, having moved away from Minneapolis to Florida, sent Christmas cards back to the employees of the company he used to own. When his former employees opened their Christmas cards they found season's greetings and a check from Robert and his wife.

It was a bonus they wanted to pay to each worker who had helped build a successful company. The bonus was $160 for *each month* of service to the company—and he prepaid the federal taxes on the bonus.

Why the generosity? Robert said he understood that a company is really its employees. He said he made a lot of money when he sold the company because those employees had helped him build something special. And he said he wanted to share his success with those that helped create it.

News reports said that Matt Majka, an employee of eleven years, got an estimated $21,000. Ann Reader, six months along with her third child, got a check for an estimated $11,000. Barbara Retie, a working single mother with two daughters, had worked for the company for four and a half years, and she received a check for $9,000. None of those employees expected it. But all of them were proud to have worked for someone who understood the value of their work for the company.

Those employees of RollerBlade are a rare group of people. They had a boss who understood the importance of the people who worked for him in the success of the company. In an age where many CEOs treat their workers like disposable tools and often send their jobs overseas, Robert Naegele knew better.

The term *great American* is overused, but Robert is a great American.

THE MAN WHO MADE KATHIE LEE CRY

As I am someone who has been concerned about the sweatshop conditions under which so many American garments are produced, it is no surprise that my path should cross that of Charles Kernaghan, executive director of the National Labor Committee, the man who has been single-handedly embarrassing global corporations to clean up their acts and their offshore sweatshops.

Now, Charles will be the first to tell you his work has only just begun, but his selfless efforts have made a huge impact by raising awareness of the harsh conditions in sweatshops around the world.

The New York Times says Charles is "the labor movement's mouse that roared." *Women's Wear Daily* said, "Charles Kernaghan and his anti-sweatshop battle have been shaking up the apparel industry like nothing since the Triangle Shirtwaist Fire."

Charles is a fascinating fellow. *The Washington Post* described him thusly: "There's something austere about Kernaghan, 57—the wire-rimmed glasses, the precision-clipped goatee, the slicked-back silver hair, the flat expression. He is coiled. He seems about to spring. He is incapable of schmoozing with his corporate targets, he admits, for he's always on-message, always ready to strike."

The National Labor Committee that Charles founded is an independent, nonprofit human rights organization focused on the protection of worker rights. NLC concentrates on the plight of young women making garments, shoes, toys, and other products in Central America, the Caribbean, China, and other developing countries. (See chapter 3.)

Charles has made it his mission to better workplace conditions around the globe since witnessing the conditions while participating in a peace march in Central America two decades ago. In 1996, during congressional testimony, he put a spotlight smack dab on the sweatshop horrors in a Honduras factory where thirteen-year-old girls were sewing pants under armed guard for Kathie Lee Gifford's Wal-Mart label for thirty-one cents an hour. Of course, the spotlight quickly turned to Kathie Lee, who threatened to sue, then burst into tears.

It was huge news, and it forced Wal-Mart and other companies to address the issue. Much of that has been lip service, but there have been improvements. I told *The Washington Post* in July 2005 that Charles Kernaghan changed the way people do business for the better. The *Post* wrote:

> That's not just hyperbole. The president of the Arlington-based American Apparel and Footwear Association says virtually the same thing—though he's careful not to appear to be giving credit to Kernaghan, who is, let's be frank, a thorn in the apparel industry's side.
>
> "We remember that every day," Kevin M. Burke says of the Kathie Lee controversy, "and that's a lesson to us, the fact that we don't want that to happen again. And as a result of that, you had an industry begin to mobilize itself to make certain that, over time, they produce their products in the most responsible manner to make certain that employees are treated with dignity and respect."

One man and a staff of four have improved working conditions around the world for thousands who may never know his name. But I thought it was important that *you* get to know them as the heroes they are.

LEO HINDERY CALLS FOR A RETURN TO INTEGRITY

I realize that hard as some of us have fought over the years for the workingman and against outsourcing, the words of a politician rarely resonate the way those of a man who has been in the trenches do. That's why I have so much respect for Leo Hindery, a former NASCAR driver. And oh yes, also the former CEO and president of companies such as AT&T Broadband, TCI, and the YES Network. Today, he is a managing partner of InterMedia Partners, a communications company.

But Leo is becoming more well-known for pointing out what has gone wrong in big business today—the fact that five media companies control 80 percent of what you see on television—and what he sees as the abandonment of integrity in big business.

He has written a book, *It Takes a CEO,* about this crisis of greed, and says CEOs should approach a career as life's meaningful work and not just a means to accumulate personal wealth. Leo, who worked his way up from poverty and through college to compete in the world's largest business arenas, has a rare perspective. He knows what it is to be poor, middle-class, and wealthy, and what he sees happening to America and America's workers worries him.

He said:

> Wal-Mart's success has come at an enormous and painful cost to our national and local economies. From its boarding-up of Main Streets to its failure to pay workers fairly, to its imposing on taxpayers welfare costs for its underpaid employees, to its material contribution to our obscene ballooning trade deficit with China, this Wal-Martization of America is leaving us with an economy increasingly characterized by a gaggle of cheap imported consumer goods, shoddy employee practices, and insensitivity to communities.
>
> It is beyond time for all Americans to wake up from this nightmare and support those companies . . . that believe that companies

and their CEOs have as much responsibility to employees, customers, and the nation as to shareholders. And it is way beyond time for us to take our support away from those companies that believe otherwise and do more to aggrandize management than to serve employees and their communities.

Leo is one of the few CEOs of stature willing to tell the truth about the damage being done to America.

LOU DOBBS—TOUGH AS NAILS

My next hero of trade is a pretty obvious one. No journalist has done more to document the ills of the loss of American jobs through outsourcing than has Lou Dobbs, whose book *Exporting America,* named after his CNN series, was the first book to really tackle the loss of American jobs. Lou's work in print and in electronic media has served as a wake-up call for America. He is on a one-man campaign to wake up America.

The opening paragraph of Lou's book hits like a blow to the solar plexus—"The power of big business over our national life has never been greater. Never have there been fewer business leaders willing to commit to the national interest over selfish interest, to the good of the country over that of the companies they lead."

Lou Dobbs knows his stuff. He graduated from Harvard University with a degree in economics. And, for the record, he is a Republican—I know there are good people in both political parties. And while economic and religious extremists have hijacked the Republican party, Lou Dobbs has refused to go along for the ride. I respect that.

In the wake of Rob Portman's appointment as U.S. Trade Representative and after the ill-advised passage of CAFTA, Dobbs noted in a column for *U.S. News & World Report:*

> Albert Einstein defined insanity as "doing the same thing over and over again and expecting different results." Yet the United

States continues to enter into similar free-trade agreements with countries and regions that allow corporate America to outsource plant, production, and jobs to other parts of the world. When those products and services are then exported back into our $11 trillion marketplace, we only add to our unsustainable trade deficit.

One of the most courageous things Dobbs has done is publicize a list of the companies outsourcing jobs. Now, I don't suppose that endears his show to potential advertisers, but it hasn't stopped him from pointing fingers at these red-faced companies. You can find the growing list with a quick Google search. Dobbs was perhaps the first to point out that some forty state governments outsource jobs to other countries!

In a 2004 Associated Press interview, Dobbs said, "I think if this trend is allowed to continue, that the United States, without being unduly alarmist, is headed toward if not a third-world category than a second-world category as a nation." He added, "There are some who simply look at this [U.S. economy] as a convenient piggy bank to loot, and the worker be damned."

I believe we are close to an awakening in America—that's what this book is all about—and when it happens, much of the credit will be due to Lou Dobbs.

THE FEISTY GODFATHER OF TRADE

Most Americans did not consider the ramifications of unfair trade until 1992, when a short-tempered, short in stature, all ears (his words) Ross Perot declared there would be a "giant sucking sound" as American jobs left the country via NAFTA. He lost a debate with Al Gore on that point, but Ross Perot was 100 percent dead-on right.

In 1993, Perot wrote in his book *Save Your Job, Save Our Country*:

NAFTA is really less about trade than it is about investment. Its principal goal is to protect US companies and investors operating in Mexico . . . Ultimately, NAFTA is not a trade agreement but an investment agreement. NAFTA's principal goal is to protect the investment of US companies that build factories in Mexico. This is accomplished by reducing the risk of nationalization, by permitting the return of profits to US businesses, and by allowing unlimited access to the American markets for goods produced in Mexico.

I never viewed Perot as antitrade. He was just sharp enough to spot inequities in the agreements and trouble on the horizon. His was a commonsense approach.

I admire the fact that early on, Perot knew that the 1991 "fast-track" legislation was a bad idea because it "gave President Bush the authority to negotiate NAFTA in complete secrecy and without the participation of either Congress or the U.S. public." Perot noted that since 1960, the Senate had approved or ratified 25 treaties and agreements of various types without "fast-track" authority.

Funny, isn't it, that fifteen years ago Ross Perot was just a curious man warning about implausible scenarios. Now, when you consider the accuracy of his predictions, you have to give him an enormous amount of credit. But one thing was obvious even then. Ross Perot loved his country. He was and is a patriot.

GOING THE DISTANCE FOR LABOR—IMPORTANT LABOR FIGURES

In today's political-economic-social climate it is not in vogue to express support for unions because unions have never been without real controversy. Greed and corruption are not foreign to unions any more than they are to Wall Street and to Washington, D.C. But, as I detailed in chapter 3, unions have played a crucial role in this democracy by leveling the playing field for the worker.

Unions have been the voice of the workers of America. While the fight for a fair share of the income for workers may have increased the labor costs in the short term for big business, their corporate vision has been too narrow to see that a thriving middle class made possible by workers who earn a fair wage is the reason the corporations have succeeded! The equation is so simple, yet it escapes the brightest minds in business. As Henry Ford understood, you have to pay your workers enough so they can afford to buy the products they make!

How many people in China and Mexico can afford the products they make? The idea that these trade agreements would open up new marketplaces has been a giant sham! But few people really grasp that.

GEORGE BECKER—A VISIONARY

One man's name is often mentioned when it comes to a commonsense approach and vision to trade and labor issues. George Becker is a member of the U.S.-China Economic & Security Review Commission whose task it is to monitor, investigate, and report to Congress about the national security implications of the trade and economic relationship between the United States and China.

How crucial is this issue? "We need to be treating trade agreements as seriously today as we did arms control agreements a decade ago," says C. Richard D'Amato, who served with George Becker on the Commission.

Becker is one of those old-school steelworkers. He moved up from being a steelworker to be elected to two terms as the international president of the United Steelworkers of America (USWA), representing 750,000 industrial workers in the United States and Canada. In that position, Becker went eye to eye with an industry bent on busting unions.

Before studying the ramifications of trade with China, George Becker was a member of the U.S. Trade Deficit Review Commission. His list of accomplishments while serving labor and government includes establishment of some of the early national health standards adopted by the U.S. Occupational Safety and Health Administration for workers exposed to lead, arsenic, and other toxic substances.

In 1999, when most of government was still asleep at the switch over the disaster NAFTA had become, George was sounding the alarm about the exploitation of workers throughout the world:

> NAFTA has failed for American workers, for Mexican workers, and for Canadian workers. They told us NAFTA would create 200,000 jobs a year and clean up the environmental degradation in the maquiladoras. It was supposed to provide a living wage for Mexican workers. These were the hollow promises that were laid out by the government spokespersons and by industry.
>
> Five years later, what do we have? Do we have 5 million new jobs? No! We've lost 600,000 industrial jobs to Mexico. In Mexico, 2 million jobs have evaporated from the landscape. Meanwhile, workers there are making less than a dollar an hour.
>
> There isn't a day that goes by that our union doesn't hear about some plant or factory that is closing down and reopening in Mexico. The workers who get these jobs are living in poverty. They can't support their families. Families are living in hovels with dirt floors, drinking water out of drums. And yet they are working in state-of-the-art plants owned by companies that are based in the U.S. They get paid $4.50 a day for working approximately nine hours, and they have no benefits, and no rights to organize.
>
> NAFTA is the greatest betrayal of workers in my lifetime. NAFTA was never intended to protect workers—NAFTA was intended to protect industrialists and bankers. The only institution that protects working people is the union movement.

Years later, those words still resonate. In many ways, when it comes to recognizing the dark vision of these lopsided trade agreements that enrich corporations and decimate labor, George Becker has been a man ahead of his time.

JOHN SWEENEY—TELLING IT LIKE IT IS

There are voices today that say the AFL-CIO is a dinosaur. I don't believe that. For decades it has been the voice of working people in America. This organization, more than any, has set the bar for workplace standards and wages. Now, even with the AFL-CIO's efforts, that bar is being lowered with the advent of global trade. It's difficult enough to organize workers in one country—but maintaining and raising the quality of life of workers in America while corporations exploit workers abroad is an even bigger challenge.

AFL-CIO president John Sweeney understands what the American worker is facing better than anyone. His focus is simple—workers need good jobs, health care, and retirement security. He says:

> Let's face it. Today's working families are on the brink of economic trauma—if they haven't already been pushed over the edge. The middle class is disappearing under the burden of job insecurity and Wal-Martization, stagnating wages, unbearable gas and oil costs, unaffordable health care and vanishing pensions. The White House and congressional leadership could not be doing a better job of enriching the wealthy while picking the pockets of working families and the poor . . .
>
> The best family security, middle-class-building tool in the world is a union card. Union workers earn better wages, receive better benefits and have a collective voice on the job—a real say in working conditions and the way the work gets done. They also have the collective power of the union movement and work together for laws and public policies that improve life for all working families.

Which, in the eyes of those in power, is precisely the problem with labor unions.

A conservative friend and I were discussing the weakening voice of

American labor, when he said matter-of-factly, "Labor is a commodity just like anything else."

I think he crystallized the argument for outsourcing jobs in eight words. But what he is also saying is that money and materialism are *more important than people*. And I think that is what philosophically separates Democrats from Republicans. Democrats believe that people are the most important factor in this equation. If it is not good for people, what is the point? Is it not the goal of any community at any level to improve the lot of the people?

This whole extreme right-wing philosophy of Dog Eat Dog and the Law of the Jungle sounds good if you are a big dog or tiger. No health care? Tough. No money for college? Dig ditches. Lost your pension? Beg, you old coot.

No, labor is more than a commodity. Honest work for honest pay is the very foundation of a successful society. No society can long survive gross inequity on this point.

I hope John recognizes this book for what it is—a defense of the American worker and a plan to create public policy in this country that values work and helps the people who get up every morning and build, create, innovate, and, yes, manufacture, fabricate, and push wheelbarrows as well. John Sweeney has been a strong, relentless voice for good jobs that pay well with good benefits in America. Has he succeeded? Not yet, but the fight isn't over. Together with Richard Trumka and other courageous leaders, John will continue the fight.

LEO GERARD—AN AGITATOR

One of the most important facets in the American labor movement is the steel industry, and in Leo Gerard the United Steel Workers of America have just a dandy leader. He is the son of a Canadian mine worker, but he sounds red, white, and blue to me.

I'll let him handle his own introduction as he made it in a 2004 speech:

What I want to tell you right now, what I am, what the Steel-workers are and what we're not. I'm the son of a union organizer and a left wing miner. I'm an agitator. And like Jim Hightower says, "the job of an agitator in a washing machine is to get the dirt out." And that's what we're going to do.

The Steel Workers Union is not middle of the road, move to the center, so-called moderate, "me, too," hard hat Republicans. We're not centrists, we're not free traders, we're not corporate apologists, and we're not new Democrats. Rather like all of you, like all of you, and millions of Steelworkers, industrial workers, public sector workers, civil rights activists, antipoverty activists, social justice activists, environmental activists, student activists, and so many more, we represent the values of fairness, of equity, of social justice, of decent jobs, of high quality universal health care, clean air, clean water. We represent equality of opportunity. We represent a fair trade policy. We represent economic and social justice for everyone.

Leo Gerard has been a voice of conscience by seeking worldwide standards for workers in the tire, rubber, aluminum, and mining industries. Gerard understands that by protecting workers abroad, he is protecting workers at home.

His concern has real merit. In November of 2005, a federal lawsuit was brought against Bridgestone Firestone for using slave labor and child labor on its rubber plantation in Liberia. (Incidentally, Bridgestone/Firestone is Japanese-owned nowadays.)

While Bridgestone Firestone denies the charges, the suit alleges, "The plantation workers are modern day slaves, forced to work by the coercion of poverty, with the prospect of starvation just one complaint about conditions away." (As of March 2006, there was no action on the lawsuit.)

It is yet another indication that the labor movement has never been more important. There is too much to be done. As Leo Gerard said in that rousing speech, "Brothers and sisters, we are the heart and soul, we are the true values of America. We are the heart and soul, and in fact, we are the blood that runs through the veins of democracy."

Indeed, what are worker rights if not democracy at its very core? This administration can talk about spreading freedom and democracy all it wants, but our trade policy is spoken in a whole different language. It is a language that tacitly approves, by ignoring, the well-documented exploitation of workers, including children.

THE IMPORTANCE OF BILL MOYERS

The political dynamics have gotten so twisted in this country a journalist can't report the truth without being accused of being liberal—as if that were a crime. The bully pulpit of the White House and propagandists like the people at Fox News and Rush Limbaugh have made it hard to be a good journalist. Get out of line, and you're in trouble.

The media deserve some of the beatings they've taken. Many reporters have proved to be sloppy, and some enjoy close relationships with those they are supposed to be covering objectively. Consolidation has badly wounded media's willingness to tackle the tough issues. That is why I have battled the Federal Communications Commission (FCC) against further consolidation. We need more voices. More perspectives.

One of the best broadcasters of our time, Bill Moyers, is no longer in the broadcast booth at PBS, but he continues to write some of the boldest, most patriotic speeches I have read, including one delivered at New York University in 2004 entitled "This Is the Fight of Our Lives." Every engaged citizen ought to read it. (Google it!)

While Moyers's focus on issues has been broad, he has devoted a good deal of time to the inequities of trade, so he is deserving of a place in this Heroes chapter. Moyers, a former spokesman for Lyndon Johnson, one of the original organizers of the Peace Corps, and senior correspondent for CBS, is the winner of ten Peabody Awards and more than thirty Emmy Awards. Moyers did an exceptional piece for PBS in

2002 called "Trading Democracy." I included an excerpt in the previous chapter (goats: Carla Hills).

In North Dakota, a bastion of common sense, I learned to trust my eyes and not my ears. The president might be telling me things are going great and America's economy is cruising along like a limousine heading down Wall Street, but when I look around, something doesn't seem right.

Bill Moyers sees it, too. And he reports it. The unvarnished truth.

In his speech at New York University, Moyers said:

> Astonishing as it seems, no one in official Washington seems embarrassed by the fact that the gap between rich and poor is greater than it's been in 50 years—the worst inequality among all Western nations. Or that we are experiencing a shift in poverty. For years it was said those people down there at the bottom were single, jobless mothers. For years they were told work, education, and marriage is how they move up the economic ladder. But poverty is showing up where we didn't expect it—among families that include two parents, a worker, and a head of the household with more than a high school education. These are the newly poor. Our political, financial and business class expects them to climb out of poverty on an escalator moving downward.

Moyers is right. What few people have figured out is how outsourcing has put downward pressure on wages. We don't expect the labor force in China to have an effect on our own. But it does. The result of this boneheaded economic strategy is obvious to anyone willing to look and raise questions.

Moyers continues:

> Until now. I don't have to tell you that a profound transformation is occurring in America: the balance between wealth and the commonwealth is being upended. By design. Deliberately. We

have been subjected to what the Commonwealth Foundation calls "a fanatical drive to dismantle the political institutions, the legal and statutory canons, and the intellectual and cultural frameworks that have shaped public responsibility for social harms arising from the excesses of private power." From land, water and other natural resources, to media and the broadcast and digital spectrums, to scientific discovery and medical breakthroughs, and to politics itself, a broad range of the American commons is undergoing a powerful shift toward private and corporate control. And with little public debate. Indeed, what passes for "political debate" in this country has become a cynical charade behind which the real business goes on—the not-so-scrupulous business of getting and keeping power in order to divide up the spoils.

Bravo! Few people in America truly understand the dangerous transformation that is being exploited in large part by international corporations. Few of those who do understand have the courage to stand against it. Thank you, Bill Moyers.

SENATOR ROBERT BYRD

Two of my greatest allies on trade issues in the U.S. Senate have been Robert Byrd and Fritz Hollings. Both have been consistent in their opposition to unfair trade agreements. Senator Byrd, a Democrat from West Virginia, is the author of an antidumping amendment signed into law by Bill Clinton in 2000. The law previously allowed U.S. companies to file antidumping petitions and have tariffs imposed and payments made to the United States, but the Byrd Amendment directed the payments to the injured companies. Of course, this has the WTO riled up, and frankly, anything that riles up the WTO can't be all bad. Unfortunately, the Republican majority in Congress has now passed legislation that will overturn the Byrd Amendment in 2008.

Senator Byrd has offered a real sense of conscience in the Senate during difficult times—and not just on trade issues. In his speech "We

Stand Passively Mute," delivered on the floor of the Senate before the president launched a war on Iraq, Robert Byrd questioned this administration's rush to war.

But his speeches in the Senate on trade policy could have also been titled "We Stand Passively Mute." He is one of the few senators who have been consistently and strongly protesting a trade policy that ships good U.S. jobs overseas.

FORMER SENATOR FRITZ HOLLINGS

When Senator Fritz Hollings retired from the Senate, South Carolina and working people lost a strong voice. A tireless fighter against the trade deficit and proponent of American labor, my former colleague enjoyed support even from the prickly Ralph Nader, who endorsed Hollings in his last election by saying:

> Hollings is a champion of fair trade, not free trade. He has been a Senate leader in fighting to keep American jobs at home and opposing the unrestrained actions of multinational corporations that move jobs overseas in search of cheap wages and lowered environmental standards, leaving our communities in tatters and our balance of trade in deficits. As a senior member of the Commerce Committee, Sen. Hollings has fought for consumers to defend our full access to the courts to hold giant corporations accountable when they manufacture defective products that injure and destroy lives. He opposes federalization of state courts in this crucial area of state personal injury law.

Naturally, these positions did not sit well with Corporate America, but Hollings witnessed firsthand the devastation of the textile industry in his state. He knew early on that the trade imbalance was a deadly serious issue that would wound our economy and result in more poverty.

Tall, with silver hair, Fritz looked like a movie actor playing a senator. He had a booming voice and a deep Southern accent, and his speeches on the floor in opposition to the recent trade agreements were something to experience. I wish he were still in the Senate fighting the battle for American jobs.

But in a note of pleasant irony, the Republican senator who replaced Fritz Hollings has the same views on trade as Hollings. Senator Lindsey Graham is a new, strong voice in the Senate for a trade policy that demands fairness and stands up for American jobs.

MARCY KAPTUR, SANDER LEVIN, AND BERNIE SANDERS—A SENSE OF CONSCIENCE IN THE HOUSE

U.S. House members Marcy Kaptur from Ohio, Sander Levin from Michigan, and Bernie Sanders from Vermont are three members of Congress who have refused to buckle under corporate and political pressure. They have fought a relentless battle against unfair trade agreements at a time when most of their colleagues were signing on to the corporate agenda on trade.

In 1996, Congresswoman Kaptur blasted the Newt Gingrich strong-arm tactics on trade legislation. Her statement represents the type of fight that she, Levin, and Sanders, along with a few other stalwarts who refused to budge in the fight to prevent bad trade deals, conducted:

> You have an accounting to do in a higher life for the votes you will cast on this issue. Commercialism—that is what has become the basis of our foreign policy in the post–cold war world in which we are living. In fact, the words of democracy, the hope for democracy, respect for the rule of law, the dignity of working people, the promotion of a sustainable environment, those are all illusions as we stand here in this chamber this evening.

Those are tough words from Congresswoman Kaptur, who, along with Levin and Sanders, has waged the all-too-lonely fight for good jobs in our country.

In 2005, before the narrow loss on CAFTA, Sander Levin made an articulate argument against the agreement in a rare op-ed piece in *The Washington Post*:

> The opposition to CAFTA cannot be dismissed as a battle between big business and big labor. It is not about free-trade Democrats going AWOL, nor is it about Democratic leaders wanting to deliver a defeat to the president. It involves issues broader than those relating to sugar or textiles.
>
> It is about globalization.
>
> As is becoming apparent in Latin America, including Central America, the benefits of globalization are not flowing broadly to its citizens. Within Latin America, which has the worst income inequality in the world, four of the Central American nations rank among the top 10. Poverty is rampant. Middle classes are weak or practically nonexistent. . . .
>
> The goal of globalization must be to expand markets and raise living standards, not promote a race to the bottom. An essential part of this leveling up is for workers in developing countries to have the freedom to join together to have a real voice at work so they can move up the economic ladder. This is not true in Central America, where State Department and International Labor Organization (ILO) reports confirm that the basic legal framework is not in place to protect the rights of workers. . . .
>
> By condoning the infringement of workers' rights and freedoms, the Bush administration's trade agreement would provide cover for maintaining an oppressive status quo in the workplace and in society at large. The president urges a vote for CAFTA on the grounds that it will bring "stability and security" to the region. Administration officials have said that Latin American dictators will "celebrate in the streets" if CAFTA is defeated. The opposite is true. Oppressive regimes are undercut when workers join together and demand a piece of the economic action. If they do so in the workplace, they will do so in the larger society.

Then there is Congressman Bernie Sanders, an Independent and tough as nails when it comes *to expressing unpopular truths*. What I like about Congressman Sanders (a favorite to win a Senate seat in the next election) is his sense of optimism. He said in an interview before the CAFTA vote:

> There has been a tidal shift in sentiment about trade in the last couple of years. A lot of it during the Clinton administration—of course, Clinton himself put pressure on Democrats to support NAFTA. Bush puts enormous pressure on Republicans, but a lot of these folks now, the Republicans, go back to the districts in the Midwest, they see industry after industry wiped out. They see good-paying jobs gone. They see the emergence of low-paying McDonald's and Wal-Mart type jobs. And even these guys are waking up and saying, "Hey, you know what? We were sold a bill of goods. It just ain't working."

WILLIAM GREIDER SPEAKS THE UNCOMFORTABLE TRUTH

There are some things so sacrosanct in America most politicians don't want to touch them with a ten-foot pole.

Perhaps the most sacred of sacred cows is capitalism. It has become a religion. To hear the right wing tell it, Social Security is a blight on the purity of capitalism. And a national health-care system? Sacrilege!

Oh, I like capitalism. But without checks and balances, capitalism is destined to play out like a game of Monopoly. So we have rules. And we try to find ways in which to improve our country with public policy that complements our free market capitalistic system.

We need the Securities and Exchange Commission to monitor Wall Street and the Enrons, Tycos, and Arthur Andersens of the world. We need a Teddy Roosevelt to bust up a monopoly now and then. Everyone knows it. It's just not politically wise to question capitalism, profit, or greed, the Holy Trinity of Wall Street.

As the media has been consolidated and compromised by the indistinguishable tangle of big business and big government, and becomes less effective in its defense of the common citizenry, I have learned to appreciate those rare individuals who consistently challenge the powers that be. Bill Greider is one of those writers who routinely speak the uncomfortable truth.

In a 2003 essay for *The Nation*, Greider says:

> On Wall Street . . . fewer than 1 million Americans manage the money. And only a relative handful of those people make the big decisions. Collectively, they are very, very powerful. Nobody elected them, but their exalted position in American life is reflected in their incomes. . . .
>
> With a few important exceptions, the agents of capital operate with dedicated blindness to capital's collateral consequences, an indifference to the future of society even as they search for the future's returns. . . .
>
> The great contradiction—and the reason reform is possible—is that Wall Street works with other people's money, mainly the retirement savings of ordinary Americans whose values it ignores, whose common interests are often trampled. In fact, the huge fiduciary institutions holding this wealth own 60 percent of America's 1,000 largest corporations and yet are utterly passive as investors—meekly following the advice of banks and brokerages rather than asserting the true self-interests of the "beneficial owners." That is a central element of all that must be changed.
>
> A transformation of Wall Street's core values is not only possible but eventually likely to occur, I predict. . . .
>
> Organized labor is widely disparaged as a weak and anachronistic force in American life, but, in one important matter, the labor movement is the vanguard: determined to reposition the capital that effectively belongs to working Americans to serve the true interests of those workers and, therefore, society's long-term interests too. Labor may be greatly weakened from its heyday, but

one thing it possesses is capital assets—the power of the $400 billion in union-managed pension funds and the trillions in public-employee pension funds, where labor unions can exercise real influence over the patterns of investment.

William Greider invigorates me. Not just because he so accurately pinpoints cracks in our democracy but more so because he offers hope, and hope seems to be in short supply these days.

JIM HIGHTOWER: "SPEAK THE TRUTH BUT RIDE A FAST HORSE"

Jim Hightower is an author, radio host, staunch government critic, former state commissioner of agriculture, and the best thing to come out of Texas since Willie Nelson. Like his Lone Star State contemporary Molly Ivins, Hightower is an expert at pointing out the absurdity of conservative politics—not that Democrats haven't felt his wrath from time to time, too. I especially appreciate that Hightower is one of those rare commentators who understand agriculture and its importance to this nation's security and well-being.

Hightower says he abides by an old Texas mantra, "Speak the truth, but ride a fast horse." He's only half-kidding.

In one of his syndicated columns, he blasted Treasury Secretary John Snow:

In 2004, the American economy bought $600 billion more in products from foreign countries—especially China—than we sold to them. This is the exact opposite of a good business plan. Yet, Snow, apparently snorting a noseful of intergalactic dust, proclaimed that this Grand Canyon of a trade gap "reflects the fact that Americans are becoming more prosperous," thus buying more foreign products. More prosperous? Hey, you Bushites are waving our middle-class manufacturing and high-tech jobs offshore, and American wages are not even keeping up with the cost of living, at the same time that your disastrous borrow-and-spend economic policies are sinking us into an unfathomable sea of federal debt. Just the interest on that debt now costs every American man, woman, and child $333 a year. This is prosperity?

As is typical of Bush and the people he puts around him, Snow blames others for the rising trade imbalance. He whines that the Europeans and Japanese are at fault because they don't buy enough American products. So his "solution" is to plead with foreign governments to change their economic policies to fit our needs. Hellooooo, Johnnie—they're our competitors. We're supposed to outdo them, not whimper at them. It's not exactly in the can-do spirit of America for our team leaders to be begging the other team to spot us some points. To bridge the trade gap, our leaders must start investing again in American workers, farmers, and entrepreneurs, restoring our grassroots competitive strength.

THE WISDOM OF WARREN BUFFETT

Like all things in great quantity, great wealth can build or destroy. A large amount of wealth and power creates the opportunity for bigger mistakes. And it can also create a bully pulpit for those willing to say what others fear to say.

One of America's business icons lives quietly in Omaha, Nebraska. He is listed as the world's second-richest man. But you'd never know it by visiting with him.

I admire Warren Buffett for a lot of reasons. While he is probably our country's most successful investor, he also has a disarming way of telling our country the truth as he sees it. He is both a patriot and a humanist. One of his goals is to minimize the nuclear and biochemical threat against this nation. But he has been a savvy observer and a strong critic of America's flawed trade strategy and fiscal policy as well.

During an interview on CNN with Lou Dobbs in 2005, he said:

We had, you know, 618-billion-dollar trade deficit last year, and it's already grown a little bit this year. The standard line is, it can't go on forever, but no one seems to give an answer of what is going to be done about it. We exported $1.1 trillion last year, and we imported over $1.7 trillion. We are running up obligations to the rest of the world, and they are buying our assets at the rate of almost $2 billion a day. And that will have consequences.

He added, "If we keep doing what we're doing—and we have shown no signs of slowing down—the world will own a substantially greater percentage of this country."

I greatly admire the fact that as an extremely wealthy man, he remains engaged, in the public policy debates. Not in a way that reflects his self-interest, but rather in a way that reflects the concern about his fellowman. And he is also refreshingly honest about his largesse, as evidenced by this exchange in that 2005 CNN interview about Social Security reform:

BUFFETT: I personally would increase the taxable base above the present $90,000. I pay very little in the way of Social Security taxes because I make a lot more than $90,000. And the people in my office pay the full tax. We're already edging up the retirement age a bit. And I would means test . . . I get a check for $1,700 or $1,900 or something every month. I'm 74. And I cash it. But I'll eat without it.

DOBBS: You will eat without it. So will literally more than a million other Americans, as well. Means testing, the idea of raising taxes, the payroll tax. In 1983, Alan Greenspan, the Fed chairman, he had a very simple idea: raise taxes. That's what you're saying here.

BUFFETT: Sure. But I wouldn't raise the 12-point and a fraction payroll tax. I would raise the taxable base to above $90,000.

DOBBS: That's a progressive idea. In other words, the rich people would pay more?

BUFFETT: Yeah. The rich people are doing so well in this country. I mean, we never had it so good.

DOBBS: What a radical idea.

BUFFETT: It's class warfare, my class is winning, but they shouldn't be.

DOBBS: Exactly. Your class, as you put it, is winning . . .

BUFFETT: The rich are winning. Just take the estate tax, less than 2 percent of all estates pay any tax. A couple million people die every year, 40,000 or so estates get taxed. We raise, what, $30 billion from the estate tax. And, you know, I would like to hear the congressman say where they are going to get the $30 billion from if they don't get it from the estate tax. It's nice to say, you know, wipe out this tax, but we're running a huge deficit, so who does the $30 billion come from?

Imagine, a man willing to vote against his own economic interest as a simple matter of conscience. That's why I am proud to list Warren Buffett as one of my heroes.

THE BARK AND BITE OF RALPH NADER

I know . . . I know . . . He's pretty well worn out his welcome with me, too. But since he burst into public consciousness in the midsixties with his seminal wake-up call about the automobile industry's disregard for passenger safety, *Unsafe at Any Speed,* Ralph Nader has remained a burr under the saddle of unscrupulous big business and a hero to many Americans. And early on he fought against the trade policies that have led us into this box canyon.

As I compiled my list of heroes for this chapter, closer examination of Ralph Nader's views on global trade found me nodding in agreement. Nader says, "There have to be some agreements (like the WTO) dealing with tariff barriers and other issues that really interfere with authentic comparative advantage. And by that, I don't mean dictatorially repressed costs such as in China or Indonesia, where global corporations go in the name of free trade, but there's no free trade because the workers can't organize and there's no market-determined cost. It's all dictatorial, repressed costs."

I agree!

Unfortunately, Ralph's two bizarre presidential campaigns in 2000 and 2004 have rubbed some of the shine off some major accomplishments. Sure, everybody has a right to run for president. But by his race in 2000 he ended up electing George W. Bush. Ralph knew that could happen, and, for his own selfish reasons, ignored the potential consequences of it. Maybe Ralph doesn't think it matters that he gave us George W. Bush, but I do.

But still, that lack of judgment aside, Nader has been a visionary in his canny understanding of the ramifications of unmanaged global trade and by his support of workers of the world. Today, there is growing recognition of the problem—and the intent of this book is to broaden that awareness—but Nader has long been ahead of the curve.

By 1996, just two years after it was signed, Nader said:

NAFTA has turned out worse than we predicted.

1. Nobody predicted that the U.S. government would have to have a package of $50 billion to bail out the crooked Mexican government regime and its billionaire oligarchs.
2. NAFTA promised us more jobs. We've lost almost 400,000 jobs because we now have moved from a trade surplus in Mexico to probably a $10 billion trade deficit. . . .
3. It's turned out badly for most of the Mexican people; they're poorer, there are more unemployed and they are ravaged by a vicious inflation.
4. The borders are a nightmare; more smuggling, more pollution, more infectious diseases. The environmental commissions are toothless.

Vintage Ralph Nader. Those were the days.

TIME FOR A CHANGE

The selection of the heroes who have bucked the tide and who keep fighting for sensible policies that will strengthen our country could have filled much more space. There are many remarkable people who have had the courage to stand up against policies that trade away American jobs.

As for the politicians who have created the policies that are the subject of this book, there are plenty of heroes and even more goats. But it is important for people to understand there is a difference between the two parties on this subject.

Many middle-class Americans voted for the Republican party, which has led the way for the corporate agenda to outsource jobs, cut overtime pay, cut veterans benefits, refused to raise the minimum wage, tried to cut Social Security, let Big Energy and Big Pharma run roughshod over consumers, and forced more of a hidden tax burden on everyone but the wealthy!

It's time for a change. The Republicans have been clever and relentless in branding their politics. I can use just nine words to describe what nearly every one of them claims their party stands for—"Less government, lower taxes, strong defense, and family values."

That's what they say they are for.

That's not the way they govern.

For example, if you track the Bush administration record (and the record of the Republican-controlled Congress) they stand for big federal deficits, outsourcing of jobs, more pollution, and tax cuts for the wealthy. Put that on a bumper sticker.

But the Republicans don't want to talk about those issues. They prefer raising the issues of gay marriage and flag burning as close to the election as possible to convince people not to pay much attention to the many issues that affect their daily lives.

In this book, I have made the case that every American should be outraged about the export of American jobs and the growing trade deficit. And the American people should hold politicians and corporations accountable for what they are doing. I'm talking about politicians from both parties. If they are wrong on jobs, they are on the wrong side of how to build a better country.

I have outlined many concerns in this book about trade and jobs. In the final chapter, I will offer solutions inspired by the heroes described in this chapter, solutions that value work and will strengthen our country.

TWELVE

FLAT WORLD? NO, FLAT WRONG!
HERE'S HOW WE FIX IT

*T*HE WORLD IS FLAT—THAT'S THE TITLE TOM FRIED-
man's bestselling book trumpets from the bookstore shelves.
With all due respect, that's just flat wrong!

The world isn't flat. Our trade agreements aren't fair. And outsourcing American jobs hurts our country.

It can't be denied—the world is becoming smaller. Breathtaking
changes in communications and technology have given us a world with
instant access to information about what is happening in all of the rest
of the world. So the world is shrinking in both time and distance. But
"it ain't flat"!

In his book, Friedman looks at Bangalore, India, and marvels that
technology allows American companies to hire engineers in India for a
fraction of the cost of an American engineer. He sees China as the in-
heritor of low-cost manufacturing opportunities because it has an
abundance of workers willing to work for very low wages. Similarly he
describes Indonesia, Vietnam, and others as countries that are becoming "manufacturing platforms," and he describes as inevitable that textile, manufacturing, technology, accounting, and finance jobs will
migrate to these countries.

He sees the opportunity to transfer both capital and technology to nearly any spot on the globe as an incentive and a benefit to corporations who seek to lower production costs. And he describes it as a boon to the consumers who reap the benefit of lower prices on the products they buy.

But there is bare mention in his book to describe how his flat world is destroying work standards and wages that we have fought for in this country for the past century. There is no real discussion about what it all means to American workers.

Well into his book, Friedman finally points out: "Critics of China's business practices say that its size and economic power mean that it will soon be setting the global floor not only for low wages but also for lax labor laws and workplace standards." But he then dismisses those concerns by saying "that is just a short-term strategy."

Short-term? Well, I've got news for him. The so-called short term for China can be decades, or even centuries. In the meantime, our jobs are gone, and the wages, labor standards, and other descriptions of fair work rules coming from their communist Chinese government are setting the standard of what U.S. companies expect when they move their jobs offshore.

Friedman describes it as a competition. But it is truly a race to the bottom.

I don't see that as a "flat" world. I see it as a world tilted in favor of the largest corporations. Minimum wages, the right to organize, the requirement to have a safe workplace, child-labor laws, environmental standards . . . all of these have improved life in our country and represent progress that has improved the standard of living for the American people. In Friedman's flat world, these rights are in full-scale retreat. Instead of honestly trying to pull other countries up, we are being set up to diminish our standards here at home in order to compete in the global economy.

The January 2006 announcement by Ford Motor Company that their plan for the future is to cut thirty thousand jobs and to close fourteen manufacturing plants in the United States in the next six years is just the latest in a string of announcements by large American companies that they are cutting jobs to meet the competition. The Ford announcement mirrors one made by General Motors just months before.

The same week of the Ford announcement, the Auto Show was going on in Detroit and a Chinese car company named Geely announced that it would begin exporting Chinese cars to the U.S. market by 2007 that will sell for less than $10,000.

When those cars hit our shores they will be subject to a $2^1/2$ percent tariff. On the other hand, when a U.S. auto company tries to ship a car to sell in China, it will be charged a 25 percent tariff by the Chinese government. Unfair, you say. Damn right it is. And our U.S. trade negotiators agreed to it. Flat world? Nonsense. This sort of thing is just flat crazy.

I do know something that's flat: American wages. And job opportunities for American workers.

My differences with Tom Friedman are that I believe our country has a right, even in a global marketplace, to determine the kind of economy and future it wants for itself. We can decide that trade is beneficial and set conditions for the kind of trade that we believe will fit the type of economy and standards we have set for our people and our marketplace.

A country also has a right to establish a reasonable admission price for entry into its marketplace. And that admission price can require a country to develop labor and environmental standards that lift their country up as a condition for being allowed to sell in our marketplace. We have a right to do that. The question is, do we have the will?

Fast-forward ten to twenty years and think about where this all leads if we continue down this path. The gains we made in the United States that have made our country great have, in large part, been made over the opposition of major corporations. On nearly every issue, from fair labor standards, to the minimum wage, to environmental standards, to standards for a safe workplace, corporations have fought against them every step of the way.

Do you really think that U.S. corporations that have moved their production to foreign countries are going to be part of a movement there to increase the regulations and standards that they opposed here at home? Of course not! They view regulations as antibusiness. Regulations increase the cost of production, they argue.

Here is a perfect example of the way that works. In November 2005, Philippine president Gloria Arroyo announced that raising the minimum wage in her country "was the right thing to do." According to Bloomberg News, the Carrier Corporation immediately said that if the Philippine government increased the minimum wage across the board, they would move their jobs to China. (Workers in the Philippines are paid between $3 and $5 a day and one-third of the 86 million people there live on less than sixty cents a day.) So, if American corporations leave the United States in search of cheap foreign labor, and then threaten foreign governments they will leave if they improve working conditions for their people, how is this strategy going to pull up the standards in other countries? The answer is, it won't.

Unless changed, we face a future of more and more U.S. jobs moved offshore and products produced under conditions we would not allow here at home. We will see relentless downward pressure on wages and benefits for jobs here in the United States. The pressure to compete on prices of products made with rock-bottom wages in China and other low-wage countries will persuade American corporations to continue stripping away pension programs and chipping away at the security for the jobs that remain here at home.

I don't believe this leads to a future of growth and opportunity for our country. I think it leads to lower growth, fewer jobs, and less opportunity here at home.

I know I've painted a pretty grim picture in this book of corporate greed, political incompetence, and a chorus of ignorance that has undermined America's ability to make progress. I haven't pulled punches. That is the way I see it, and it isn't pretty.

But through it all, I still have a deep reservoir of hope about the future.

This is a county filled with a basic goodness. People want to do the right thing.

That is what causes such turmoil when citizens see their government veering off track. Oh, they have the patience to wait for a while to see if something will work. But if it doesn't, they will grab the American steering wheel and change direction.

The inescapable conclusion I have reached while researching and writing this book is that unless trade enhances the lives of common people, it is a failure. That's what all the fuss is about as workers here and abroad protest the policies of megacorporations and the governments that allow the exploitation. Trade isn't about numbers on a spreadsheet. It's about people. When a job is lost in America that is a real person with a family to support. When a worker is exploited in China, literally worked to death, it is more than a statistic. When a five-year-old child becomes a slave, weaving exotic rugs locked in a warehouse in Asia for blithely unaware Americans, it is a sin by anyone's standard.

Now, it is in vogue in America today for economists, politicians, and CEOs gleefully to project a brave new world of wonders to come as a result of global trade.

It's easy to get confused in the abstract, but silently and insidiously, real American jobs are being lost because companies and workers cannot compete on the tilted playing field of international commerce. Sure, we hear about the big layoffs, but when twenty-five jobs are lost here, and fifty there, it doesn't make headlines. But it is happening every day. And unless we wake up, it is going to get worse.

MANAGING TRADE FOR OUR BENEFIT!

Before I go any further, let's make sure our steel-toed work boots are firmly grounded in reality. Global trade is going to continue. We couldn't stop it if we wanted to. And I don't want to. What I do want to do is bring an element of reason and compassion to our trade policies. We have to begin managing trade for our benefit.

First, let's start by rejecting the propaganda that our current trade strategy is strengthening our country. It's not true. In fact, it is weakening our nation.

Do you remember the story about Mark Twain traveling from Hannibal, Missouri, to Virginia City, Nevada? It's reported he wrote back to his friends in Missouri, and said, "You'll never guess what I've found down here in Nevada. Why there is drinking going on . . . there are wild women . . . and there is gambling. This is certainly no place for a Presbyterian . . . And I did not long remain one!"

I see some of that in the U.S. Congress these days. Oh, it's not women or drinking. It's the gambling . . . betting on our country's future with this radical, wrongheaded economic strategy.

Now, you might think I have teed off on some Republicans in this book. Good. You were paying attention. But I know that in our political system, one party is not all bad and another party all good. We have two grand political parties, and both have contributed to the building of our country.

The thing is, right now the Republicans are in complete control. They're the ones responsible for these policies. And I believe these policies are hurting our country. So when Republicans complain about the direction of the country, I say, "Hey, you're driving!"

Republicans used to be recognizable by their flinty serious look . . . the grey suits and wire-rimmed glasses gave them that conservative appearance as if they had just swallowed a lemon. And they used to live up to their name. They could always be counted on to demand balanced budgets, and they reacted to deficits and debt like a bad rash. I miss those Republicans. I embrace fiscal responsibility, but I'm feeling as lonely as the Maytag repairman these days.

It's a new crowd in Congress, and it's like we've played musical chairs. "Deficits don't matter," Dick Cheney says. Budget deficits and trade deficits ($1.2 trillion in 2004 and about the same in 2005) don't even make them blink. Oh, how times have changed. A friend and I were talking about the financial train wreck being engineered by the Republicans one day, and as we were discussing the need for fiscal discipline, he said, "You know, I would join the Republican party . . . if I could find it."

It's clear to me that America is off track. And few in positions to do something about it seem to care. The theology of so-called free trade, pumped up and supported by the corporate beneficiaries with cheer-leading by the major news organizations, has made a thoughtful debate about it almost impossible.

The Washington Post and *The New York Times* relentlessly push the message of free trade on their editorial pages, and seldom allow an alternative voice on their op-ed pages. Still, even though these papers are full of propaganda by the missionaries for free trade, one would think that as time moves on, all the evidence of the failure of this strategy might produce a change in tone and message. Wrong! Could those who are pushing this strategy of shipping U.S. jobs overseas be "under the influence"? Sure. But it is not moonshine. It is the influence of Corporate America. They are the creators of this strategy because it is good for them even if it isn't good for their country. Any great sales pitch will tell you what's good for you, but the question to ask is what's in it for the seller. Consider the source.

From time to time, I've entertained the thought that maybe I'm the one who is wrong about all of this. Maybe this is a road paved with gold. Maybe it will all work out for the better. But facts keep getting in the way. We are running a trade deficit of over $700 billion a year, the biggest in the history of the world. We've lost over 3 million jobs that have been moved overseas in just the past five years.

The Bank of Korea holds $200 billion of our currency.

The Bank of Japan holds $800 billion of our currency.

The Chinese hold $750 billion of our currency.

Taiwan holds $250 billion of our currency.

These Asian countries are our largest creditors financing our trade deficit. And I haven't even mentioned the Europeans, Canadians, Mexicans, and the growing list of countries with which we have bloated trade deficits. They, too, along with the Asian banks own more and more of America every day

The world is changing, and we have to change with it, the pundits say. We shouldn't expect to continue to live forever as an Island of Plenty in a Sea of Poverty. You can't say that and get elected, but that is the premise behind the strategy of this administration and their corporate backers.

It is true things are changing. But there are some things that remain the same. We share this planet with 6 billion neighbors. And many live in poverty. One-half of the earth's population has never made a phone call. (Of course, if we give them all phones, the first call they get will be from a telemarketer.) One-half of the people live on less than $2 a day.

And somehow, we ended up living on this unique spot on the planet called the United States of America. And there's only one spot like it. We are living with the greatest opportunities on earth. We shouldn't be ashamed that we've done so well. We built this place—we built something special here. We accomplished what we have with hard work, by taking risks, and, finally, by doing the right thing.

So let's reach out and help pull others up. But it makes little sense to build up our neighbor's house with bricks from ours.

Consider: What was it that made our place on this earth so special in the first place? We created an environment where effort, risk, and reward were related. It was a place where everyone could go to school and be whatever their God-given talents allowed them to be. From this fertile ground, amazing things sprouted. Our country made breathtaking progress in so many areas. We split the atom, spliced genes, invented the silicon chip, the computer, the telephone, television, cured polio and smallpox, built airplanes and learned to fly them, built rockets and walked on the moon.

But the greatest accomplishment is what we did for humanity. Democracy could never have flourished if Americans had not had the vast opportunities of a thriving, fair marketplace. But more than that, we also decided that freedom meant people had rights. That applied to all people. *Workers* had rights—the right to bargain collectively, the right to work in a safe workplace, the right to a fair wage—the right to live and work in dignity.

And from those lofty ideals sprang forth the world's strongest economy.

When I arrived in the U.S. Congress in 1981, the oldest congressman there was a man named Claude Pepper from Florida. I went to his office one day to meet him. At the time, Representative Pepper was in his eighties and his office was a museum of collectables from his career. However, I was most struck by two framed photographs behind his desk. The first was a photo of the Wright Brothers' first airplane flight December 17, 1903. It was autographed on the bottom to Congressman Pepper "With admiration to Claude Pepper." It was signed by Orville Wright. Just below it was a photograph of Neil Armstrong stepping on the surface of the moon July 20, 1969. It, too, was autographed to Congressman Pepper. Claude had met the first person to fly and the first person to walk on the moon. What a distance in one man's lifetime!

I thought about what those two photographs represented . . . what our country had achieved in a relatively short time. Those two pictures on the wall were only six inches apart. But they measured a remarkable distance traveled in the growth of knowledge and quality of life.

MANUFACTURING MATTERS . . .

As America grew into the world's preeminent economic power, its economic engine combined a foundation of manufacturing innovation and capacity that was unparalleled.

These days, as our manufacturing jobs are shipped overseas, the popular refrain by the free traders is that manufacturing doesn't matter all that much. Oh really? Maybe a little history would help.

At Tehran, Iran, late in 1943 Joseph Stalin from the Soviet Union proposed a toast: "To American production, without which this war would have been lost." Now, you won't often find me invoking Stalin, but he was right on this count. By 1942, things did not look good for the Allies. German and Japanese forces had destroyed over sixteen hundred ships with Japanese and German air power and the German wolf pack submarines.

It was at that time that industrialist Henry J. Kaiser, at age sixty, having just acquired shipyards on the West Coast, began to introduce new techniques in shipbuilding that would allow mass production of shipping. William Manchester's *The Glory and the Dream* describes one of the greatest productive feats in American history: "From an initial keel-to-delivery time of over two hundred days, he cut the average work time on a liberty ship to forty days . . . In 1944 he was launching a new escort aircraft carrier every week . . . and they were turning out entire cargo ships in seventeen days . . . During the first 212 days of 1945 they completed 247 of these, better than one a day."

Henry J. Kaiser's revolutionary manufacturing and fabricating techniques, combined with a workforce that for the first time included "Rosie the Riveter," resulted in the unparalleled mass production of ships and planes that truly saved democracy.

When American workers turned their attention to building airplanes, they created production lines in the factories that were nearly unbelievable in their ability to mass-produce new airplanes.

Here is the way Manchester put it in his book:

On May 10, 1940, when the Wehrmacht burst through the Lowlands and the Ardennes, its historic blitzkrieg was supported by the 3,034 aircraft, 2,580 tanks, 10,000 artillery pieces, and 4,000 trucks.

In the five years following the French collapse, America turned out:

Warplanes	296,429
Tanks	102,351
Artillery Pieces	372,431
Trucks	2,455,964
Warships	8,762
Cargo ships	5,425

And that is why Stalin said that without American production "this war would have been lost." So, is manufacturing important? Ask the World War II veterans who saw the tanks, the planes, and the ships—the might of American manufacturing—on the battlefield and sailing the high seas.

There is no greater illustration that a strong manufacturing base is not just the foundation of good jobs, good wages, and the foundation of our middle class. It is an essential part of this country's national security.

Amidst the clamor about terrorism and homeland security, we have not seen the forest for the trees. By addressing trade and outsourcing, we can shore up both our economy and national security. When we outsource the manufacturing of components critical to our military technology, we not only lose jobs, we weaken our national security and preparedness. But when we take steps to keep that manufacturing here at home, we keep our jobs here and invest in our security. It is astonishing to me that with all the brainpower in Washington, D.C., no one seems to have grasped this crucial fact.

Instead, our country is in danger of having the world's strongest manufacturing and industrial base destroyed. And no one seems to think it matters much. I believe it is urgent that we take action to protect our economic interests. There, I said it. The four-letter word (well, seven actually) of trade—*protect*.

The free traders have so co-opted the language of trade that it is considered inappropriate to use the word "protect" when discussing our interests in trade. It's not really four letters—I was using "fuzzy math"—but it is still regarded as a dirty word in the arena of trade. So, let me plead guilty to wanting to protect U.S. economic interests. And shame on those who don't.

A CHANGE IN DIRECTION . . .

So what do we do now? What next? What can we do besides complain? Plenty! The first step is to awaken from our deep sleep and decide that when you are trading away your jobs and your economic strength, you have to find a way to change course.

This book is the result of my passion to awaken America to this crisis. It is easy to become distracted by the barrage of diverse conflicting information. It is easy to file our concerns in the back of our minds as we run faster and faster on our treadmills, trying to keep up without considering why we are working harder and falling farther behind.

But it is not hopeless. We can change policies and turn things around here in our country. We can start protecting our own economic interests even as we reach out to help others. But it will require that we take our country back from those economic interests that now pull the strings and call the shots.

Here are the strategies that I am pushing to do just that. Will I be successful? I don't know. But, if the American people rise up as one and demand change, we can make it happen. All the power in America is in the power of one, one person casting one vote on one day. That's how *We the People* get change and reform.

So, here's a long menu of what we have to do to take our country back and start building opportunity once again.

1. Develop an American Fair Trade Plan
2. Merge the seventeen federal agencies that deal with trade into one Federal Trade Department
3. Make an assessment of the national security implications of trade
4. Eliminate our trade deficit through a plan of Import Certificates
5. Repeal the tax break for exporting jobs
6. Prohibit imports from companies that abuse overseas workers
7. Set a ceiling on trade deficits
8. Make Normal Trade Relations (NTR) with China a year-to-year decision rather than a permanent condition
9. Encourage stronger labor unions
10. Tackle health-care costs and education excellence
11. Put the brakes on outsourced pollution

A great strength of America's political system is the peaceful transfer of power through regular elections. The reins pass from Democrats to Republicans (and hopefully back again soon!) without riots, coups, and anarchy. Yet this system also has drawbacks. One party may be heading the country in a particular direction, but in one or two elections, all that can change. As I have said earlier, many American politicians are shortsighted—planning from election to election—while international corporations can be even more shortsighted, living from quarter to quarter. None of this is good in the long run.

Still, I believe there is enough common ground on some issues that members of opposing parties, business and labor leaders alike, can stand together and plan for the long-term welfare of the country—a plan that transcends elections and quarterly reports.

America needs a long-term, consistent trade policy that demands fair trade and reflects our national interest.

Create a Fair Trade Plan

I propose we form a National Emergency Commission on Trade comprised of members from both major political parties as well as top labor and business leaders to develop a Fair Trade Plan. Its charter would be to set long-term goals for trade and develop a new strategy that would emphasize "fair trade."

On my wish list would be goals to balance trade deficits, address worker wages and conditions here and abroad, secure our infrastructure, and seek ways to encourage companies to employ Americans and provide affordable health care and retirement benefits. Compromises would need to be made, but I believe that with thoughtful planning we can develop a long-term plan that lifts us out of this hole. I also believe if we put our minds to it, we can develop an approach that is flexible enough to react to changing economic and political pressures yet provides a vision and a plan for the future—which we do not have now.

Make no mistake, there is an economic struggle going on in this country and across the globe in which we all have a stake. Yet we have no plan, no strategy. We're too damn busy living in the now to think about the welfare of the country. And our children will suffer for our selfishness.

Let me draw an analogy to WWII. Though there were many Allies united in a common cause, it required a Supreme Commander, Dwight D. Eisenhower, to organize and manage the distractions, disputes, and overall military effort. He succeeded because the Allied political leaders were able to compromise when they needed to, and the goal was clear. That goal did not change when FDR died, and it would not have changed had a Republican been elected in 1944. We had a mission. We were all in it together.

We still are. And though bullets aren't flying on the trade front, there are human casualties. Today, we glorify CEOs for actions that weaken our country because the bottom line looks good. They are rewarded on Wall Street with higher stock prices. But in another time, they would have been exposed for injuring our country. If we flounder economically, we flounder militarily, and if America sinks, so do her ideals for freedom and human rights. Yes, it's business, all right. But it is serious business, and if we ignore this challenge, our future as a nation will be grim indeed.

Merge the Seventeen Federal Agencies That Deal with Trade into One Department of Trade

We now have seventeen federal agencies that have their hands in trade policy. That makes no sense.

The Commerce Department, for example, is supposed to be facilitating trade and at the same time it is supposed to enforce trade agreements. Of course it does little to enforce agreements. It's too busy trying to encourage trade. So our country signs new trade agreement with countries like China, and then no one cares whether China complies with the conditions of the agreement.

We have a dangerous and growing trade deficit with China of over $200 billion a year, and yet in the U.S. Commerce Department there are only twenty-three people whose job it is to enforce our trade agreements with China. And we have a huge trade deficit with Japan and there are only eleven people whose job it is to make sure that Japan is complying with our trade agreements. It shows how little interest there is in the U.S. government about standing up for our interests and requiring our trade partners to do what they promised.

The U.S. Trade Ambassador's Office is out making new trade deals. And a dozen more agencies have their hands on trade matters. Some are selling, some are cheerleading, some are enforcing (not much), and some are just ruminating. In many cases they not only have no coordination, but they actually work at cross-purposes. Is it too much to ask that our country have a plan? One that we all work toward.

The only way that is going to happen is if we consolidate all trade issues in one Department of Trade that will follow the plan we develop to get our country out of this deep hole.

Make a Comprehensive Study of the National Security Implications of Trade

Here is where I believe both political parties have common ground. Despite the rhetoric and demagoguery we hear from talk-show mavens, both Republicans and Democrats support the concept of a strong national defense. Senator Joseph Lieberman, D-CT, has sounded the alarm over the flight of high-tech manufacturing to other countries. It is a vital concern, for it is America's technology that has been the key to making us the world's greatest military and economic power. There are constant worries that the selling of cutting-edge technology to other countries and the outsourcing of the production of critical components of military weapons to other countries can have a negative impact on our national security.

Ultraconservative Republican Oliver North grouses:

> Ever since the Global War on Terror began in 2001, one of the key weapons in the U.S. arsenal has been the Joint Direct Attack Munition (JDAM)—the remarkably accurate high-altitude, guided

bomb that allows a precision attack on a specific target with minimum chance of collateral damage.

Thousands of JDAMs have been used in Afghanistan and Iraq over the course of the last three years. Some of the Special Operations troops who participated in Operation Enduring Freedom maintain that the Taliban might still control Kabul if it weren't for the JDAMs delivered in support of their ground campaign. . . .

Unfortunately, a crucial component of the JDAM was manufactured by a Swiss company, Micro Crystal. Because the Swiss opposed the war in Iraq, the government in Berne ordered the company to stop shipment of any more JDAM elements. It took several months for the Defense Department to find alternative sources for the critical parts.

One might hope that the "international" experience with the JDAM would have been instructive to the Pentagon's procurement wizards; but apparently not.

. . . the Defense Department awarded a $6 billion contract to a consortium lead [*sic*] by Lockheed Martin to build a new Aerial Common Sensor (ACS) reconnaissance aircraft for the Army and Navy.

By the way, the airplane the consortium will use will be a Brazilian Embraer design with major parts of the plane built in Brazil and Chile.

Now, I would say Joe Lieberman and Oliver North are a good distance apart on the political spectrum, but both see some serious problems from the private and military sector when it comes to outsourcing and the transfer of key technologies. That ought to concern us all. These examples are just the tip of the iceberg. According to the Center for Public Integrity, "While most of the top seven hundred contractors were American corporations, nearly 100 were foreign-owned."

I wonder what message it sends to the troops when our leaders need to outsource the weaponry. Check the sidearm of a military man. It's a Beretta. Italian-made.

I believe our Department of Homeland Security must, as part of its mission, do a comprehensive inventory of key industries vital to our national security—certainly food supply and the energy, technology, and manufacturing base must be a focus. And we must review what additional protections are necessary to defend our national interests.

Balance Our Trade Through a Plan of Import Certificates

The plan that I believe we should employ to tackle these dangerous trade deficits and stop the wholesale export of American jobs is one offered by Warren Buffett. He is a wealthy man, but he is so much more than that. Warren Buffett is one of our nation's original and creative thinkers, and someone with the credibility to be taken seriously.

So, when he calls our growing trade deficit and, the demise of our manufacturing sector dangerous, it is important to take note.

The proposal he has advanced is simple, fair, and, more important, would work. It is a proposal that would lead to balanced trade and would, more than anything that has been done previously, finally force open foreign markets.

Here is the Buffett proposal in summary. It would achieve balanced trade by issuing Import Certificates (ICs) to U.S. exporters in the amount equal to the dollar value of their exports. Each exporter would be able to sell the ICs to others in their country who want to import goods into our country, or they might sell the ICs to exporters from other countries who wish to ship into the U.S. market. Here is the way Warren Buffett describes his plan:

> To import $1 million of goods, for example, an importer would need ICs that were the byproduct [*sic*] of $1 million of exports. The inevitable result: trade balance.
>
> Because our exports total about $80 billion a month, ICs would

be issued in huge, equivalent quantities—that is, $80 billion certificates a month—and would surely trade in an exceptionally liquid market. Competition would then determine who among those parties wanting to sell to us would buy the certificates and how much they would pay. (I visualize that the certificates would be issued with a short life, possibly of six months, so that speculators would be discouraged from accumulating them).

For illustrative purposes, let's postulate that each IC would sell for 10 cents—that is, 10 cents per dollar of exports behind them. Other things being equal, this amount would mean a U.S. producer could realize 10% more by selling goods in the export market than by selling them domestically, with the extra 10% coming from his sale of ICs.

In my opinion, many exporters would view this as a reduction in cost, one that would let them cut the prices of their products in international markets. Commodity-type products would particularly encourage this kind of behavior. If aluminum, for example, was selling for 66 cents per pound domestically and ICs were worth 10%, domestic aluminum producers could sell for about 60 cents per pound plus transportation costs in foreign markets and earn normal margins. In this scenario, the output of the U.S. would become significantly more competitive and exports would expand. Along the way, the number of jobs would grow.

Foreigners selling to us, of course, would face tougher economics. But that's a problem they're up against no matter what trade "solution" is adopted—and make no mistake, a solution must come. (As Herb Stein said, "if something cannot go on forever, it will stop.") In one way the IC approach would give countries selling to us great flexibility, since the plan does not penalize any specific industry or product. In the end, the free market would determine what would be sold in the U.S. and who would sell it. The ICs would determine only the aggregate dollar volume of what was sold.

To see what would happen to imports, let's look at a car now entering the U.S. at a cost to the importer of $20,000. Under the new plan and the assumption that the ICs sell for 10%, the importer's cost would rise to $22,000. If demand for the car was exceptionally strong, the importer might manage to pass all of this on to the American consumer. In the usual case, however, competitive forces would take hold, requiring the foreign manufacturer to absorb some, if not all, of the $2,000 IC cost. . . .

I believe that ICs would produce, rather promptly, a U.S. trade equilibrium well above present export levels but below present import levels. The certificates would moderately aid all our industries in world competition, even as the free market determined which of them ultimately met the test of "comparative advantage." . . .

Would this start another Smoot-Hawley tariff war? Hardly. At the time of Smoot-Hawley we ran an unreasonable trade surplus that we wished to maintain. We now run a damaging deficit that the whole world knows we must correct.

For decades the world has struggled with a shifting maze of punitive tariffs, export subsidies, quotas, dollar-locked currencies, and the like. Many of these import-inhibiting and export-encouraging devices have long been employed by major exporting countries trying to amass ever larger surpluses—yet significant trade wars have not erupted. Surely one will not be precipitated by a proposal that simply aims at balancing the books of the world's largest trade debtor. Major exporting countries have behaved quite rationally in the past and they will continue to do so—though, as always, it may be in their interest to attempt to convince us that they will behave otherwise.

I have quoted Warren Buffett extensively about his plan because it's his idea. It is new, fresh, and interesting. And I support it. His point is not that we must have a neutral trade balance with every country. But rather, it is in the aggregate that we must strive to have a balance in our trade when we measure it against all of the countries with whom we trade. This type of plan would have to be phased in over a certain time, but it can be done and would put us back on track toward balanced trade.

I know the trade purists will have a seizure over this. (And that will be good for the pharmaceutical industry.) Trade purists don't think that the notion of "balanced" trade is particularly important.

And in any event, the strategy to get to some kind of balance requires that trade be "managed." The concept of managed trade is something we should know about because most of our trading partners practice some kind of managed trade. In other words, they set goals and manage toward those goals. It is exactly what the free traders adamantly oppose.

Probably the best way to describe the importance of the current imbalance of our trade and the burden of our record trade deficits is to turn again to Warren Buffett. He describes it in a story about two isolated islands of equal size called Thriftville and Squanderville. Warren's simple and clever description is a useful primer to understand the consequences of all of this. Here's how he describes it:

> Land is the only capital asset on these islands [Squanderville and Thriftville], and their communities are primitive, needing only food and producing only food. Working eight hours a day, in fact, each inhabitant can produce enough food to sustain himself or herself. And for a long time that's how things go along. On each island everybody works the prescribed eight hours a day, which means that each society is self-sufficient.
>
> Eventually, though, the industrious citizens of Thriftville decide to do some serious saving and investing, and they start to work 16 hours a day. In this mode they continue to live off the food they produce in eight hours of work but begin exporting an equal amount to their one and only trading outlet, Squanderville.
>
> The citizens of Squanderville are ecstatic about this turn of events, since they can now live their lives free from toil, but eat as

well as ever. Oh, yes, there's a quid pro quo—but to the Squanders, it seems harmless: All that the Thrifts want in exchange for their food is Squanderbonds (which are denominated, naturally, in Squanderbucks).

Over time Thriftville accumulates an enormous amount of these bonds, which at their core represent claim checks on the future output of Squanderville. A few pundits in Squanderville smell trouble coming. They foresee that for the Squanders both to eat and pay off—or service—the debt they are piling up will eventually require them to work more than eight hours a day. But the residents of Squanderville are in no mood to listen to such doomsaying.

Meanwhile the citizens of Thriftville begin to get nervous. Just how good, they ask, are the IOUs of a shiftless island? So, the Thrifts change strategy: Though they continue to hold some bonds, they sell most of them to Squanderville residents for Squanderbucks and use the proceeds to buy Squanderville land. And eventually the Thrifts own all of Squanderville.

Do you get the picture? Warren Buffett has captured with devastating simplicity what is now happening (and has been happening for over a decade) to weaken our country. We are the Squanders and we are putting our IOUs in the hands of other countries in increasingly dangerous amounts. In short, we are selling about $2 billion worth of our country to foreigners each and every day.

For most of the life of our country we were Thriftville in the Buffett tale. But in the late 1970s it changed. Now, other countries own about $2.5 trillion more of our country than we own of theirs. That adds up to about 5 percent of our national wealth, according to Buffett. That is now increasing by over *1 percent* a year! In short, we are selling our country with a trade strategy that serves the corporate interest, but not our national interest. We have to deal with this. The question isn't whether; it is how. And I like the Buffett Plan.

The free traders who are the architects of our current policy will say it is a giant retreat toward protectionism. Nonsense. It is a giant step toward common sense.

Repeal the Tax Break for Exporting Jobs

We have to repeal the insidious and perverse tax incentives that reward the companies that move their manufacturing jobs overseas. This isn't rocket science. But how do you stem the tide of U.S. jobs leaving our country if our official government policy is to reward the companies that are moving those jobs with tax breaks? It's true that the Congress has voted on this previously and refused to put an end to this tax break for exporting jobs, and multinational corporations will howl and fight it like a pack of wolves.

But the American people should insist on it. And I intend to keep trying.

If the politicians now in the Congress aren't willing to do what is right, then they should be replaced by those who will. Maybe we should consider "outsourcing" those who aren't willing to stand up for America's jobs. But first, give them another chance to do the right thing.

Just a brief review is in order. Our tax code tells U.S. corporations that if they make their income here in the United States, they pay taxes on it now. However, if they make their money overseas, they can delay paying taxes on it until they bring the money back home. And then we offered them a $5^{1}/_{4}$ percent tax rate when they repatriated the dollars in 2005! By the way, that is about *one-half* of the tax rate the lowest-income American taxpayers shell out. Some sweet deal.

You may be surprised to learn that the first suggestion to shut down this tax reward for doing your business overseas came from John F. Kennedy in 1961. Back then, not many companies were moving their jobs overseas, but he could envision a wave washing jobs out to sea. It has become a tsunami. Companies are aggressively moving their jobs out of the United States and are being rewarded for it by this insidious tax break.

Now it's up to the American people to set the politicians straight. They can, and I hope will, force the change that will abolish these perverse rewards for destroying American jobs.

Prohibit Importation of Goods from Companies That Abuse Overseas Workers and Infringe on Human Rights, and Allow U.S. Companies to Take Their Competitors to Court When They Exploit Foreign Labor to Lower Their Costs

If we're going to encourage the spread of democracy and human rights, the U.S. Congress should enact legislation prohibiting the importation of goods from companies that are engaged in gross violations of the labor laws of those countries. And the legislation should allow U.S. companies to take their competitors to court if they abuse their overseas workers.

We know that there are children and other workers employed in some third-world countries in slavelike conditions. I have described many of them in this book. Many more go unreported. It's time for our country to say that there is an admission price to the American market. The price of admission requires that imports not be produced by exploited or abused workers.

In a debate about outsourcing, the proponents will argue that our trading partners do have their own labor standards. China, for example, does have minimum wage and other requirements. That's true. But what's also true is they don't enforce these standards because they don't want to do anything that would discourage foreign investment. The result is workers are exploited by being required to work long hours for little pay.

My proposal would prohibit a company from importing products into the U.S. market if they were produced by overseas companies that were engaged in "gross violations" of the labor laws of those countries. (I would explicitly define "gross violations.")

With this one rule, we can do more to elevate living standards around the world and simultaneously protect our own workforce and economy. That doesn't mean American businesses and workers don't have to compete. It does mean they get fair opportunity to do so.

In addition I believe that U.S. companies that are producing here and trying to compete with companies that are importing the products from abroad should have a remedy for unfair trade. In other words, if their competitors are selling products made by foreign workers who are being abused, the U.S. company should have the right to take its competitors to court. America's textile industry is one of those that could experience a revival, given the opportunity to compete on a level playing field.

On the human rights front, I have concerns about American-based technology companies helping Chinese officials to repress free speech—specifically Yahoo!

The Washington Post columnist Richard Cohen (1/19/06) wrote, "When the Chinese government asked the company who among its many users was sending out certain embarrassing e-mails, Yahoo! provided the name—Shi Tao—and he is now serving a 10-year prison term at what amounts to hard labor."

If we're in the business of spreading democracy, then let's do it. If we're in the business of spreading commerce, well, then, let's just admit it instead of trotting out the "spreading democracy and freedom" argument every time a new trade proposal appears on the table.

Set a Ceiling on Trade Deficits

But if our country does not have the will to adopt a balanced trade plan, we should, at a very minimum, move to set a trade deficit and trade debt ceiling just as we establish a debt ceiling for our budget deficits.

Occasionally, you hear that the Congress is debating an increase in the debt limit. That refers to the accumulated debt of the United States that grows worse each year when the country is running budget deficits. Congress is *required* to vote on increasing the debt limit. Limiting the amount of debt is one way of forcing the issue of confronting the annual budget deficits and accumulated debt that the country is experiencing. It's not a revolutionary idea. American families and companies have been managing debt and budgeting successfully for a long time!

Because there is no similar requirement for the trade debt, it can grow and grow, and no one has to be accountable for it or cast a vote to allow it to increase. That's convenient for the politicians, but not good policy for the country. And that's the problem. We've got a country that needs to focus on a long-term plan, but we have politicians thinking in two-, four-, and six-year increments. We have corporations that are even more shortsighted. Too many of them are interested only in the next quarterly results.

There should be limits on the yearly trade deficits and the accumulated trade debt related to our total yearly economic output. When we exceed that limit, it should trigger a requirement that Congress take action to reduce it. I propose that we set a limit so that whenever our foreign debt reaches 25 percent of our GDP or when the yearly trade deficit exceeds 5 percent of our Gross Domestic Product it would trigger our use of the provision in our international trade agreements allowing member countries to impose temporary tariffs when there is a balance of payments crisis.

The trade purist will call that protectionist. Pundits will say that it is a giant step backward and will undermine our leadership in pushing to open up foreign markets and reduce foreign country tariffs. But we are facing a crisis and we have a right to take action.

Article XII of the GATT (General Agreement on Tariffs and Trade) states that any country "in order to safeguard its external financial position and its balance of payments, may restrict the quantity or value of merchandise permitted to be imported."

It's time to implement that provision and take action to protect our economy and our jobs.

Make Normal Trade Relations with China a Year-to-Year Decision to Exert Pressure on Them to Open Their Markets and Engage in Fair Trade

Because China alone accounts for nearly one-third of our trade deficit and has intentionally undermined good faith trade agreements, I believe we should revoke the permanent approval that gave China Normal Trade Relations status and make it an annual determination once again.

Only in that way can we put the kind of pressure on China that is necessary to bring our trade into some kind of balance. China's leadership manipulates its currency valuation, it looks the other way on piracy and counterfeiting, and it continues to make it difficult for U.S. producers to have unfettered access to the Chinese markets. All the while our trade deficit with China grows to alarming levels.

In the one month of September 2005 for example, we imported $23 billion in products from China while we were able to export only $3 billion in products to China.

This disparity will continue until China decides we are serious about demanding fair trade rules and enforcement. Prior to China joining the WTO, the United States took action to remove the year-by-year certification that was previously required for China to receive Normal Trade Relations status. That requirement was discarded when China was given permanent NTR status in 2000 at the request of President Clinton. But it hasn't worked out the way it was advertised.

It is time to revoke the permanent NTR and restore the year-by-year certification vote by Congress. Technically, it would require the Congress to reinstate China under the Jackson-Vanik Amendment so that China would be denied normal trade relations status unless specifically authorized by the Congress each year. Only with this action will we have the leverage to push China to stop the unfair trade practices they routinely employ and begin to understand that our trade relationship must be mutually beneficial.

Encourage Stronger Unions

Why encourage stronger unions? Hasn't their day come and gone, you ask. Well, there is a reason I included a chapter discussing the history of the labor movement (chapter 3). You see, what unions did in America and in Poland and around the world has a great deal to do with true freedom and democracy.

Over the course of this book, I have spoken about the need for balance. What labor unions did and can do again is provide a natural balance to large-scale corporate power. If you have healthy unions, it works much as the checks and balances of the three branches of American government. When one branch starts to dominate—as we see with the unprecedented strength and power of global corporations or even with an "imperial presidency"—there needs to be a check on that power.

So what happened to unions? Unchecked globalization gave corporations an opportunity to exploit workers in other nations because workers in America are harder to exploit, thanks to unions and laws to protect workers. Now, I don't think this is intended to be particularly malicious. It is just business. Commerce chooses the path of least resistance just like water or electricity. Both can lead to a nasty shock.

While more than a third of American workers were union members fifty years ago, and wielded great influence over the whole political and social spectrum, now powerful corporations have filled that vacuum. Union membership has dropped to just over 12 percent of the workforce today, so their negotiating power has been eroded.

When it comes to American jobs, I'll confess—I want to try to protect good jobs here at home. And we ought not to grant favors to companies who send American jobs overseas.

But here's the catch. Just as labor unions wielded substantial political power in past decades, these days it is the corporations that have the clout to dismantle laws that impede their financial progress. So they are pushing to diminish health care, pensions, salaries, and work standards, all in the name of being able to compete. But compete against what? The competition they have created by moving their jobs overseas?

There's a common sentiment that labor unions had it coming. We've all heard stories (some true) about unreasonable union rules that burdened businesses with inefficiencies. So, yes, in some respects, labor unions caused their own problems. They got fat. They pushed people around, and now they pay the price. I can't dispute one word of that argument. But the labor movement has changed. And if there is a misuse of power in our country today, it is by some large corporations that use, abuse, and discard their workers at will.

Damn right, we should expect unions to put their house in order, but our country needs organized labor to stand up for the rights and interests of working people. We need the counterbalance to corporate power.

Labor unions have been vilified over the past several decades by the very interests that have wanted to weaken the labor movement. And yet, unions have been very successful. And as more and more families moved into a middle-class life in part because of the work of unions, they were less inclined to think they needed a union any longer to help them bargain for their wages and their jobs. As a result the union movement lost membership. But with the challenge of corporations moving jobs overseas at a record pace these days, this is the time when we need a resurgence of a strong labor movement.

I don't believe it is public policy that will accomplish that result, but as more and more Americans see their jobs, pensions, and wages eroding because of the global economy, I expect more people to understand the need to organize in order to protect themselves.

Tackle Health Care and Education in America

When Maryland lawmakers voted in early 2006 to enact a law requiring companies that employ more than ten thousand Maryland workers (Wal-Mart) to spend at least 8 percent of their payroll on health care, Wal-Mart detractors were doing back flips. I won't go that far. As tough as I have been on Wal-Mart, the measure is a finger in a leaky dike. It is not a permanent solution.

If we really want to see American industry competitive and minimize outsourcing, we must take some of the responsibility of excessive health-care costs off the backs of American industry. I'm not suggesting that businesses should not have a responsibility here, but the current system imposes a huge burden on employer-based health-care coverage in a system whose costs are spiraling out of control.

We desperately need to develop an affordable national health-care plan—just like every other industrialized country with whom we compete in trade.

Companies like General Motors are handicapped when they must grant competitors a fifteen-hundred-dollar head start (the cost of health care that goes into each vehicle). Ironically, Corporate America is opposed to the very solution that could lessen that burden. It's because they are concerned about paying higher taxes for some type of national health-care system. That could be true, but it would be far less than the escalating costs of the flawed and inefficient system we have now.

I'm not proposing a Canadian style health-care system. Americans want a fee-for-service approach to health care where they have their own choice of doctors. I understand that. But we must develop a comprehensive, national plan to bring health-care costs under control. These costs are crippling companies and workers alike. And in the process, the economic health and future of the country. Unless we have political courage to tackle the problem, we will discover we don't have enough fingers and toes for the holes in the dike.

Part of the national health-care solution harkens back to the days of President Kennedy's national fitness plan. Americans must bear much of the responsibility for an increasingly sedentary lifestyle, which leads to the medicine chest far too often. A national wellness program could have a huge impact, especially if those Americans making the effort were rewarded with *significantly lower* premiums.

By the way, the United States spends more, *far more,* per capita on health care than any other country in the world. Yet we rank forty-eighth in life expectancy. Something's seriously wrong with our health-care system.

Finally, we have to rethink our education system and retool it for the decades ahead. I hear Bill Gates and others tell us that in order to compete in international trade in the future we need to change our education system fundamentally. They say our schools are failing. We are told they aren't teaching the things students need to be competitive in the new global economy. Some of that is valid. We do need to improve our education system. But I wonder if some of it isn't just an excuse. How do you educate someone to compete with people who will work for pennies an hour?

Of one thing I am certain. The best hope for an American youth is a stellar education. Emphasis on literacy and a national push for excellence in the disciplines of math and science and engineering is essential if we are to continue our edge in innovation and technology.

Several years ago President Bush demanded accountability with his No Child Left Behind program, but it remains an unfunded mandate, still leaving the success of individual schools largely dependent upon the local tax base. So, we must fund the program.

I agree that we need accountability in our public schools. And we should aspire to excellence in every classroom in the country. And we must fix failing schools rather than abandon them. There will always be those who cannot escape failing schools. The solution is not flight. The solution is fight. We have to fight harder to fix the broken schools.

And when it comes to higher education, our country ought to make it available to every student who meets the admission criteria. My Senate colleague John Kerry proposed a program I like. It is an annual four-thousand-dollar College Opportunity Tax Credit. He also offered a Service for College plan, which would allow students to earn the equivalent of their state's four-year public college tuition in exchange for community service in AmeriCorps, a program in which students travel to communities to help educate students in troubled school districts, fixing and building infrastructure, working with the National Park Service, and doing countless other tasks that build character and help communities and people who need it. This is an approach that will strengthen our country.

With the education these students earn, they will be better equipped to face the challenges and opportunities rapidly unfolding in this global economy. We are not just educating a labor force, but developing leaders, and that is what America so sorely needs right now.

Put the Clamps on Outsourced Pollution and Manage Resources

As I discussed in chapter 9, pollution is really everyone's problem. We are sharing oceans, air, and pollution, so when we allow goods to enter this country that are produced in a manner that would not be allowed here, we not only encourage unfair competition that costs American jobs, we encourage global pollution that ultimately costs lives.

There is enough hard science to conclude that the earth is undergoing climate change and that it is likely that man's impact on the earth is a contributing factor. But even if global warming is a natural phenomenon, it should not preclude us from trying to clean up our messes. It is undeniable that pollution kills and decreases life expectancy of all living creatures.

On the domestic front, it is imperative that this president or the next take the lead in preparing this country for increasingly severe storms and rising ocean levels spawned by climate change. The ocean's rise, spurred by polar ice melt, affects salinity and, quite likely, ocean currents—and that will certainly continue to affect weather. Hurricane Katrina exposed our lack of preparedness. Rising ocean levels combined with storm surges have put coastal cities in peril, yet there is no plan, no public acknowledgment of even the possibility of a problem by our leaders. And even if you don't believe in global warming or climate change, improving our response to disaster just makes sense.

While we are on the topic of oceans, one trade issue that seems to always be on the back burner is over fishing. Many countries share the ocean, and one in five of earth's inhabitants are dependent on the sea for protein. A UN report cites a Food and Agriculture Organization (FAO) estimate that over 70 percent of the world's fish species are either "fully exploited or depleted."

The UN report warns, "The dramatic increase of destructive fishing techniques worldwide destroys marine mammals and entire ecosystems." FAO reports that illegal, unreported, and unregulated fishing worldwide appears to be increasing as fishermen seek to avoid stricter rules in many places in response to shrinking catches and declining fish stock.

When it comes to tackling global pollution, we can't solve the problem overnight. But the bar should incrementally be raised as a part of our trade agreements. In the cases where American jobs are being lost because of unfair practices related to pollution, that bar ought to be raised faster.

Yes, there will be an outcry—but much of the whining will come from international corporations and their lobbies, with a lot less noise coming from the citizenry of these countries. In South America, we are witnessing a historical backlash against America and capitalism because we are viewed as fat, wealthy industrialists willing to exploit both the people and land. And while our focus has been on domestic ills caused by bad trade agreements, we have been slow to recognize that it isn't all roses for the workers in these poor countries whom our pro-traders proclaim we are rescuing. If they are being rescued, they certainly don't seem to appreciate it!

In Washington, there's a lot of talk about how global trade is spreading democracy, and I believe *equitable, measured* trade can do just that, but the facts illustrate that something else is happening right now. There are massive, popular protests in country after country against these global trade agreements that ordinary people see as threats to their lives. Certainly, some of the backlash is related to international politics—most notably, the war in Iraq—but a good deal of it is a direct reflection of the experiences people in these neighboring countries have had with global corporations.

If American workers are not winning . . . if workers in other countries are not winning . . . then we ought to question the assertions of the free trade evangelists that this is Capitalist Heaven in the making.

So insisting on labor and environmental standards from our trading partners should not be regarded as some sort of repression. It is a matter of requiring everyone involved in global trade to act in a responsible manner. When other countries see Americans taking the high road, then, and only then, will they conclude that democracy and capitalism is the most rewarding path.

IT'S UP TO US . . .

The evidence is all around us that our current trade policies aren't working. But it still won't be easy to push the president or the Congress to take the action that is necessary to deal with it.

But this hemorrhaging of red ink and good jobs just can't continue. The only question is how and when it stops. Who will finally convince the president and the Congress that their interest must be in the well-being of the United States?

We have inherited a great legacy in this country. But it has become too easy to take it all for granted. Too easy to believe that it will always be this way. We need to understand that it is our challenge to make the right decisions that will lead to a future of increasing opportunities here in America.

In the David McCullough biography about John Adams, he described the letters that Adams had written to his wife, Abigail, when he was traveling abroad in England and France representing our country's interests.

In his letters Adams seemed to be asking, where will the leadership come from to form this new country? Who will be the leaders we can count on as we try to form a new nation?

Then he would lament that "there is only us—me, Washington, Jefferson, Franklin, Mason, Madison." But in the rearview mirror of history, we know they were some of the most extraordinarily talented and visionary leaders who have ever lived.

Every generation of Americans for the past two centuries has asked the same questions. Who will provide the leadership for our country? Where will our leaders come from?

And each generation has been blessed with those who have stood up in every corner of our country to provide that leadership. From Lincoln, to Roosevelt, to Kennedy and from school boards to the presidency, our democracy has been guided by leadership from extraordinary people from ordinary places.

And if there were a Hall of Fame for business leaders that have been the builders in the private sector during the past two centuries, it would include some of the most extraordinary American creators and inventors that have ever lived. Edison . . . Ford . . . Carnegie . . . Gates . . .

We need leadership once again in America—leadership that will have the vision and courage to begin taking care of things here at home. Yes, our world is increasingly global. And for our own vital interests, we must be engaged and involved in international affairs. We cannot retreat from our international obligations.

But we still all live here, and we want good jobs and the prospect of a better life and an improved standard of living here. Huge budget and trade deficits threaten our future. Incompetent trade agreements threaten our jobs and undermine our manufacturing base. If these are left unchecked, the land our children will inherit will be a weaker country with fewer good jobs and less opportunity.

Some years ago, I led an American delegation of senators and congressmen to meet with members of the European parliament. Our discussion was to be about the trade disputes that exist between the

United States and Europe. There were about a dozen members of our delegation and a like number of theirs.

We sat around a rectangular table and talked for nearly an hour about the difficulties we were having. The discussions ranged from hormone-treated U.S. beef to European subsidies of grain sales. Finally, the head of their delegation, a Frenchman and a member of the European parliament, leaned across the table toward me and said this:

"Mr. Senator, we have been talking for an hour now about the differences between us. I want to tell you how I feel about your country. I was a fourteen-year-old boy standing on a street corner of Paris, France, when your liberation army marched in and drove the Nazis out. A young, black American soldier reached out his hand and handed that boy an apple as he marched past. Mr. Senator, I will go to my grave remembering that moment . . . remembering what your country did for me, for my family, and for my country."

I sat back in my chair, kind of stunned at what he had just said. Of course, I knew what our country had done. But sometimes it takes hearing it from others to understand fully what our country has accomplished and what we mean and have meant to others. I have said we have inherited a legacy. It is a grand one, and one we must continue to nurture.

The United States of America is the world's longest and most successful democracy. But, in the history of civilization, we have existed in just a blink of an eye. In that blink, we built the world's strongest economy and a standard of living envied by much of the rest of the world. And we have been the first to answer the call for help from others around the world. It didn't happen by accident. It took leadership in both government and business. Leaders with courage and vision, who understand that what has been built in the blink of an eye can disappear as quickly.

Some of the solutions I have proposed are direct remedies for the trade imbalance. Others address an attitude—a return to the guiding principles that built America. America cannot survive many more "Me

Generations." We can only be great when our inherent sense of right and wrong and of compassion and charity rises above materialism and greed. "Me Generations" crumble like the marble columns of Rome. "We Generations" endure forever.

I believe it is the heart of America from which change will come because it is in the very nature of Americans to face things squarely and set things right. It is the American way to do the right thing.

And that gives me hope.

INDEX